SOCIAL POLITICS
IN THE UNITED STATES

SOCIAL POLITICS IN THE UNITED STATES

BY

FRED E. HAYNES

AMS PRESS
NEW YORK

Reprinted from the edition of 1924, Boston
First AMS EDITION published 1970
Manufactured in the United States of America

International Standard Book Number: 0-404-03168-4

Library of Congress Card Catalog Number: 70-126648

AMS PRESS, INC.
NEW YORK, N.Y. 10003

211520

PREFACE

STUDIES begun in the nineties and published in two volumes, "Third Party Movements Since the Civil War," in 1916, and "James Baird Weaver," in 1919, convinced the writer that social and economic factors had played a much more important part in our politics than was realized. These factors explained the origin of minor parties and gradually were bringing about a socialization of our politics. A comprehensive survey of the principal parties, organizations, and movements involved in this process of socialization has been the underlying motive. The selection of subjects to be considered has been determined as the study progressed, the connecting link being the fact that they grew out of economic and social conditions and contributed to what may in a broad sense be described as "social politics." Some things may have been included which might have been omitted and the reverse may be true. The work has been a growth.

No attempt has been made to give exhaustive or complete references. Some chapters, especially the ones covering more recent subjects, contain a considerable number of footnotes. Every chapter is followed by a list of "Selected References," which represent in the main the materials used and suggest additional sources of information for students and readers.

The thanks of the author are due to Professor Benjamin F. Shambaugh, the Superintendent and Editor of the State Historical Society of Iowa, who has so kindly consented to the reprinting of parts of two chapters from the author's "Third Party Movements Since the Civil

War," published by the Society. In addition the research facilities of the library of the Society have been most generously placed at the author's disposal.

To Professor Richard T. Ely the thanks of the author are due for his interested and enthusiastic encouragement in the completion of the study. Dean Chester A. Phillips, of the College of Commerce, has relieved the writer of some of his teaching work and has aided by advice and counsel. Professor R. W. Stone, of the College of Commerce, has read some of the chapters on Labor. Many others have contributed by advice, by the furnishing of materials, and by suggestions as to treatment or arrangement.

FRED E. HAYNES

THE STATE UNIVERSITY OF IOWA
IOWA CITY, IOWA

CONTENTS

CHAPTER I

CHAPTER II

CHAPTER III

CONTENTS

CHAPTER VI

CHAPTER VII

CHAPTER VIII

CHAPTER IX

CHAPTER X

CHAPTER XI

CHAPTER XII

CHAPTER XIII

CHAPTER XIV

CHAPTER XV

SOCIAL POLITICS IN THE UNITED STATES

·.·

CHAPTER I

ECONOMIC CONDITIONS AND AMERICAN DEMOCRACY

"THROUGHOUT the century our political contests have been based almost wholly on economic differences, and they have revealed an increasing tendency to develop clear-cut divisions between economic classes." [1] Early manifestations of this tendency appeared in Berkshire County in Massachusetts during the years from 1775 to 1780 in the contest over the formation of a constitution for the State. Berkshire County on the extreme western frontier of that period opposed the plan of the old and wealthier parts of the State to continue for a time the form of government inherited from the period before independence had been declared. The more conservative classes urged the postponement of constitution-making till the end of the war, but the democrats of Berkshire stood their ground till they forced compliance with their demands by almost open rebellion and threats of secession. The line of division was an economic one — the conservatives were the well-to-do of the older communities, while the radicals were the poor farmers on the frontier.

Again the same line of division appeared in the contests in connection with the formation and ratification of the

[1] Ghent: *Mass and Class*, pp. 24, 25.

Federal Constitution from 1787 to 1789. In Massachusetts in 1788 on one side were the ministers, the lawyers, and the judges, while opposed to them were the small farmers, the petty traders, and the inhabitants of the country villages and towns. The hostility of the latter was directed not so much against the Constitution as "against the men who made it and the men who praised it. They were sure some injury was plotted against them. They knew the system was the work of the ambitious and the rich. 'These lawyers,' exclaimed one of their representatives, 'and men of learning and moneyed men that talk so finely and gloss over matters so smoothly to make us poor, illiterate people swallow down the pill, expect to get into Congress themselves. They mean to be the managers of the Constitution. They mean to get all the money into their hands, and then they will swallow up us little folk like the great Leviathan, just as the whale swallowed up Jonah.'" Language of this kind was heard every day in the convention. Every member from the country districts who spoke indulged "in harsh words about lawyers and judges, rich men and rulers. One cautioned the House to be very jealous of rulers. Another reminded it how all the godly men of Scripture had failed, and declared that for himself he 'would not trust a flock of Moseses.' At last, as the session drew to a close, a weather-beaten face and a pair of sunburnt hands came to be looked upon as the outward signs of an Anti-Federalist." [1]

These Berkshire Constitutionalists and Anti-Federalists were the forerunners of the later Republicans who rallied around Thomas Jefferson, and these divisions mark the beginnings of the party system as we know it in the United

[1] McMaster: *A History of the People of the United States*, vol. I, pp. 477, 478; Libby: "The Geographical Distribution of the Vote of the Thirteen States on the Federal Constitution," in *Bulletin of the University of Wisconsin*, Economics, Political Science Series, vol. I, no. I.

States. Party names and platforms have changed, but the fundamental differences have continued. The Whigs succeeded the Federalists and they in turn gave way to the Republicans. The Democrats are the direct descendants of the Anti-Federalists and Republicans of Jefferson's day. The sentiments of 1788 sound wonderfully like those of the campaigns of 1896 and 1912. Differences, based upon economic and industrial conditions, determined upon which side people would range themselves. (Political discussions emphasized constitutional differences of opinion, but the real explanation of the political divisions is to be found in economic and industrial divergences of interests. At bottom the dividing line in our politics has been and is an economic one.)

SIGNIFICANCE OF THE FRONTIER IN AMERICAN HISTORY

The first work in the economic interpretation of the history of the United States was done by Professor F. J. Turner, then of the University of Wisconsin, now of Harvard University. It was presented in the form of a paper read before the American Historical Association in 1893. The title of the study was "The Significance of the Frontier in American History," and it was intended to aid in "an understanding of the relations between the political history of the United States, and the physiographic, social, and economic conditions underlying this history. . . . It is believed that many phases of our political history have been obscured by the attention paid to State boundaries and to the sectional lines of North and South. At the same time the economic interpretation of our history has been neglected. In the study of the persistence of the struggle for State particularism in American constitutional history, it was inevitable that writers should make prominent the State as a political factor. But, from the point of view of the rise and growth of sectionalism and nationalism, it is much more important to note the existence of great social and economic areas, independent of State lines, which have acted as units in political history, and which have changed their political attitude as they changed their economic organization and divided into new groups."

Professor Turner introduced his paper with a reference to a statement made in a bulletin of the Superintendent of the Census for 1890 to the effect that "up to and including 1880 the country had a frontier of settlements," but that by 1890 the unsettled area had been "so broken into by isolated bodies of settlement" that there could hardly be said to be a frontier. "This brief official statement marked the end of a great historic movement. Up to our own day American History has been in a large degree the history of colonization of the Great West. The existence of an area of the free land, its continuous recession, and the advance of American settlement westward explain American development."

"Behind institutions, behind constitutional forms and modifications, lie the vital forces that call these organs into life and shape them to meet changing conditions. The peculiarity of American institutions is the fact that they have been compelled to adapt themselves to the changes of an expanding people . . . to the changes involved in crossing a continent, in winning a wilderness, and in developing at each area of this progress out of the primitive economic and political conditions of the frontier into the complexity of city life . . . American social development has been continually beginning over again on the frontier. This perennial rebirth, this fluidity of American life, this expansion westward with its new opportunities, its continuous touch with the simplicity of primitive society, furnish the forces dominating American character. The true point of view in the history of this nation is not the Atlantic coast, it is the Great West. Even the slavery struggle, which is made so exclusive an object of attention by some historians, occupies its important place in American history because of its relation to westward expansion."

After a general reference to the influence of the frontier upon the course of American history, Professor Turner proceeded to consider in some detail the stages of frontier advance, and the effect of each of the different kinds of frontier — the Indian trader's, the rancher's, and the farmer's. "Each of these areas has had an influence in our economic and political history; the evolution of each into a different industrial stage has worked political transformations. Wisconsin . . . in the days when it lacked varied agriculture and complex industrial life, was a stronghold of the granger and greenback movements; but it has undergone an industrial transformation, and in the presidential contest of 1896 Mr. Bryan carried but three counties." John C. Calhoun went with his father to the upland regions of the Carolinas — the frontier of his day. His young manhood was "thoroughly western in its nationalistic and loose-construction characteristics. But the extension of cotton culture . . . superseded the pioneer by the slaveholding planter. Calhoun's ideas changed with his section, until he became the chief prophet of southern sectionalism and slavery."

Next, Professor Turner considered briefly the influence of the frontier upon the East and upon the Old World. Of these effects the promotion of democracy was the most important. The frontier was productive of individualism and the frontier conditions prevalent in the colonies were important factors in the American Revolution, where individual liberty was sometimes confused with the absence of all effective government. The same conditions help to explain the difficulty of establishing a strong government in the time of the Confederation. Frontier individualism has from the beginning promoted democracy. The frontier States, admitted during the first quarter of a century after 1789, had democratic suffrage provisions and inevitably had reactive effects upon the older States. The rise of democracy as an effective force in the nation came under the leadership of Andrew Jackson, and it meant the triumph of the frontier with both good and bad results. Democracy, "intolerant of administrative experience and education and pressing individual liberty beyond its proper bounds, has its dangers as well as its benefits." It has allowed a laxity in "governmental affairs which has rendered possible the spoils system," and all the other evils that follow from the lack of a highly socialized civic spirit.

Another evidence of the democratic influence of frontier conditions appeared in paper-money inflation and wild-cat banking. "The colonial and revolutionary frontier was the region whence emanated many of the worst forms of paper currency. The West in the War of 1812 repeated the phenomenon on the frontier of that day, while the speculation and wild-cat banking of the period of the crisis of 1837 occurred on the new frontier belt of the next tier of States. Thus each one of the periods of paper-money projects coincides with periods when a new set of frontier communities had arisen, and coincides in area with these successive frontiers, for the most part." The Populist movement of the nineties was another illustration of the same tendencies.

The frontier as a force in the nationalization and development of the Federal Government has been of the greatest importance. The legislation which has most developed the powers of the National Government, and which has formed the largest part of its activity, was conditioned by the frontier. The tariff, land, and internal improvements have been discussed as subsidiary to the slavery question. In reality, the slavery question was incidental and the growth of nationalism was dependent upon the settlement of the West. The pioneer needed the commodities produced upon the coast, and consequently internal improvements and railroad grants developed with profound nationalizing effects. Over these measures great debates occurred, and great constitutional questions were discussed. Sectional groupings appeared in the votes, and "loose construction increased as the nation marched westward." But it was not enough to bring the farm and the factory together by better means of communication and transportation. Under the lead of the West protective tariffs were passed and the influence of Federal legislation broadened.

Again, the disposition of the public lands has had a profound influence upon the development of the powers of the Federal Government. The purchase of Louisiana was probably "the constitutional turning-point" in the history of the United States, because it afforded "a new area for national legislation and the occasion of the downfall of the policy of strict construction. But the purchase of Louisiana was called out by frontier needs and demands. As frontier States accrued to the Union, the national power grew. . . . 'In 1789 the States were the creators of the Federal Government; in 1861 the Federal Government was the creator of a large majority of the States.'" The policies followed in the disposal and sale of the public lands were determined by the needs of the frontier. Efforts to make the public domain a source of revenue, and to withhold it from settlers in the attempt to prevent too rapid advance, failed because of the demands of the frontiersmen. The East was powerless, and this legislation was framed under the lead of western statesmen like Benton and Jackson.[1]

---

[1] Turner: "The Significance of the Frontier in American History," in the *Annual Report of the American Historical Association*, 1893, pp. 197–227.

In spite of the original and suggestive work of Professor Turner, begun thirty years ago, and emphasized and enlarged by him from time to time, surprisingly few efforts have been made in the way of following up the many leads indicated by him in his pioneer paper. Although the importance of his work has been recognized by many students of American history, especially in the West, its results have not been applied to the study of American history at large in any comprehensive way, and there has certainly not been that detailed analysis which it deserves.

Economic Interpretation of the Constitution of the United States

In 1913 Professor C. A. Beard, of Columbia University, published a volume with the title of "An Economic Interpretation of the Constitution of the United States," and in 1915 a volume upon the "Economic Origins of Jeffersonian Democracy." He undertook in his first volume to apply the theory of the economic interpretation of history to the period of the formation of the Federal Constitution. He attempted to discover "what classes and social groups existed in the United States just previous to the adoption of the Constitution, and which of them, from the nature of their property, might have expected to benefit immediately and definitely by the overthrow of the old system and the establishment of the new. On the other hand, it must be discovered which of them might have expected more beneficial immediate results ... from the maintenance of the existing legal arrangements." The Constitution was the result of the work of a certain number of men, and it was opposed by another group. If it were possible to know the economic circumstances of all those persons connected with its drafting and establishment — probably about 160,000 men in all — we could make a scientific analysis and classification. Such information should include a list of real and personal property, lands, houses with encumbrances, money at interest, slaves, and capital invested in shipping and manufactures, and in State and Continental securities.

If it could be shown from the classification of the men who supported and opposed the Constitution that "substantially all of the merchants, money-lenders, security-holders, manufacturers, shippers, capitalists, and financiers and their professional associates are to be found on one side in support of the Constitution and that substantially all or the major portion of the opposition came from the non-slave-holding farmers and the debtors — would it not be pretty conclusively demonstrated that our fundamental law was ... the product ... of a group of economic interests which must have expected beneficial results from its adoption?"

There had been no attempt before Professor Beard's to make a survey of the distribution of property in 1787. Much of the material necessary for a complete study has, of course, disappeared, but enough remains to throw a great deal of light upon the economic conditions of the time. The Treasury Department at Washington contains much unpublished and unworked material. Shortly after the establishment of the Federal Government the old debt was converted and consolidated into a new or funded debt, and holders of State and Continental securities brought their papers to their State loan office or to the Treasury to have them recorded and converted into the bonds issued by the new Government. The records of this great transaction are unfortunately far from complete, but enough remain to enable the investigator to obtain a good deal of the information desired, which can also be supplemented by an examination of the same kind of documents preserved in some of the States.

Speculation in western lands was another leading activity of the moneyed men of the period. The chief obstacle to the rapid rise of these lands was "the weakness of the National Government which prevented the complete subjugation of the Indians, the destruction of old Indian claims, and the orderly settlement of the frontier." The leading capitalists fully understood the relation of a new constitution to the rise in value of western lands; Washington himself was an owner of such lands and would be benefited by their increase in value. "The materials for the study of land operations exist in enormous quantities, largely in manuscript form in Washington," and a careful examination of these records would afford important information in regard to these influences.

Without doubt sufficient sources are still in existence to enable the careful investigator to make a scientific study of the economic and social influences of the period of constitutional development leading up to the establishment of the new Government in 1789. Such a study would involve years of the most thorough and laborious research. Pending such an investigation, Professor Beard sketches "the broad outlines . . . which must be filled in and corrected by detailed investigations." This work was confined almost entirely to the records in the Treasury Department at Washington.

Professor Beard declares that "no one can pore for weeks over the letters, newspapers, and pamphlets of the years 1787–1789 without coming to the conclusion that there was a deep-seated conflict between a popular party based on paper money and agrarian interests, and a conservative party centred in the towns and resting on financial, mercantile, and personal property interests generally." Much of the controversy was concerned with various features of the Constitution; but the authors of "The Federalist" gave careful attention to the fundamental elements as well as to the incidental details. The literature of the contest in the States where the struggle over ratification was most severe gave the frankest "recognition of the fact that one class of property interests was in conflict with another." This recognition appeared "not so much in attacks on opponents as in appeals to the groups" which had the most at stake in the result of the contest. There was, however, much virulent abuse of debtors and paper-money advocates. Merchants, money-lenders, public creditors were constantly urged to support the Constitution on the ground that their economic security depended upon the establishment of the new National Government.

In his final summary of conclusions, Professor Beard brings together the important results which his study appeared to warrant. The movement for the Constitution was begun and carried through largely by four groups whose interests had been adversely affected by the conditions existing under the Confederation; the four groups were made up of money-lenders, owners of public securities, and those with investments in manufactures and in trade and shipping. The first steps in the formation of the Constitution were taken by "a small and active group of men interested through their personal possessions in the result of their labors." No popular vote was taken upon the proposal to call the Convention which drafted the Constitution. "The members of the Philadelphia Convention . . . were, with a few exceptions, immediately, directly, and personally interested in, and derived economic advantages from, the establishment of the new system. The Constitution was essentially an economic document based upon the concept that the fundamental private rights of property are anterior to government and morally beyond the reach of popular majorities. The major portion of the members of the

Convention are on record as recognizing the claim of property to a special and defensive position in the Constitution. ... The leaders who supported the Constitution in the ratifying conventions represented the same economic groups as the members of the Philadelphia Convention; and in a large number of instances they were also directly and personally interested in the outcome of their efforts. In the ratification it became manifest that the line of cleavage for and against the Constitution was between substantial personality interests on the one hand and the small farming and debtor interests on the other."

Economic Origins of Jeffersonian Democracy

In his second study, "Economic Origins of Jeffersonian Democracy," Professor Beard undertook to determine "whether there was any connection between that party and the large body of citizens who opposed the establishment of the Constitution." As the country was sharply divided over the adoption of the Constitution along fairly definite economic lines, it would be "natural to assume that these divisions did not disappear when the new Government began to carry out the specific policies which had been implied in the language of the instrument and clearly seen by many as necessary corollaries to its adoption. It was hardly to have been expected that the bitter animosities which have been aroused by that contest could be smoothed away at once and that men who had just been engaged in an angry political quarrel could join in fraternal greetings on the following morning. Many of the older historians assumed, therefore, without a detailed analysis of the facts in the case, that the party division over the adoption of the Constitution formed the basis of the Federalist-Republican antagonism which followed the inauguration of the Government."

If there was no relation between the party division of 1787 and 1788 and that which followed the establishment of the new Government, we should expect to find the men, who were upon opposite sides in the constitutional conflict, distributed fairly equally between the Federalist and Republican parties. Of the fifty-five members of the Convention of 1787, forty-three supported the Constitution and lived several years after its adoption. Of these six cannot be satisfactorily classified, leaving thirty-seven, of whom twenty-five became loyal Federalists, and twelve became Republicans, although seven of the latter did not adopt their new party relation until the important fiscal measures had been adopted. Not one of the opponents of the Constitution in the Convention became a Federalist. They fought the establishment of the Constitution; they went into the opposition early, and they remained Republicans to the end of their public careers. The men who drafted the Constitution and were active in obtaining its ratification formed the dominant group in the new Government organized under it. "The spokesmen of the Federalist and Republican parties, Hamilton and Jefferson, were respectively the spokesmen of capitalistic and agrarian interests." The Republicans charged the Federalists with building up "a moneyed aristocracy," and thus drew to themselves the support of the farmers and of a considerable portion of the smaller tradesmen and mechanics of the towns.

DEMOCRATIC INFLUENCE OF THE WEST

Professor Turner's suggestive work and Professor Beard's studies of the economic influences that led to the establishment of the Federal Constitution, and shaped the policies of the new Government under Hamilton and Jefferson, make clear that American democracy has been modified by economic and social conditions from the very beginning of our national existence. As we investigate more carefully later periods we find the same forces at work.) The democratic influence of the West was first felt conspicuously in national affairs in the contests for the Presidency in 1824 and 1828. Adams represented the conservative, commercial interests of the East, while Jackson personified the new democracy of the West of his day, just coming to political consciousness. The ideas of the Anti-Federalists and of the Jeffersonian Democrats had found a new and larger field in the West. Adams was accused of aristocracy and corruption. The new democracy wanted a man of the people — one of themselves — in the White House, and Jackson was swept into office on the top of the democratic wave. Efficiency in government gave way to the demand for government by the people. The "spoils system" came in with the attempt to sweep out of office every supporter of Adams and every opponent of the people. The war upon the National Bank, as an institution in league with moneyed men and business interests, followed as a part of the campaign waged by Jackson against those supposed to be opposed to the new western democracy.

During the early years of the Republic the Government was in the hands of the aristocracies of Virginia and New England. The first serious attack upon this situation came with the accession to power of Andrew Jackson in 1829. From that time to 1860 large classes, before indifferent or unable to exert an influence, began to take an effective part in governmental affairs. All property qualifications were swept away. Officials, formerly appointed, were made subjects for election by the people. Even the judges came to be popularly elected for limited terms. State constitutions were amended in accordance with the new democratic ideas. Legally there was government by the people in a completer sense than had ever existed.

Naturally this new democratic movement turned its attention to slavery which came to be a subject for discussion after 1840. As a matter of course it was anti-slavery. The new anti-slavery democracy of the West reinforced the moral and religious leaders, Garrison, Phillips, and Whittier, who in the East were denouncing slavery. The real decisive battle with slavery was fought and won in the West. Without the West, the issue might have been doubtful: with nine free States in that section added to the free States of the East, the victory for freedom was assured. The Civil War and the abolition of slavery mark the crest of the democratic wave in the United States. The slavery question was itself, of course, an economic and social problem, and its abolition was determined by economic and social forces arrayed against it as a result of the settlement of the West. Again in a great crisis of our national history the forces largely controlling events were economic and social even as they had been in the days of Washington, Hamilton, Jefferson, and Jackson.

It is also interesting to note that, during the thirties and forties, a wave of humanitarianism and social reform swept over the country, which desired "to apply the public lands to social amelioration," and which was "eager to find new forms of democratic development." According to Professor Commons, "A dozen colonies of idealists, like the Brook Farm philosophers, went off by themselves to solve the problem of social existence in a big family called a phalanx. . . . Robert Owen called a 'world's convention' on short notice, where a dozen different 'plans' of social reorganization — individualistic, communistic, incomprehensible — were submitted in all solemnity. It was the golden age of the talk-fest, the lyceum, the brotherhood of man — the 'hot-air' period of American history." This democratic movement "suddenly disappeared in the slavery contest," and one cannot help wondering "what might have been the present condition of American democracy if there had been no race issue and its irrepressible conflict? For . . . there was emerging in the forties a class of idealists and a spirit of social progress more promising even than those of other nations. This idealism was exhausted in the Civil War, and it needed another generation to come upon the scene and to learn anew the social problems which the intervening years had intensified." [1]

A new significance is given to the slavery conflict and the democratic influence of economic forces is seen from a new point of view when the relation of Jacksonian democracy, utopian socialism, and the anti-slavery agitation is understood. Is it not a suggestive fact that the first great contribution of the West to American life should have been a widespread democratic movement which resulted in the bringing to an end of a situation in which the great Republic of the United States had been the last stronghold of slavery as a great economic and social institution? Is it not splendid testimony to the truth of Professor Turner's emphasis upon the democratic influence of the frontier upon American life?

After the war industrial development delayed the revival of the democratic movement. The small employer gave way to the great factory or mill with its hundreds and sometimes thousands of hands. The captain of industry came to be the most striking feature of modern business; the individual worker shrank into insignificance. Autocracy in industry replaced the comparative democracy of earlier times. The trust was the most conspicuous manifestation of the anti-democratic tendency in industry. Side

[1] Turner: "Social Forces in American History," in *The American Historical Review*, vol. XVI, p. 228; Commons: *A Documentary History of American Industrial Society*, vol. VII, pp. 19, 20; vol. IX, pp. 19, 20.

by side with political democracy there developed one-man rule in industry. It was inevitable that this change should react upon government and law. The influence of big business has been in favor of increased efficiency, but hostile to democracy. Consequently there has been a receding of the democratic tide since the Civil War — at least until a comparatively recent date. Wealth and industrial prosperity progressed with leaps and bounds, but the gains for democracy were few. Great individual fortunes, the industrial combination, and the material development of the West absorbed attention.)

(And yet, with all these anti-democratic influences at work, there were clear evidences of the persistence of democratic forces, even though concealed and obscured. From 1872 to 1912 a succession of minor parties, or reform movements within the two major party organizations, asserted new democratic demands with ever-increasing emphasis and with greater and greater political strength, until in 1912 a considerable majority of the voters endorsed them. Evidently the democratic influences of the West were still active.)As Professor Turner declared in 1910, the Granger, the Greenback-Labor, and Populist parties were continuing expressions of deep-seated forces rather "than fragmentary and sporadic curios for the historical museum." These democratic tendencies gradually emerged, first in the form of the so-called "third parties," just mentioned, and later captured the Democratic Party under the lead of Mr. Bryan and the Republican Party under the direction of Mr. Roosevelt. The Progressive Party of 1912 was a temporary merger of all these elements. What might have happened had not the great European War begun in 1914 must remain unanswered. The events of 1912 make it plain that democracy has still place and power in the settled and developed West of the twentieth century even as it had in the thirties and forties of the last century.

ORGANIZATION OF LABOR

(Another influential factor in democratic development in the United States has been the organization of labor.) Beginning soon after 1800 in a small way in New England, New York, and Pennsylvania, it has grown with the development of industry until the American Federation of Labor and the Railroad Brotherhoods have been able to negotiate with the Federal Government as representative of millions of workers. The organization of labor has been an accompaniment of our industrial progress — it represents another result of the working-out of economic forces in this country. As workmen have increased in numbers and importance, they have demanded a larger share in the control of the conditions under which they are required to work. Parallel with the growth of industrial absolutism has developed the demand for industrial democracy — for that self-government in industry that shall match and complete political and religious democracy.

The organization of labor has been most conspicuous in the older industrial communities of the East and in the great cities from the Atlantic to the Pacific. The political activities of labor organizations have been subordinated to their industrial relations, except in comparatively few instances, since there has not been in the United States the formation of labor parties as in many European countries. In 1878, in 1888, and again in the nineties, more or less successful efforts were made to bring about a merger of the democratic forces originating in the West, and similar forces growing out of the industrial situation in the East and the great cities. But these undertakings brought about no permanent amalgamation. Each has worked independently in its own field. Certain superficial differences have prevented their coöperative action. In spite of this failure to get together and work in open union with Western democracy, organized labor has been the second great force urging us on toward real democracy in the United States. It has supplemented the efforts of minor parties and, while rarely openly coöperating, it has usually been sympathetic and helpful.

INFLUENCE OF SOCIAL WORK

(A third factor in democratic progress in the United States has been the influence of a generation of social work) Beginning in organized form with the Associated Charities of Buffalo in 1877, and with the Social Settlement in New York and Chicago in 1889, the experience of social workers gradually developed a social programme which was largely adopted by the Progressive Party in 1912. This programme was the result of a thorough study of the social and industrial conditions in the great cities, and involved the application of European experience to the American situation. It had been gradually evolved by social workers in the course of dealing with concrete industrial and social problems. They had progressed from remedial to preventive measures, and finally reached a stage where they realized that society must take a hand. Hence their programme for social and industrial justice — a scheme of legislation aimed to meet in a constructive way the many needs they had wrestled with individually and in groups.

As in the case of the minor parties and of the organization of labor, this work of preparation and education was done outside of the great political organizations and has accomplished its results by a process of permeation. Gradually the two major parties have had forced upon their attention social and industrial issues and they have been compelled to give them a large place in their platforms. They have had to give up, somewhat reluctantly, exclusive consideration of political and constitutional questions, and to recognize more and more plainly the fundamental importance of the social and economic forces that have shaped our political parties from the beginning, although for many years the political and constitutional emphasis concealed the real nature of the political situation.

✗ (The great campaigns of 1896 and 1912 made it clearly evident that our democracy must be socialized. The real, vital progress toward social democracy in the United States is going on within the ranks of the two major political parties, and the initial impetus in each party has come from outside; it has come from the democratic spirit of the West, from organized labor, and from the experience of a generation of social work. All these influences are social and economic in their origin and they have consequently carried us well along the road toward a reasoned and hopeful social democracy.)

SOCIALIZATION OF POLITICS

✗ (This socialization of the Democratic and Republican parties under the leadership of Bryan, Roosevelt, and Wilson explains the insignificance politically of organized socialism in the United States. So long as the two major parties and their leaders remain so amenable to permeation from outside, no socialist party will have more than temporary importance or success. Social democracy will come, and is coming rapidly, and its advent has been hastened by the great European upheaval, but that social democracy will prove to be only an orderly progress from one reform to another, and will be no more revolutionary and disturbing than the changes through which we are now passing.) In spite of the disappointments of the Russian Revolution and the curious blindness of our own socialists, social democracy does not necessarily mean stupidity nor an inability to penetrate beneath the surface of things. The chief reason why organized or scientific socialism remains after forty years an exotic in the United States is because it was and is a foreign importation, introduced by persons who are themselves unacquainted with American conditions. (Social democracy is really coming in the United States as an orderly development out of the political, constitutional, economic, and industrial progress of the country. The democratic West has been a chief source as it has marched across the continent, but its impulse has been strengthened by other influences such as that of the organized working-men and of the social workers in our cities.)

SELECTED REFERENCES

1. Turner: "The Significance of the Frontier in American History," in the *Annual Report of the American Historical Association* for the year 1893, pp. 199–227. Also in Turner: *The Frontier in American History*, pp. 1–38.
2. Turner: *The Frontier in American History*.
3. Turner: "Social Forces in American History," in *The American Historical Review*, vol. XVI, pp. 217–33.
4. Turner: "The Problem of the West," in the *Atlantic Monthly*, vol. LXXVIII, pp. 289–97.
5. Turner: "Contributions of the West to American Democracy," in the *Atlantic Monthly*, vol. XCI, pp. 83–96.
6. Beard: *An Economic Interpretation of the Constitution of the United States*.
7. Beard: *Economic Origins of Jeffersonian Democracy*.
8. Libby: "The Geographical Distribution of the Vote of the Thirteen States on the Federal Constitution, 1787–88," in *Bulletin of the University of Wisconsin*, Economics, Political Science History Series, vol. I, no. 1.
9. Wilson: "The Proper Perspective of American History," in *The Forum*, vol. XIX, pp. 544–59.
10. Common's *Documentary History of American Industrial Society*, vol. VII, pp. 19–44; vol. IX, pp. 19–51.
11. Simons: *Social Forces in American History*.
12. Ross: *Changing America*, chap. IX.
13. Ghent: *Mass and Class*.
14. Nicholson: *The Valley of Democracy*.
15. Schlesinger: *New Viewpoints in American History*.

CHAPTER II

UTOPIAN SOCIALISM IN THE UNITED STATES

SOCIALISM before 1850 was a humanitarian rather than a political or economic movement. The utopian socialists did not understand the new industrial system, and acted upon the general principle that the evils arising from it were "arbitrary deviations" from natural law due to the acts of the dominant powers in society. They believed, with the eighteenth century philosophers, that governments were made and unmade by the deliberate acts of men, as described by Rousseau in his "Social Contract," and they therefore usually planned a form of society which would be free from the evils of the existing system and urged its adoption. Frequently, the plan was presented in the form of a description of an imaginary country with a government and manner of life free from the evils of the contemporary social organization.

The "Utopia" of Sir Thomas More was the model for many of these reformers, and they hoped by a limited test of their plans in a small community to convert gradually the entire world to their proposed systems. Hence the utopian socialists frequently were responsible for the establishment of such communities as social experiment stations. In fact the principal concrete manifestations of this phase of socialism are to be found in a great number of communities that were undertaken both in Europe and the United States from 1820 to 1850, as the result of the activities of Robert Owen, Charles Fourier, Étienne Cabet, and other utopian socialists.

Communistic Experiments

For a number of reasons the United States was the chief theater of these communistic experiments, which needed large tracts of cheap land in places at a distance from the evil influences of existing industrial conditions. There was, of course, an abundance of such land in North America down to the middle of the nineteenth century, and in addition the political and religious situation naturally attracted those who were inspired by dreams of a new social order. Hillquit, in his "History of Socialism in the United States," estimates that several hundred communities were established, and that the number of persons who participated in them ran into hundreds of thousands.

But the establishment of communities in the United States was not confined to the efforts of the utopian socialists. Even earlier religious or sectarian communities were founded in which communism was incidental or subordinate to religion. Among these sectarian communities was the "Rappist community," made up of German immigrants, who came to this country in 1804, and settled first in Pennsylvania, and later moved to Indiana where they bought the property which they sold in 1824 to Robert Owen.

The most remarkable of these religious communities was the Amana Society, which originated in Germany early in the eighteenth century, and which removed to America in 1842, and settled near Buffalo, New York. In 1855 they purchased land in eastern Iowa, and established there a settlement which now consists of seven villages with a population of 1800. These people own twenty-six thousand acres of "the richest bottom-land and the most fertile upland in all Iowa — including that variety of surface and soil requisite for meadows, grain fields, pastures, and vineyards, in addition to an abundant supply of water. Besides, there are the well-timbered hills which have furnished most of the building materials and all of the fuel for the entire community for over half a century without any present indication of ever being completely stripped." [1]

Like other communities of this kind, the socialistic elements are merely accidental, adopted after arrival in America to meet immediate needs. The Amana Community is the strongest of the surviving societies in point of numbers and in wealth. Its continuance depends, however, far more upon its religious and racial composition than upon its communistic or utopian form of government.

The existence of these religious communities is an indication that such a form of organization was not original with nor confined to the utopian socialists. It represented a rather widespread tendency of the period, and it was a manifestation, too, of the belief in a golden age, or in an ideal form of society, which has hovered before the eyes of men and women through the ages.

There were two periods of activity of utopian socialism in the United States. One group of communities was founded either by Robert Owen directly, or under the influence of his agitation. These communities were the first to be organized in this country in support of a general social theory and for purposes of general propaganda. As many as twelve are known to have been founded, and probably many more may have existed for a brief time. They were undertaken chiefly during the years from 1825 to 1830. The second group was the result of the activity of the American followers of Charles Fourier, and his so-called "phalanxes" were the principal features of the first socialist system in the United States to become national in its character. The agitation lasted from 1840 to 1850, and produced over forty communities in different parts of the

[1] Shambaugh: *Amana: The Community of True Inspiration*, p. 93.

country. Still another community, Icaria, and its numerous offshoots, grew out of the work of another Frenchman, Étienne Cabet. It was founded in 1848 and by a process of schisms and migrations, prolonged its existence for about half a century. It was confined almost entirely to Frenchmen, and had little general influence upon American social development.

ROBERT OWEN AND NEW HARMONY

In 1824 Robert Owen purchased the town of Harmony, Indiana, from the Rappite Community for $150,000, for the purpose of establishing a community of the kind which he had worked out during his experience as a cotton manufacturer at New Lanark, near Glasgow, Scotland. In 1817, when invited by a committee of the House of Commons to state his views on the cause of increasing pauperism and to propose measures of relief, Owen had proposed the establishment of industrial communities on the basis of mutual coöperation. The communities were to consist of from one thousand to fifteen hundred persons who would produce all the necessaries of life, and who were to be housed in buildings belonging to the community. There was to be common ownership of property and common enjoyment of the proceeds of community industries. Owen believed that the cause of poverty was to be found in the competition of human labor with the new machinery, and that the only remedy was through the united action of men, and the subordination of machinery. His plan was rejected as too radical, but he continued his agitation, and awaited a favorable opportunity to undertake the experiment with his own resources. The desire of the Rappites to sell the town of Harmony seemed to offer the kind of opportunity he needed, and he purchased it.

Upon his arrival in the United States, he exhibited models of the proposed communities, and delivered addresses in many American cities where he found many interested listeners among the most intelligent classes. To give the widest possible publicity to his plan and views, he secured the use of the Hall of the House of Representatives in Washington, and there on the evenings of February 25 and March 7, 1825, delivered long addresses to distinguished audiences. Among his auditors were the President, the President-elect, all the justices of the Supreme Court, and many Senators and Representatives.

From Washington, Owen went directly to Harmony, to which he had invited "the industrious and well-disposed of all nations" to come, and in April, 1825, he met a motley crowd of men and women in the old Rappite Church, which he called New Harmony Hall. He formed a preliminary society of New Harmony, established a constitution which was to continue three years, and left the management of affairs in the hands of a committee. There was no objection to these arrangements, for the people there were really his guests, and everything had been provided by and belonged to Owen. "At his expense one hundred and thirty children were boarded, clothed, and taught, and a band maintained in order that the people might dance every Tuesday and listen to a concert every Friday evening."

After making these preliminary arrangements, Owen went back to England and did not return to New Harmony till January, 1826. He found a situation which required immediate reorganization. Consequently, he drafted a new constitution for what he now called the New Harmony Community of Equality, which provided for "freedom of speech, absolute equality of rights and equality of duties, common ownership of property, coöperation to the fullest extent, and a rigid practice of economy." To secure these ends, six departments were created — agriculture, manufacture, and mechanics; literature, science, and education; domestic economy; general economy; commerce." Under the new organization and under Owen's personal control, the community for the first time showed signs of prosperity. To the town had come also men of marked ability, who believed in the community system and in its ultimate success.

Owen's first reforms had been cheerfully accepted, but his next proposals caused trouble. He decreed uniformity of dress, prescribing for men an outer garment consisting of "a collarless jacket, drawn on over the head, pantaloons buttoned to the jacket, and a belt around the waist." The women were required "to wear pantalets and a sleeveless frock that came down to the knees." Many refused to wear the new costume and would have nothing to do with those who did. Owen patiently bore with the recalcitrant, whom he regarded as the fruit of the irrational system in which they had been trained.

In July, 1826, he made a "Declaration of Mental Independence" which shocked and horrified far more people than it ever converted. "Man, he said, up to that hour, all the world over, had been a slave to a trinity of the most monstrous evils that could possibly be combined to inflict mental and physical evils on the whole race. One was private or individual ownership of property; another was absurd and irrational systems of religion; the third was the marriage tie, which, he declared, ought to be made without any ceremony and terminated at the pleasure of those concerned. This was too much. His theories about property and coöperation, the arrangement of building, and the education of the children were matters of opinion. In a land of toleration he might hold any religious belief or none. But the moment he touched the marriage rite he touched public morality, and his views were denounced from one end of the country to the other. Newspaper after newspaper attacked him. People whose friends, sisters, daughters, had gone to New Harmony were shocked and alarmed." In vain did leading members declare that no immorality or vice existed there. The prosperity of the community was destroyed, and in a little while three hostile factions existed. In less than six months New Harmony was taking on all the characteristics of a village of the ordinary sort; before a year had passed, Owen, discouraged with the conditions he saw around him, left his followers to their fate.

OWENISM AFTER NEW HARMONY

After the failure of New Harmony, Owen made three visits to the United States in the interest of socialism. In 1845 he called an international socialist convention to meet in New York, but it was an insignificant affair. The next year he was at Albany explaining to the Constitutional Convention his theory of the formation of human character. His four sons became American citizens, and his oldest son, Robert Dale Owen, was the foremost exponent of his father's theories in the United States. This son was twice elected to Congress and drafted the act under which the Smithsonian Institution was established. As a member of the Indiana Constitutional Convention, he had a share in the enactment of liberal provisions for women's rights and for the introduction of the free-school system. A letter written by him to President Lincoln is said to have been a potent influence in bringing about the proclamation abolishing slavery. All of Robert Owen's sons were talented and achieved reputation in their chosen occupations. [1]

While the history of New Harmony was developing, other

---

[1] McMaster: *A History of the People of the United States*, vol. v, pp. 88–102; Spargo: *Americanism and Social Democracy*, p. 5.

communities of a similar kind, and inspired by Owen's propaganda, were springing up in various places. At Nashoba in Tennessee one was established which in many ways exceeded all others in interest. The founder was Frances Wright, one of the early advocates of women's rights. She was born in Scotland, and, while a young girl, she spent two years in New England. She then returned to England, greatly impressed with society and conditions in America. From England she went to France, and lived three years in the family of Lafayette where her admiration for the United States was naturally increased. In 1824 she again visited this country, and discovered for the first time that slavery existed. She set herself the problem of finding some way by which slavery could be gradually abolished, and undertook to apply to the negro the same system of education that Owen had made use of in dealing with the laboring classes in Scotland. Accordingly, she visited the Rappites, studied the system of the Shakers, was at New Harmony when the Rappites left and the Owenites began to arrive, and by 1825 had determined upon a plan of action.

She proposed that sections of the public domain should be purchased in the Southern States; that colonies of one or two hundred slaves should be settled on each; that coöperative labor on the community plan should be introduced and the negroes educated and fitted for freedom. The labor of each slave was to be estimated at its full market value; the cost of food and clothing was to be deducted, and the surplus set aside to form a fund to purchase his freedom and that of his children. As an example of such a community, Miss Wright, in the fall of 1825, purchased twenty-four hundred acres, thirteen miles from Memphis, and founded there a town which she named Nashoba. Money was freely given and the experiment tried, but it shared the fate of New Harmony, and in 1829 the founder took her negroes to Hayti. Later she was associated with Robert Dale Owen in reform propaganda, and had a part in the formation of a Working-men's Party in New York, which elected four of its candidates to the Legislature in 1830.

Thus the Owenite agitation was linked up with early labor and social reform movements in the United States. After the War of 1812 the Industrial Revolution had begun, and the development of the factory system was producing on a small scale the same kind of problems which were later to appear on a larger scale. Especially, the growth of cities, like New York and Philadelphia, each of which had in 1820 over one hundred thousand people, and Boston and Baltimore with more than forty thousand inhabitants, forced upon these communities some attention to the needs of the increasing class of factory workers with their conditions of life and labor. The condition-of-the-people question began to emerge as it has in every part of the world as the effect of the Industrial Revolution has come to be recognized.

Anti-slavery agitation, the woman's rights movement, temperance, and other reforms were also under discussion by different groups. Everything was still vague and indefinite, but some real evils were leading to increased unrest. Into such an unsettled and undeveloped situation the Owenite propaganda came, and formed a nucleus around which much of the incipient unrest gathered. Had not all of these agitations been drawn into the anti-slavery movement later, some real social progress might have resulted, although it is probable that conditions were not then ripe for real reform, and the Owenite propaganda was not clear as to its aims and purposes. Owen himself destroyed all prospects, even of temporary or partial success in the United States, as he had already in England, by unnecessary attacks upon religion and by his radical expressions about marriage. The latter views were particularly unfortunate because they were so entirely opposed to the example set by his own domestic life. Owen's utopian socialism, and his relation to contemporary agitations in the United States, are interesting episodes in our social history, but have no vital connection with later movements.

FOURIERISM IN THE UNITED STATES

The second group of communities to be established in the United States under the inspiration of the utopian socialists was the result of the activities of the American followers of Charles Fourier, a French socialist whose life covered the years from 1772 to 1837. The different movements for social reform which agitated the country during the decade of the forties were variously known as "Association, Fourierism, Agrarianism, Socialism, and Community System." Socialism during this period was understood to imply the community of property advocated by Owen; the word "communism" had not yet come into general use. Later on socialism was used to describe any scheme of social organization which was not competitive. The followers of Fourier called themselves "Associationists." [1]

The social principles of Fourier were introduced into the United States by Albert Brisbane (1809–90), the only son of a well-to-do New York landowner, who received a thorough and liberal education, and who spent his early manhood traveling in Europe and Asia. He became interested in the work of the utopian socialists, and after the collapse of the St. Simonian school, he found in the doctrines of Fourier an idea which he had never met before — "the idea of *dignifying* and *rendering attractive* the manual labor

[1] Commons: *A Documentary History of American Industrial Society*, vol. VII, p. 147.

of mankind; labor hitherto regarded as a divine punishment inflicted on man." He went to Paris in 1832 and remained there two years, studying the more intricate features of the system, partly under Fourier's personal guidance, and also taking part in the propaganda which was just beginning to be undertaken. After his return to the United States, he carried on his work quietly until 1840, when he published his exposition of Fourier's system under the title of "Social Destiny of Man." About one half consisted of extracts from Fourier, while the remainder was devoted to comments and illustrations suitable to American conditions. The book was written in a popular style, and had an immediate and great success. It was published at a time when the country was suffering from the effects of the first great crisis experienced in the United States, that of 1837 and the years directly after, and when, consequently, an unusually large number of persons were interested in social problems.

Brisbane's book was not only widely read, but it also secured the support of Horace Greeley, who was just then at the beginning of his great career as a journalist. His interest in social reforms was already aroused, for he had been engaged in the relief of the distress in New York City, which had resulted from the crisis of 1837. Two years after the publication of Brisbane's book, when the "New York Tribune," founded by Greeley in the mean time, had obtained a considerable circulation, its columns were opened to the discussion of the new doctrines. The arrangement provided for the use of a column daily on the first page of the paper "by the advocates of association, in order to lay their principles before the public." Its editorial direction was stated to be "entirely distinct from that of the 'Tribune.'" Brisbane edited the column until he went to Europe again in the summer of 1844. At first the articles attracted "little attention, and less opposition," but gradually "Fourierism became one of the topics of the time," and was quite widely discussed, receiving support as well as criticism and disapproval.

Greeley's share in the agitation was not limited to the sale of space in the "Tribune." Sometimes he referred to the subject editorially, and always in such a way as to attract attention. He spoke whenever and wherever there was opportunity, and he took a very active and influential part in the meetings of the Fourierists, and in the attempts to establish "phalanxes." His most famous undertaking was a discussion carried on in the columns of the "Tribune" and the "New York Courier and Enquirer" with the editor of the latter paper, Henry J. Raymond. The debate lasted six months, beginning November 20, 1846, and ending May 20, 1847. It attracted much attention, and the twenty-four articles of which it consisted were later published by Harpers in a "pamphlet of eighty-three closely printed, double-columned pages," which had a considerable sale, and had long been out of print in 1868, when Parton's "Life of Horace Greeley" was first published.

After Brisbane and Greeley, the most important person in the movement, was Parke Godwin, associate editor of the "Evening Post," and son-in-law of its editor, William Cullen Bryant, the poet. A pamphlet published by him in 1843, under the title of "Democracy, Constructive and Pacific," is described by Hillquit as "one of the most effective weapons in the literary arsenal of Fourierism. The pamphlet contained but little more than fifty pages, but in brilliancy of style, power of argument, and soundness of views, it excelled everything else written in this country in defense of Fourierism. Parke Godwin was one of the first American socialists to divine the tendencies of the capitalist mode of production, and he came very near the modern socialist conception of the class struggle. His appeal was addressed principally to working-men." Godwin also published a "Popular View of the Doctrines of Charles Fourier" and a "Life of Charles Fourier." [1]

Fourierist societies were formed in Massachusetts, New York, New Jersey, Pennsylvania, Ohio, Illinois, Indiana, Wisconsin, and Michigan. State conventions were held from time to time, and in April, 1844, a national convention met in New York City. George Ripley, the founder of Brook Farm, was elected president, and among the vice-presidents were Greeley, Brisbane, and Godwin. It was described as a "most noteworthy and enthusiastic gathering." Many resolutions were adopted, most of them dealing with the organization of associations. Communities modeled upon the plan of Fourier's "phalanxes" were declared to be the universal remedy for all social evils, but members were warned against experiments undertaken on too small a scale and with insufficient preparations. The convention decided to form a permanent national organization with an official organ and an executive committee. It also favored the international coöperation of Fourierists, and appointed Brisbane to confer with European representatives. The period immediately before and after the national convention was the time of greatest prosperity in the Fourierist movement in the United States.

Fourier maintained that a "phalanx" could not be made a success unless it had a membership of from fifteen hundred to two thousand persons, and a capital of about one million francs. Brisbane reduced the number of persons required to four hundred, but believed that a capital of four hundred thousand dollars was necessary. The leading Fourierists in the United States warned the enthusiasts

[1] McMaster: *A History of the People of the United States*, vol. VII, pp. 142-45.

against hasty experiments with insufficient capital and members, but very little attention was paid to the warning. Phalanxes grew rapidly, and were undertaken by any number of persons with small amounts of capital, and sometimes without any at all. Soon the States in which the movement had taken root were covered with a "veritable network." The history of these attempts was "one monotonous record of failure." The only phalanxes that seemed at any time to justify an expectation of permanent success were the North American Phalanx in New Jersey, the Brook Farm Phalanx in Massachusetts, and the Wisconsin Phalanx. Of these the first lasted over twelve years, and the others five and six years respectively. The average life of all other undertakings was about fifteen months.

BROOK FARM AND TRANSCENDENTALISM

Brook Farm, the most famous of these phalanxes, was located at West Roxbury, nine miles from Boston. Its greater fame is due chiefly to the fact that it attracted to itself a number of persons who later achieved reputation and standing in literature. It did not begin as a Fourieristic experiment, but grew out of a philosophical and humanitarian movement which existed in New England in the thirties of the last century. A group of people, many of whom lived in Boston and vicinity, came to be known as the "Transcendental Club." They were enthusiasts and advocates of all the social, political, and religious reforms of the time. George Ripley, their leader, declared that they were called Transcendentalists because they believed in an order of truth that transcended the sphere of the external senses. One of their critics spoke of them as persons who "dove into the infinite, soared into the illimitable, and never paid cash." A result of the activity of the Transcendentalists was a magazine of high literary standard called

"The Dial," which was published irregularly, and contained contributions from the pens of the famous men and women connected with the movement.

In 1840 Ripley decided to establish a community in which a practical application of the principles and theories of the Transcendentalists could be made. A site was chosen in the spring of 1841, and about twenty persons, including Ripley, his wife and sister, John S. Dwight, Nathaniel Hawthorne, and William Allen, established themselves at Brook Farm. The official name was "The Brook Farm Institute for Agriculture and Education," and the object, as formulated by its founders in the Articles of Association, was "to more effectually promote the great purposes of human culture; to establish the external relations of life on a basis of wisdom and purity; to apply the principles of justice and love to our social organization in accordance with the laws of Divine Providence; *to substitute a system of brotherly coöperation for one of selfish competition;* to secure for our children, and to those who may be entrusted to our care, the benefits of the highest physical, intellectual, and moral education which, in the present state of human knowledge, the resources at our command will permit; to institute an attractive, efficient, and productive system of industry; to prevent the exercise of worldly anxiety by the competent supply of our necessary wants; to diminish the desire of excessive accumulation by making the acquisition of individual property subservient to upright and disinterested uses; to guarantee to each other the means of physical support and of spiritual progress, and thus to impart a greater freedom, simplicity, truthfulness, refinement, and moral dignity, to our mode of life."

It was also agreed that the property of the community should be in the form of shares and that all shareholders should be provided with employment suitable to their abilities and preferences. There was to be a uniform rate of compensation for all labor; a maximum working day of ten hours; free support of children under the age of ten, of persons over seventy, and of those unable to work because of sickness; education, medical attendance, and the use of library and bath were to be free to all.

The principal feature of the new community was its school, which was divided into four departments, and provided for children of all ages from under six to those ready to enter college. A wide range of sciences and arts was taught, and equal attention was paid to physical and mental development. Many men, who later took an important part in the literary and political life of the country, were educated in the Brook Farm School.

In the course of three years the membership of the community grew to about seventy, but the financial success was only moderate, and life was "full of toil and devoid of earthly comforts." And yet the Brook Farmers understood how to lighten their burdens by good fellowship, games, dances, music, excursions, and literary and scientific discussions in their leisure hours. Life was also made more attractive by the visits of friends from the outside world, among whom were Margaret Fuller, the Channings, Theodore Parker, Miss Peabody, and others.

Soon after the national convention in New York in 1844, Brook Farm declared itself a Fourieristic community and became the "Brook Farm Phalanx." The change was not a radical one, as a reference to the Articles of Association and the mode of life will show, but it led to the development of Brook Farm as the center and head of the Fourieristic propaganda. The publication of the weekly magazine, the "Harbinger," was established there, and its columns opened a new field for the literary talents of the Brook Farmers. They also sent out some of their members upon lecture tours to urge the advantages of Fourierism to the outside world. The Association was incorporated and it was determined to build a large unitary building, or phalanstery.

Brook Farm was in its period of greatest prosperity. It was widely known and its visitors numbered thousands every year. It had many applications for membership and its finances were gradually improving. After two years of work, the new phalanstery was nearing completion, and it was expected thát the large building would enable the Association to admit members who had been kept out because of lack of room, and that the resources and efficiency of the community would be greatly increased thereby. Just as these anticipations were about to be realized, the large new wooden structure caught fire through some negligence of the workmen and was totally destroyed. The loss proved fatal, and, after a hopeless struggle through the spring and summer of 1846, the Association broke up in the autumn. The "Harbinger" was transferred to New York, and the property sold.

Étienne Cabet

Another French socialist, Étienne Cabet, was responsible for a series of communities, or rather for one community with a number of offshoots. Cabet, who was born in 1788, was affiliated from an early age with the secret revolutionary societies which abounded in Paris at that time. He was active in the revolution of 1830, and at first received preferment under the monarchy of Louis Philippe. His intense democracy, however, led him into the opposition and he was banished for five years. He went to England, and while there he worked out a system of communism quite similar to that of Robert Owen. In 1839, he returned to France, and published his "Voyage en Icarie" (Voyage to

Icaria). The book was in the form of a novel, and was much like More's "Utopia." Its success was extraordinary, and it appealed especially to the working-men, who were in a constant state of unrest and discontent during the years between 1830 and 1848. By 1847 Cabet was said to have had a following of four hundred thousand.

His enthusiastic supporters urged the establishment of a community in which his theories might be tested. Accordingly in May, 1847, he issued a proclamation to the French working-men, urging them to go with him to "Icaria," which he proposed to found "somewhere in America." Following the advice of Robert Owen, he purchased a tract of land in Texas, and sent out the first settlers early in 1848. The "advance-guard" found that Cabet had been deceived by the American land agents, and the first site, therefore, had to be abandoned. Late in 1848 Cabet himself arrived at New Orleans, and in March, 1849, with about two hundred and eighty persons, located at Nauvoo, Illinois, the site of the Mormon colony before its removal to Utah. For a number of years the Icarians were fairly prosperous, and received new settlers from France and the United States, until their membership had nearly doubled. For a time Cabet exercised his power as president discreetly, but as he grew old, he became narrow and arbitrary. Gradually, two parties developed, and finally in October, 1856, Cabet was formally expelled from the community, and with a faithful minority of about one hundred and eighty persons went to St. Louis, where he died early in November, 1856, as the result of a sudden stroke of apoplexy.

The group which left Nauvoo with Cabet later settled on an estate six miles from St. Louis where it remained until its dissolution in 1864. Those who were left in possession at Nauvoo decided, after Cabet's expulsion, to remove to a site near Corning in Adams County in southwestern Iowa, where they had already in 1852 purchased three thousand acres of land. The transfer was made in 1860, and for a number of years the community endured great hardships because of the isolation and the privations of pioneer life. After a time, the Civil War and the buildings of railroads enabled them to sell their surplus farm products to a better advantage, and thus to improve their financial condition. For a number of years they enjoyed moderate prosperity, but again two parties gradually developed, and in 1877–78 the controversy was taken into court. The community never recovered from the effects of the split. One group removed to California where they established a new settlement which lasted only from 1884 to 1887. The other group struggled to revive the old community, but without much success, and it was finally dissolved in 1895.[1]

UTOPIAN SOCIALISM AND LATER MOVEMENTS

The communities established by the utopian socialists during the first half of the nineteenth century had little influence upon the later forms of socialism either in Europe or in the United States. Occasionally, we find some connection between the earlier and later movements, but these instances are usually exceptional and are not indications of any vital or important relations.

Some of the Fourierists took a sympathetic interest in the development of later socialism, but as a rule they did not have any important place, and with some radical views did not long survive the disappointment of their hopes in social reform. Brisbane lived until 1890, but he spent much of his time in Europe, and lived the life of a scholar and artist. He was a sympathetic but passive observer of the progress of modern socialism. Godwin lived until 1904,

---

[1] Teakle: "History and Constitution of the Icarian Community," in *The Iowa Journal of History and Politics*, vol. xv, pp. 214–86.

but there is no evidence of any social interest upon his part after the passing of Fourierism.

Horace Greeley remained a radical to the end, and Professor Commons has worked out a very interesting theory which compares his relation to "the social revolution of the forties" with that of "Thomas Jefferson to the political revolution of 1800." [1] Whether we accept this suggestive explanation or not, it is true that Greeley's activities after the forties were in other fields than those of modern socialism. His paper, the "Tribune," was the spokesman of the plain people of the country, and its energies, as theirs, were absorbed in the anti-slavery conflict and reconstruction down to his death in 1872. Furthermore, since the recent socialist movement dates only from about 1876, we have no way of knowing what would have been his attitude to later movements. The Republican Party of his day was in many ways a radical party, and probably represented quite fully and completely his ideas as to political and social development.

Utopian socialism failed to leave any strong impression because it appealed chiefly to persons above the laboring-classes. It received support largely from the middle, well-to-do, literary, and professional classes, from people who felt somehow that there was need of reform, and who were breaking away from old established conventions and customs. These people were eager for all sorts of new things, and the wonderful changes in industry were beginning to attract their attention. Utopian socialism was intellectual and moral rather than social and political. It did not so much wish or undertake to reform political and social life generally. Its advocates preferred to retire from the world

[1] Commons: *A Documentary History of American Industrial Society*, vol. vII, pp. 20–44. The same article is in the *Political Science Quarterly*, vol. xxIV, pp. 468–88.

into a community, and to work out a better social order for themselves and their companions. American conditions favored the acceptance of liberal ideas of many kinds, but the social and industrial situation was not yet ready for such economic analysis as Karl Marx applied to English society in the middle of the last century, and from the study of which he evolved his socialism. Modern socialism was to develop later in the United States as the result of "the observed and experienced variance" between the theory of our law and the facts, and would attempt "to make the facts correspond to the theory" — in other words, "to add the social function to democracy." [1]

SELECTED REFERENCES

1. Kirkup: *A History of Socialism*, chaps. II, III, IV.
2. Hillquit: *History of Socialism in the United States*, part I, chaps. I-IV.
3. Shambaugh: *Amana: The Community of True Inspiration.*
4. Swift: *Brook Farm: Its Members, Scholars, and Visitors.*
5. Codman: *Brook Farm: Historic and Personal Memoirs.*
6. Frothingham: *George Ripley*, chaps. III, IV.
7. Shaw: *Icaria: A Chapter in the History of Communism.*
8. Commons: *A Documentary History of American Industrial Society*, vol. VII, pp. 20–44.
9. Commons: "Horace Greeley and the Working-Class Origins of the Republican Party," in the *Political Science Quarterly*, vol. XXIV, pp. 468–88.
10. Lockwood: *The New Harmony Movement.*
11. Parton: *The Life of Horace Greeley*, chap. XIV.
12. Bushee: "Communistic Societies in the United States, in the *Political Science Quarterly*, vol. XX, pp. 625–64.
13. Mumford: *The Story of Utopias.*
14. Hertzler: *The History of Utopian Thought.*

---

[1] Vedder: *Socialism and the Ethics of Jesus*, p. 235; Addams: "The Subjective Necessity for Social Settlements," in *Philanthropy and Social Progress*, p. I.

CHAPTER III

MARXIAN SOCIALISM

THE beginnings of modern scientific or Marxian socialism are to be found among the emigrants from Germany during the first half of the nineteenth century. The larger part of this emigration was composed of working-men, but it also included a considerable number of men of education. The revolutions of 1830 and 1848 added "political refugees."

Large German colonies were established in France, England, Switzerland, and Belgium. Under the influence of French utopian socialism they formed secret revolutionary societies and organized clubs for the discussion of social problems. In this way arose the Communist Club, for which Karl Marx and Friedrich Engels drafted the famous "Communist Manifesto" in 1848. Many Germans also emigrated to the United States, and by 1830 they were quite numerous in Pennsylvania, Ohio, New York, and Maryland.

The same influences were felt in the United States as in the German colonies in European countries, and organizations were formed to gather together the political refugees, and to prepare them to return to Germany when the next revolution should break out in that country. These organizations were of little importance until the arrival of William Weitling in 1846, who came upon the invitation of a group of German Free-Soilers. Weitling was born in 1808, and became a socialist at an early age as a result of his travels in France as a journeyman tailor. He was associated with Marx and Engels in Paris and Brussels, and was the author of three socialistic books, published between 1838 and 1846. In the main Weitling was a utopian socialist,

but he had glimpses of the conception of modern socialism in his recognition of class distinctions between the
"poor" and the "wealthy." He seems to have been an influential figure in the German colonies in Europe during
the forties of the last century.

Weitling's first visit to the United States lasted only a
year when, because of rumors of an approaching revolution
in Germany, he hurriedly returned to Europe. After the
failure of the revolution of 1848, he came back, and found
for a few years a wide and fruitful field of activity. He immediately undertook the work of centralizing the social
and labor organizations among the German immigrants.
For this purpose he began the publication of a magazine,
which appeared monthly during 1850, and was converted
into a weekly in April, 1851.

Under his leadership "Central Committees of United
Trades" were formed in New York and other cities. This
movement attracted favorable and unfavorable criticism,
and soon spread beyond the German labor organizations
with which it originated. In September, 1850, a call for a
general working-men's convention, urged by Weitling, was
issued, and in October it was actually held in Philadelphia.
This was the first national meeting of German working-
men in the United States, and is therefore of considerable
significance in the history of the socialist movement in this
country. About forty delegates represented a membership
of 4400, distributed among forty-two organizations in ten
cities, including St. Louis, Baltimore, Pittsburgh, Philadelphia, New York, Buffalo, and Cincinnati.

The political views of the convention were stated in the
motto, "Equal Rights and Duties," and its platform was
composed of twelve planks, most of them borrowed from
the programme of the Free-Soil Party. The delegates also
provided for a central committee in each city to act to-

gether in State and national elections, and they also adopted resolutions in favor of the extension of education, and of the organization of communistic settlements.

The convention failed to designate an official name for the combination of organizations represented, and the body was somewhat vaguely referred to as "the association," or "the union of cities," until the name "General Working-Men's League" was settled upon by general use. The period immediately following the Philadelphia Convention marked the height of the influence of Weitling, and was succeeded by a rapid decline. An attempt by his followers to realize his colonization scheme by founding a settlement, called "Communia" in Clayton County, Iowa, failed disastrously. Finally, Weitling's methods and his self-assertiveness provoked the hostility of many prominent members of the League, and after a violent quarrel he withdrew to private life. The remainder of his life, until his death in 1871, was passed as a clerk in the Bureau of Immigration in New York City. Only once was his retirement broken when he appeared at a joint meeting of the New York sections of the International in January, 1871, three days before his death. The League continued its existence for some years after Weitling's withdrawal, but it never attained the importance which its beginnings seemed to promise.

Several other attempts were made by German leaders to spread the doctrines of Marxian socialism in the American labor movement, but only local success in New York and a few other cities was attained. A Communist Club was organized in New York in 1857, but little is known of its history. Its membership seems to have been made up chiefly of men of the middle classes who had received a good education in Germany. All of these efforts were made by persons who had been associated with Marx and Engles in

European revolutionary circles. Political revolution, the organization of labor, and developing socialistic theories were indiscriminately mixed up in these early undertakings.

The German socialists were actively interested in the anti-slavery movement, and the abolition of slavery was always one of their political demands. As the Civil War became more and more imminent, this issue assumed greater practical importance, and when war finally came in 1861, it absorbed their attention as it did that of all other radical and humanitarian movements. Each of the various socialist groups furnished its full share of soldiers for the Union army. Active propaganda was suspended of necessity during the contest, and it was not until 1867 that the movement began to recover.

The International in the United States

The history of the socialist movement in the United States during the years immediately after the Civil War was very closely connected with the career of the European International of Karl Marx. The influence of this organization was exerted through two distinct channels: (1) through the native American labor movement, especially in connection with the National Labor Union, (2) by means of actual socialists, chiefly of foreign birth, affiliated directly with the International by branch organizations.

After the close of the Civil War a strong trade-union movement began to develop in the United States. Many local and national organizations were formed, but there was no common bond between them. In 1866 a convention was held at Baltimore for the purpose of consolidating the labor forces of the country, at which over sixty organizations were represented. During the debates a German socialist, a follower of Ferdinand Lassalle, first proposed the formation of an independent labor party. He represented the German Working-Men's Association of Chicago and his address is described by Hillquit as "eloquent and persuasive." As an argument for the organization of an independent labor party he pointed out that if the Free-Soil Party had not been formed, Lincoln would never have been President of the United States. His appeal made a deep impression, and he was elected vice-president at large as an indication of "appreciation of his views and abilities."

The first direct reference to the International was made at the second convention of the National Labor Union held in Chicago in 1867. The convention was attended by over two hundred delegates, and the interest in its proceedings was greatly increased by the presence of a real leader, William H. Sylvis, who had shown his ability by the formation of one of the strongest and most prosperous labor organizations in the country at that time — the Iron Molders' National Union. He had also had an active part in the establishment of the National Labor Union, although sickness had prevented him from attending the first convention.

Sylvis brought up again the plan of forming an independent labor party and he urged the establishment of official relations with the International. The convention, however, defeated the first proposal by a close vote and disposed of the second by the adoption of some resolutions, expressing sympathy with the "efforts of the working-classes in Europe to acquire political power, to improve their social conditions, and to emancipate themselves from the bondage under which they were and still are."

Again, in 1868, Sylvis was the leading spirit of the convention of the National Labor Union, and his particular interest — the establishment of an independent labor party — was finally realized by the organization of the National Reform Party, of which he was made president, and for which he drafted the platform. This document was modeled upon the Declaration of Independence, and considerable space was devoted to monetary reforms according to the ideas of the Greenback Party, under the influence of which Sylvis had come. He was very active for the next few months in the work of building up the new party — "a working-men's party — for the purpose of getting control of Congress and the several States legislatures."

At the same time Sylvis had been in correspondence with leading members of the International, and had shown marked inclination in the direction of modern socialism. As a result of this correspondence, the International in May, 1869, addressed an open letter to the National Labor Union in which, after some references to the probable influence of the Civil War upon the progress of the working-class in the United States, it extended a formal invitation to that body to send delegates to the next meeting which was to be held at Basle in August, 1869. The invitation was accepted by the National Labor Union, and a delegate was elected, who attended the convention of the International and made a very exaggerated report as to the strength of the American organization. A closer affiliation was probably not made because of the sudden death of Sylvis in July. His death not only ended any progress toward closer arrangements with European socialists, but made the continuance of the National Labor Union itself very unlikely unless a new leader was found to replace Sylvis. After a lingering existence of a few years, the Union and its political counterpart, the Labor Reform Party, shared the fate common to all independent political parties formed by American labor organizations before and since.

The other connecting link between American and European socialism during this early period was found in the German labor organizations in the United States, which maintained relations both with the National Labor Union and the International. These German socialists formed the first organizations directly affiliated with the International in this country in 1869. They formed small societies in New York, Chicago, and San Francisco, which were described as "sections" of the International. The "first strictly Marxian organization of strength and influence on American soil" was the "General German Labor Association," which grew out of the activity of the New York "sections." The present socialist movement, according to Hillquit, may be said to date from the formation of that organization. The platform was a sort of a compromise between the principles of the National Labor Union and those of the International. A definite line of demarcation had not as yet anywhere been established between socialism and trade-unionism.

In 1870 the New York sections of the International, by direction of the General Council, constituted themselves into a provisional Central Committee for the United States. By taking advantage of a number of events during that year the new organization succeeded in making substantial progress. The number of sections increased from six to thirty and the cities included in its activity also became more numerous. The membership grew to about five thousand. The press devoted considerable space to its proceedings; its views and methods were widely discussed, and even Congress, in the course of a debate upon the appointment of a commission to investigate labor conditions, paid some attention to its activities.

The rapid growth and widespread interest had some disadvantages, as it attracted all sorts of reformers to its membership. Consequently, conflicts arose and divisions were formed which became so serious that they had to be referred to the General Council for decision.

The first national convention of the International was held in New York City in July, 1872, at which twenty-two sections were represented. The official name of North American Federation of the International Working-Men's Association was adopted, and an executive committee of nine, called the Federal Council, was appointed. A new impetus was given to the movement about the same time by the transfer of the seat of the General Council of the European International from London to New York to avoid its possible control by the anarchists led by Bakunin. F. A. Sorge, a veteran of the German revolution of 1848, and a personal friend of Marx and Engels, was made general secretary. He had come to the United States in 1852, and, while the International continued, he was the leading spirit in the organization. After its dissolution he went into retirement where he remained until his death in 1907.

In April, 1874, a second national convention was held at Philadelphia. The chief topic of discussion related to the policy to be followed in the future by the International. A large number of members, including some of the most active, urged that greater attention should be given to the labor movement at home than abroad, and that coöperation should be permitted with portions of the labor movement which could not be regarded as strictly socialistic. The older and more influential members, however, insisted upon the maintenance of the established policy and refused to make any concessions to the minority. The result was the formation of rival socialist parties in New York and Chicago. The New York organization took the name of the Social Democratic Working-Men's Party of North America and it had a part in the formation of the Socialist Labor Party.

The last convention of the International was held in Philadelphia in July, 1876. It was composed of ten delegates from the United States and one who was supposed to represent a group of German members. Under such circumstances it was apparent that the existence of the organization was only nominal, and the delegates at once proceeded to dissolve it formally. Before adjourning, the convention adopted an address to their "Fellow Working-Men," in which they explained the reasons for their action, and urged that the principles of the International should be guarded until the time came again when the conditions were favorable for the formation of a new organization. The address closed with the cry: "Proletarians of all countries, unite!"

The Social Democratic Working-Men's Party of North America was formed in July, 1874, by several New York sections of the International which had withdrawn earlier in the year. In conjunction with them were some radical labor organizations of New York, Philadelphia, and a couple of smaller cities. The founders of the party were mainly German socialists who had come under the influence of Ferdinand Lassalle. They attached greater importance to political methods than did the adherents of Karl Marx.

As the International declined in the United States, the new party gained a certain amount of strength and influence. Its second convention was held in Philadelphia in July, 1875, and was well attended. The most important act of this convention was the passing of a resolution, instructing the executive committee to use its influence to bring about a union of all the socialist organizations in the country. Out of this action came, more or less indirectly, the Socialist Labor Party, which was for twenty years the dominant factor in the American socialist movement.

Conferences of socialists held during the fall of 1875 did not make any real progress toward union. Meanwhile an effort was being made to revive the National Labor Union, and a convention for this purpose was called to meet at Pittsburgh in April, 1876. The socialists determined to capture this convention and, accordingly, representatives of their various organizations assembled at the same place on the eve of the proposed meeting. The socialists easily carried out their plan, for they were organized, had well-defined views, and knew how to present them, while the other delegates to the convention were a heterogeneous lot, unorganized and broken up into many different groups.

The success was of no practical significance, as the convention adjourned without definite results, but the socialist representatives at Pittsburgh, about twenty in number, agreed upon a plan of union and arranged to hold a convention to complete arrangements within a few months. The proposed meeting was held in Philadelphia from July 19 to 22, 1876.

The convention was composed of seven delegates, representing four organizations with a membership of about three thousand. The four organizations were the North American Federation of the International Working-Men's Association, the Social Democratic Working-Men's Party of North America, the Labor Party of Illinois, and the Socio-Political Labor-Union of Cincinnati. Representatives from a Philadelphia, a Cincinnati, and a Milwaukee organization were refused seats on the ground that their organizations had not been represented at Pittsburgh.

The work of the convention was begun by the consolidation of the four organizations into the Working-Men's Party of the United States. Provision was made for an executive committee of seven, subject to the control of a "board of supervision" of five members. The headquarters of the committee were placed in Chicago, while the board of supervision was located in New Haven. The platform was a "somewhat abstract exposition of the cardinal points of Marxian socialism."

The Socialist Labor Party

At its second meeting in December, 1877, the new Working-Men's Party of the United States changed its name to the Socialist Labor Party of North America, and from that time for twenty years it remained the most important socialist organization in the country. Its history from 1877 to 1897 is the history of American socialism during that period.

The difficulties before the Socialist Labor Party, as the first socialist party on a national scale, were very great. Besides the obstacles in the path of every radical reform movement in the early stages of its development, the new party was handicapped by one great disadvantage peculiar to it. It is estimated that no more than ten per cent of its members were native Americans. The most active and influential leaders were foreigners, unacquainted with the conditions, institutions, and opinions of the country in which they were living, and frequently unable to speak its language. Under the circumstances the special mission of these early advocates of socialism was "to acclimatize the movement and to leave its further development to the American working-men. The endeavor to 'Americanize' the socialist movement is the main keynote of the activity of the Socialist Labor Party throughout its entire career." How to accomplish this result was "the subject of the most animated discussions and heated controversies within the party, it shaped its policy, determined its action, and was at the bottom of most of its struggles."

The founders of the new party discovered two main avenues of approach to American working-men — the trade unions and political activity. Their efforts, however, directed through these two openings, did not meet with the success that they expected.

The situation in the United States differed from that of Europe where socialism had to a certain extent created the trade-union movement. In this country the organization of labor made its appearance before the socialist movement and the Socialist Labor Party found it just entering upon a period of great prosperity. The Knights of Labor held their first general assembly in 1878, and from that date to 1893, under the leadership of T. V. Powderly, who became head of the order in 1879, they enjoyed a phenomenal growth. Three years later, the Federation of Trade and Labor Unions was formed, which, under the name of the American Federation of Labor, after the decline of the Knights of Labor, succeeded to its place and leadership.

These two bodies seemed to the Socialists their natural allies, and they tried to bring the two movements into close coöperation with each other. In spite of these efforts and of the natural sympathy between radical organizations, the Socialist Labor Party failed to exert much influence upon the labor movement. The Socialists were too few in numbers to permeate effectively the widely scattered groups of working-men, and as their failure became evident some of them protested against further work as a waste of time. Especially during periods of industrial depression when labor organizations were greatly weakened, indifference and even hostility developed among the Socialists. The gradual recognition of the futility of their efforts on the part of the Socialists led finally to complete estrangement and open enmity between the two kinds of organizations.

Success through the other avenue of approach — political activity — was no more satisfactory in its results. Among the Socialists two groups existed based upon differences of attitude in regard to participation in politics. One group, made up of native Americans and a number of former followers of Lassalle, advocated political activity, while the other group urged the postponement of such activity until the party was strong enough to make a respectable showing at the polls. According to the political and industrial conditions at any given time one group or the other gained influence in the shaping of party policy. These controversies led to splits in the organization which weakened its efforts even more than its small numbers made inevitable. These splits finally ended its usefulness and led to its replacement by a new party after 1897.

The long period of industrial depression which followed the crisis of 1873 created a sentiment favorable to radical movements. Unemployment and wage reductions led in 1877 to a series of strikes, the most significant of which was that of the railroad employees. Between 1873 and 1877 the wages of railroad workers had been reduced nearly twenty-five per cent and in June, 1877, another reduction of ten per cent was announced. This last reduction provoked the great railroad strikes of that year which extended over seventeen States and in which three hundred lives were lost, one thousand persons injured, and property to the amount of from $12,000,000 to $15,000,000 destroyed. The most serious disturbances occurred in Pittsburgh and St. Louis.

The Socialists had no part in the agitation which brought about the labor troubles of 1877, but they took advantage of the opportunity to spread their doctrines among the excited working-men. Great mass meetings were held in Philadelphia, New York, and Chicago; speakers were active everywhere and printed matter was distributed in all industrial centers. During 1876 and 1877 twenty-four newspapers were started, eight in English, fourteen in German, and two in other languages. Among these papers were eight dailies. Of course most of them survived only for a short time.

The activity of the party resulted in its rapid growth until, early in 1879, there were nearly one hundred sections in twenty-five States, with an estimated total membership of ten thousand. At the convention held in December, 1877, when, as already stated, the Working-Men's Party of the United States took the name the Socialist Labor Party, there were thirty-eight delegates, representing thirty-one sections compared with the seven delegates from four organizations which met the preceding year.

Early in 1878 the "New Yorker Volkszeitung" was established as a daily devoted to socialist and labor interests. It was edited by a staff made up from the ablest journalists in the American socialist movement and it maintained its high position for many years. Its wider influence, however, was limited by the fact that, as its name suggests, it was printed in German.

Industrial prosperity gradually returned, beginning in 1879, and with the coming of better times the new party disintegrated rapidly. Conditions were not yet ready in the United States for the development of a strong socialist movement. Consequently, the membership declined, many sections disbanded, and the party press largely failed for lack of supporters.

Under these discouraging circumstances the second national convention of the Socialist Labor Party was held at Allegheny City, Pennsylvania, December 26, 1879. Twenty-four delegates represented twenty sections; the membership had declined from the estimated ten thousand in 1877 to numbers varying from fifteen hundred to twenty-five hundred. The chief topic of discussion was in regard to the participation of the party in the presidential election of 1880.

Socialists had taken no interest in the Greenback Party as long as it limited its agitation to currency matters, but after 1878, as the new party came into closer relations with the labor movement, their attitude became more friendly. Some sections supported the Greenbackers in the elections of 1878 and 1879, but their support was unofficial and local in character. The national authorities of the party merely tolerated it.

There were three distinct currents of opinion in the meeting. One group stood for a compromise with all liberal and labor organizations in the selection of candidates and in framing a platform. Another group favored the sending of delegates to a Greenback conference to be held in Washington in January, 1880, while a third group urged the nomination of candidates without reference to any other party. The convention decided to name three men to be voted upon by the party membership, the one getting the largest number of votes to be the presidential candidate, and the next, the vice-presidential candidate. No delegates were appointed for the Washington conference, but the party was unofficially represented. By a referendum vote the party reversed its action as to independent nominations and decided to send delegates to the Chicago Convention of the Greenback Party.[1]

As soon as this action had been determined upon, the national executive committee issued a call to all sections and trade unions in sympathy with it to send delegates to a conference in Chicago on August 8, 1880. The national nominating convention of the Greenback Labor Party was to meet in the same city, August 9, 1880, and the Socialist Labor Party conference of the preceding day was to be a

[1] Commons: *History of Labor in the United States*, vol. II, pp. 284–86.

caucus of the delegates of the party who expected to attend the convention. About ninety representatives attended the conference, nearly half of whom were residents of Chicago. Among the delegates were a number of prominent members of the Socialist Labor Party, including Philip Van Patten, the party's secretary, Dr. Adolph Douai, P. J. McGuire, Albert R. Parsons, and T. J. Morgan.

The Socialist conference decided to apply for admission to the Greenback Convention as a body and to vote as a unit upon all questions. It insisted upon the admission of from twenty to fifty delegates and upon the appointment of seven Socialists on the platform committee. The spokesman of the caucus presented these demands to the convention "in behalf of 100,000 voters represented by the Socialist Labor Party," who wished to make common warfare against the money power. The Socialists were given the representation asked for upon the platform committee and were allowed forty-four delegates in the convention. Later in the sessions, a ruling requiring all votes to be taken by States, was opposed by the Socialists, and after its adoption, they abstained from voting.

As the Socialists were too weak numerically to play an important part in the convention, they concentrated their efforts upon the inclusion in the platform of a plank declaring that land, light, air, and water were the free gifts of nature, and that monopolization by any person to the detriment of the rights of others ought to be condemned and abolished as soon as possible. Even this vague and general statement proved unacceptable to the Greenback leaders. By a skillful use of parliamentary methods, they prevented a vote upon it until after the platform had been adopted and the nominations made. Then it was adopted by a large majority as a special resolution, but it was not to be regarded as a part of the platform.

The results of the work of the Socialist delegates in the convention were not satisfactory to many members of the party. The Greenback candidates were endorsed by 608 votes to 396, and the platform by 521 votes to 455. In order to meet the objections made by opponents, Van Patten, the national secretary, wrote General Weaver, the presidential candidate, inquiring whether he accepted the land plank. According to the "Des Moines Register," General Weaver replied in a letter in which he declared his approval of the "Socialist land resolution." [1] But this expression of opinion failed to satisfy many of the objectors. The New York section by resolution stated that the land plank was not socialistic, that Van Patten's letter was uncalled for, and that, therefore, the Socialists ought not to vote for the Greenback candidates.[2] Immediately after the election, the alliance was dissolved and the Socialists took no part in politics in a national way until 1892, when they nominated a presidential candidate of their own.

Late in 1880 and early in 1881 the Socialist Labor Party received temporary reënforcement from the arrival of political refugees from Germany, who had been driven out by the Government in its efforts to enforce the Anti-Socialist Law passed in 1878. The new arrivals were warmly welcomed by their Socialist comrades and public meetings were held for their reception. This general influence in favor of socialism was supplemented by the sending to the United States by the Social Democratic Party of Germany of two representatives to give information in regard to the situation in that country, and to collect funds to carry on the campaign to elect Socialist members to the Reichstag. These delegates reached the United States in February, 1881, and addressed large mass

[1] *Des Moines Register*, August 6, 1880.
[2] Commons: *History of Labor in the United States*, vol. II, pp. 286–90.

meetings in New York, Boston, Philadelphia, Milwaukee, and Chicago. These meetings were made the occasion for general socialist propaganda, and helped to cause a temporary revival of the American socialist movement, but soon after the close of the tour of the German visitors, the Socialist Labor Party relapsed into its previous condition of weakness.   Under these conditions its third convention was held in New York in December, 1881. Seventeen sections were represented by about twenty delegates, most of whom were from New York and Brooklyn. No action of importance was taken, and it was admitted by officials that a majority of the socialists in the United States were outside of the party.

While the Socialist Labor Party was in such a weakened state, it had to face a new and threatening danger from extremists in its own ranks and from others outside of it. At the convention in 1879 a division appeared between the moderate and radical elements; in November a number of members from New York sections left the party and formed a Revolutionary Club, which adopted a platform in which some anarchistic statements were included in a document largely modeled upon the German Socialist programme of 1875.

Similar clubs were formed soon after in Boston, Philadelphia, and Milwaukee, but the most important manifestation of the new tendency occurred in Chicago, where a national convention was held late in 1881, and the Revolutionary Socialist Labor Party was formed. The new organization wavered between a more radical socialism and outspoken anarchism. It lacked a leader until the arrival of John Most in December, 1882.

JOHN MOST

Most, who is described by Robert Hunter in his study of

"Violence and the Labor Movement" as "the most fiery personality that appeared in the ranks of the anarchists after the death of Bakunin," was born in 1846 in Augsburg, Germany. After a cheerless and unhappy childhood and youth, he traveled in Germany, Austria, Italy, and Switzerland, finally locating in Vienna in 1868. While in Switzerland he came in contact with the International and was afterwards continually active in revolutionary movements. In 1870 he was arrested for revolutionary propaganda and sentenced to five years' imprisonment. He was, however, released after a few months in the course of a general political amnesty, and a little later he was expelled from Austria and returned to Germany, where he edited a paper and belonged to the most radical wing of the Social Democratic Party. During 1873 he spent eight months in jail, and upon his release he was elected to the Reichstag. Again in 1877 and 1878 he was arrested, the last time in connection with the attempted assassination of Emperor William I. After his release he was compelled to leave Germany, and in December, 1878, he went to London where he began to publish a weekly, "Die Freiheit."

His views became so extreme and violent that Liebknecht, who with Bebel for many years guided the German Social Democratic Party, felt obliged to repudiate Most and his paper in the interest of his party. The same year saw Most converted to anarchism through the influence of a friend, a former supporter of Bakunin, and he was formally expelled from the German Social Democracy at the party convention in 1880. Bebel declared that Most was "one of the victims of Bismarck's savage policies," because his expulsion from Germany removed him from the influence of his friends, who might have moderated his extreme views and saved his undoubted abilities to the socialist cause.

In March, 1881, when Alexander II of Russia was killed, Most wrote an editorial praising the deed, for which he was sentenced in London to sixteen months in jail. Upon his release in October, 1882, he determined to go to the United States and he reached New York in December of the same year. The revolutionary faction of the socialists received him with open arms, as the "victim of bourgeois justice," and as a martyr to the cause. His tour through the country, beginning with a mass meeting at the Cooper Union in New York, "resembled a triumphal procession," according to Hillquit. His meetings were large and enthusiastic, they were extensively reported by the press, and a number of anarchistic "groups" were organized as a result of his agitation. After the close of this tour, which took place early in 1883, Most settled in New York and renewed the publication of "Die Freiheit."

A joint convention of revolutionary socialists was held in Pittsburgh in October, 1883. It was attended by representatives of twenty-six States and among the delegates was John Most. Letters of interest and encouragement were received from revolutionary groups in the United States and from a number of European countries. A national organization was created under the name of "International Working-People's Association," with a general "Information Bureau" for purposes of communication between the different local groups, with headquarters in Chicago.

The most important accomplishment of this convention was the adoption of a declaration of principles, which came to be known as the "Pittsburgh Proclamation," and which is still regarded as a classic exposition of communistic anarchism. It was a peculiar mixture of the theories of Marx and Proudhon and the philosophy of the French encyclopedists of the eighteenth century.

The Pittsburgh convention, and the frequent lecture tours of Most and other prominent anarchists, made their propaganda familiar to the radical circles of the labor movement in the United States, especially among the German-speaking members. The revolutionary groups gained steadily in numbers; "Die Freiheit" increased its circulation; some socialist papers deserted the old party, and several new organs were established.

The growth of this new anarchistic movement led by Most still further depleted the weakened ranks of the Socialist Labor Party. Efforts were made by some of its members after the Pittsburgh Convention to consolidate formally the old party with the new organization. The reason for such a proposal is to be found in the fact that the "Pittsburgh Proclamation" was more moderate than had been expected and seemed to offer some hope of common action between the two wings of the movement.

The leaders, who were striving for common action, addressed a letter to the Chicago groups, in which they urged the wisdom of united action and the similarity of the fundamental views of the two organizations. The answer advised the dissolution of the older party into autonomous groups which could be affiliated with the International Working-People's Association in the same way as the groups already attached to it.

Under these depressing circumstances the fourth national convention of the Socialist Labor Party met at Baltimore in December, 1883. Only sixteen delegates were present, and of these, four came from Baltimore and ten from New York City and its vicinity. The principal significance of the convention was the drawing of a sharp line of division between socialism and anarchism. Henceforth all attempts at reconciliation were given up and there was open war between the two groups of radicals.

The controversy between the socialists and the anarchists was carried on by means of the press and by public discussions. In May, 1884, a public debate was held at Chicago between John Most and Paul Grottkau, the latter a representative of the Socialist Labor Party. Hillquit describes it as "the most notable" of these debates and "a well-matched contest," as both men were practiced speakers and ready debaters. The debate was reported stenographically, published in book form and widely circulated. Its influence, however, was limited by the fact that it was in German.

Lecture tours were arranged by the Socialist Labor Party for the particular purpose of combating anarchism. In addition a systematic campaign of education was conducted which resulted in a steady growth. In October, 1885, the fifth national convention met at Cincinnati, where forty-two sections were represented by thirty-three delegates as compared with only sixteen two years before.

Although the Socialist Labor Party had somewhat recovered from the attacks of anarchism, it had by no means gained as rapidly as the revolutionary organization opposed to it had done. Compared with the approximately sixty sections of the older party, the younger organization had about eighty groups, with an enrolled membership of seven thousand, and eleven papers — seven German, two English, and two Bohemian.

THE CHICAGO ANARCHISTS

The main strength of the revolutionary socialists was in Chicago where they had twenty groups with a membership of three thousand, while New York City and its vicinity had the larger number of the more moderate socialists. John Most, however, made New York City his headquarters and published his paper from that point. He was generally regarded as the representative of the doctrines of the Black International, or anarchistic wing of the revolutionary movement, in the United States. His greatest influence seems to have been in Chicago, and from it there developed the Haymarket catastrophe of 1886, which was its most significant result, and which also proved to be its concluding event.

The blending of anarchism and trade-unionism produced a kind of syndicalism which was not unlike the French syndicalism of twenty years later, and which also was closely allied to the familiar activities of the Industrial Workers of the World of recent years. The doctrines of this movement were propagated locally by August Spies and Albert R. Parsons from 1883 to 1886. Their views of trade-union action, political action, and the use of violence might easily pass for a syndicalist programme of the twentieth century. The general labor upheaval of 1884 to 1887 gave an opportunity for the development of this programme in a practical manner. The industrial depression during these years made conditions favorable for labor agitation and revolutionary propaganda.

Labor troubles were numerous during 1885 and 1886, and in connection with these the Knights of Labor, then at the height of their power, exercised a strong influence. Another organization, the Federation of Trades and Labor Unions of the United States, which had been formed in 1881, determined in 1884 to assume the leadership in a national movement for the eight-hour day, and May 1, 1886, was selected as the date for the inauguration of the new movement. The activities of these two national labor organizations provided the background out of which the Chicago drama developed. It illustrated very vividly the intertwining of the labor, socialist, and revolutionary movements in the earlier years of their existence.

In Chicago considerable interest was manifested in the proposed reduction of hours. An Eight Hours Association was formed which received the support of the Trade and Labor Assembly, the central body for organized labor in the city. At first the revolutionary socialists were indifferent to the agitation and discouraged it, as a mere compromise plan and as a hopeless undertaking, but as it assumed larger proportions they gradually changed their attitude and finally supported it. Albert R. Parsons, August Spies, Samuel Fielden, Michael Schwab, and other revolutionary socialists became the most active leaders in the eight-hour movement. At their meetings, as well as in their papers, they emphasized the importance of violence and they advised the working-men to provide themselves with arms on the first day of May. The anarchistic doctrine of the propaganda of the deed received its first and final exposition in the United States.

The first serious trouble began among the striking employees of the McCormick Harvester Works, who had been "locked out" in February as the result of the demand of the men that the company stop its discrimination against those who had been identified with an earlier strike. This struggle shaded into the eight-hour agitation and was made more bitter by the employment of armed Pinkerton detectives to protect the strike-breakers.

On the 3d of May, some of the strikers held a mass meeting near the works to discuss a proposal to be presented to their employers. Spies was addressing the men when the strike-breakers began to leave and were attacked by some of the bystanders. The police were summoned and appeared in large numbers. They were received with stones and fired into the crowd, killing four and wounding many others.

Spies, who was the editor of the "Verbote," one of the

two papers in Chicago representing the revolutionary socialists, rushed to his office where he prepared and issued "a call for revenge which contained the words: Workingmen, arm yourselves and appear in full force." This call, known as the "Revenge Circular," was printed in German and English and five thousand copies were distributed.

A meeting was held at Haymarket Square, on the evening of the following day, to protest against the "murder of our fellow workers." At the beginning of the meeting two or three thousand persons were present, but a threatening storm dispersed the larger part of the crowd, leaving only a few hundreds to listen to the last speaker who happened to be Samuel Fielden. Spies and Parsons had already addressed the meeting.

Mayor Carter Harrison, who had attended to use his influence against violent action, left at the same time with the bulk of the crowd and expressed the opinion that no trouble would occur. While Fielden was speaking, a squad of one hundred and eighty police arrived, formed in line, and began to advance upon the crowd. Fielden protested that the meeting was a peaceable one. Suddenly a bomb was hurled at the police, killing a sergeant and throwing about sixty to the ground. The police fired, and as a result of indiscriminate firing on both sides, seven policemen were killed and sixty wounded, and among the workmen four were killed and fifty wounded. It has never been definitely determined as to who threw the bomb which precipitated the Haymarket "massacre," and the question was not really seriously considered in the trial that followed.

Very naturally the revolutionary socialists were held responsible for the tragedy and there was a popular demand for their punishment. A veritable reign of terror developed. The police broke up all labor meetings and arrested many persons connected with socialist and revolutionary organizations. On May 17, 1886, the grand jury indicted ten men, charging them with the murder of the policeman who was killed by the bomb. These men were "not only the backbone of the local anarchistic movement, but were among the most prominent and influential leaders in the eight-hour agitation, and generally popular in the labor movement in Chicago." One made his escape, one turned State's evidence, and the remaining eight were placed on trial: August Spies, Michael Schwab, Samuel Fielden, Albert R. Parsons, Adolph Fischer, George Engel, Louis Lingg, and Oscar W. Neebe.

The trial began June 21, 1886, and lasted forty-nine days. The defendants were not charged with personal participation in the murder of the policeman. The prosecution maintained that they had "by speech and print advised large classes of the people to commit murder, and that in consequence of that advice somebody not known had thrown the bomb." The jury was not chosen in the usual way, but the judge appointed a special bailiff to summon such jurors as he might select. None of the jurors were working-men and many of them admitted that they had a preconceived opinion as to the guilt of the defendants. The most important witnesses for the State were the man who had turned State's evidence and detectives and newspaper reporters. The trial was conducted in a partial manner by the judge, who in his charge to the jury emphasized the fact that personal participation was not necessary to establish the guilt of the defendants.

Spies, Fielden, Schwab, Parsons, Fischer, Engel, and Lingg were condemned to death, while Neebe was sentenced to imprisonment for fifteen years. Later the sentences of Schwab and Fielden were commuted to life imprisonment and Lingg committed suicide in his cell. Spies, Parsons, Fischer, and Engel were hanged November 11, 1887. Six years later Governor John P. Altgeld pardoned Fielden, Neebe, and Schwab. His "Reasons for Pardoning Fielden, Neebe, and Schwab" contained a thoroughgoing analysis of the trial and a scathing arraignment of the unfair and partial methods of the judge. Judge Joseph E. Gary replied in defense of the verdict, pointing out that the defendants had been sentenced, not as anarchists, but because they were parties to the murder. They had "advised large classes to commit murder" and had left "the commission, the time, and place, and when, to the individual will and whim or caprice . . . of each individual man who listened to their advice, and that in consequence of that advice, in pursuance of that advice, and influenced by that advice, somebody, not known, did throw the bomb" that caused the policeman's death.[1]

A few of the more discerning men of the period interpreted this outbreak in its true relations; they viewed it as merely a violent incident in what was on the whole a peaceful agitation for the reduction of the hours of labor. The efforts of men like Henry D. Lloyd to have the anarchists treated with justice was beyond the comprehension of the dominant opinion of the time, and was treated, as was the later pardon of the survivors by Governor Altgeld in 1893, as the act of persons either mentally unbalanced or criminally inclined. Probably it was too much to expect men of that period to see things as clearly as they can be seen after the lapse of years. That we have gained in social vision was illustrated in the trial of the Lawrence strike leaders when compared with the methods used in dealing with their Chicago predecessors. In both cases the violence was an incident, perhaps an inevitable incident, for which society, as well as the individuals, was responsible.

[1] Gary: "The Chicago Anarchists of 1886," in the *Century Magazine*, vol. XLV, pp. 803-37 (April, 1893).

REVIVAL AND DISINTEGRATION

The Chicago tragedy destroyed the influence of anarchism as an active factor in the labor and socialist movement in the United States. Henceforth it was confined to a few unimportant groups. The socialists could now renew their more moderate propaganda without serious opposition from the extremists.

The work of revival was aided in the fall of 1886 by the visit to this country of William Liebknecht, the German socialist leader, 'who was accompanied by the daughter of Karl Marx and her husband. The visitors addressed about fifty meetings in all the principal cities, Liebknecht speaking in German, while the others used English.

The sixth national convention of the Socialist Labor Party was held at Buffalo in 1887, and was attended by thirty-seven delegates, representing thirty-two sections. Altogether seventy sections were reported to exist in the country. The chief topic discussed was that of political action. There was a good deal of difference of opinion upon the advisability of coöperating with political labor parties, of entering the political field independently, or of abstaining from politics entirely. A compromise was agreed upon recommending that members support the most progressive labor party.

The compromise action of the convention by no means disposed of the controversy. One group continued to oppose political action and urged concentration upon trade-unionism, while the other advised the formation of an independent socialist political party. The antagonism grew so pronounced during the next two years that it finally resulted in open hostilities.

The national officials of the party favored independent political action, while the opposition, which was represented by the "New York Volkszeitung," believed in a trade-union policy. In September, 1889, the national officials were deposed and new elections held. The deposed officials refused to recognize the validity of their removal and called a convention to meet in Chicago at the end of September. The "control committee" of the party suspended both sets of officials, took temporary charge of affairs, and postponed the convention to October 12th. The faction supporting the deposed officials refused to accept the new date and met as originally planned. Their meeting was poorly attended and remnants of this faction later merged into the Social Democratic Party.

The "Volkszeitung" faction assembled early in October with twenty-seven delegates in attendance, representing thirty-three sections. Its most important work was the drafting of a new platform which was readopted with slight modifications at every subsequent convention of the Socialist Labor Party.

Nevertheless, in spite of this internal strife, the progress of the party continued for a number of years. In 1889 there were said to be seventy sections; by 1893 one hundred and thirteen new sections had been organized, of which forty-three were German, thirty-nine American, fourteen Jewish, and the remainder made up of Poles, Bohemians, Frenchmen, Italians, and other nationalities. These organizations were distributed over twenty-one States. In 1896 two hundred sections were reported from twenty-five States.

The same year the ninth national convention was held in New York City. It remained in session seven days and was attended by ninety-four delegates, representing seventy-five sections in twelve States. The most significant action was the passage of a resolution condemning trade unions as hopelessly corrupt, which was adopted by a vote of 76 to 6. This was a radical departure from the established policy of the party and destined to have an important influence upon its future.

During the three years from 1896 to 1899, the number of sections increased to over three hundred and fifty, and the party was active in thirty States. By 1899 it had reached its greatest strength. In spite of its growth and apparent prosperity, its disintegration had already begun. The split of 1889 and the break with the trade unions in 1896 made inevitablé the failure of the party as a vital factor in the life of American working-men.

The Formation of the Socialist Party

About the middle of the nineties a new socialistic movement developed outside the ranks of the Socialist Labor Party. It was scattered all over the country, but its greatest strength was in the Middle West. It found its leader in Eugene V. Debs in 1897. He had always had radical views on social questions, and his experiences in the management of the great railroad strike of 1894 naturally intensified his views. He devoted his enforced leisure in jail in 1894 and 1895 to a study of socialism. He supported Bryan in 1896, but in January, 1897, he publicly announced his conversion to socialism.

In June, 1897, the scattered socialist groups in the West met at Chicago and organized the Social Democracy of America; its aims were crude and indefinite, but its main purpose was the promotion of a plan of colonization. The purpose was to establish a colony in some Western State, capture the State Government, and introduce a socialist régime in the State. In 1898 announcement was made of arrangements to acquire over five hundred acres in the Cripple Creek region of Colorado. No practical steps seem to have been taken to carry out the plan.

Within the new organization there were practical social-ist elements that did not believe in the colonization plan, and these elements, under the leadership of Victor L. Berger, of Milwaukee, undertook to substitute a practical programme for the rather fantastic schemes that were under consideration.

In June, 1898, the Social Democracy of America held its first national convention since its organization at Chicago; seventy delegates, representing ninety-four branches, were present. The question of ordinary practical socialism *versus* colonization was brought before the con-vention by the report of the platform committee. Two reports were submitted — a majority report which favored the abandonment of the colonization scheme, and a minor-ity report retaining the plan as the chief activity of the new organization. After a long debate, the vote resulted in fifty-three delegates supporting the colonization plan and thirty-seven opposing it. As soon as the vote was taken, the minority withdrew, as they had previously planned to do if defeated, leaving the field clear to the other faction. This group established two insignificant commu-nistic colonies in the State of Washington and ceased to exist.[1]

The thirty-seven bolting delegates formed a new party under the name of "Social Democratic Party of America." They eliminated all utopian planks from their platform, and elected a national executive committee consisting of Eugene V. Debs, Victor L. Berger, Seymour Stedman, and two others. The party grew rapidly during the next two years, nominating State or local tickets in Massachusetts, New Hampshire, New York, Connecticut, Maryland, Illinois, Wisconsin, Missouri, and California. As a result of

[1] Bushee: "Communistic Societies in the United States," in the *Political Science Quarterly*, vol. xx, pp. 635-39.

its activities in these nine States, in the fall of 1899 it elected two representatives to the Massachusetts Legislature and mayors in two Massachusetts cities. It also elected other local officials in Massachusetts and Wisconsin.

When the first national convention assembled in Indianapolis in March, 1900, the question of union with the Rochester wing of the Socialist Labor Party was the "all-absorbing topic." A committee, consisting of Max Hayes, Job Harriman, and Morris Hillquit, were present to urge the amalgamation of the socialist forces of the country and they were enthusiastically supported by the great majority of the sixty-seven delegates.

The Rochester branch of the Socialist Labor Party had been the result of one of the periodic controversies which marked the history of the organization. Since 1892 the party had been in the control of Daniel De Leon (1872–1914), who followed a very aggressive policy. Under his leadership was adopted the programme of hostility to labor organizations in 1896. He also carried on a process of "purification" of the members of the party by which those who criticized the officers were expelled and under which insubordinate sections were suspended. This "reign of terror" continued for several years and finally in 1889 reached an acute stage.[1]

As usual there was an "administration faction" and an "opposition faction." The split came over the election of new delegates to the general committee of the New York section to which the convention of 1896 had delegated the power to elect and recall the national secretary and the national committee. The election was consequently of more than local importance and it resulted in a victory for the opposition. The new committee met, and it became

[1] Brissenden: *The I.W.W.: A Study of American Syndicalism*, pp. 48, 80–82, 238–41.

at once apparent that the opposition was in control. The nomination of a temporary chairman precipitated a violent conflict and the meeting broke up in disorder. A couple of days later the opposition delegates assembled by themselves, deposed the old officials, and elected new ones in their places. Again as ten years before there were two sets of officers, each claiming to be legal representatives of the Socialist Labor Party.

In 1899 both factions nominated candidates for office in New York, each claiming its ticket represented the party. The contest was taken into the courts and was decided in favor of the faction headed by De Leon, the administration faction, although apparently the opposition had the support of a large majority of the membership of the party. To put an end to the confusion and uncertainty, the opposition national committee called a special convention to meet at Rochester, New York, to reorganize the party on the new basis. Fifty-nine delegates responded and remained in session five days.

One of the first acts of the new Rochester wing of the Socialist Labor Party was to declare its sympathy with trade unions. It also adopted a new platform and passed a resolution preparing the way for union with the Social Democratic Party. A committee of nine was appointed "to act as a permanent committee on Socialist Union," and this committee was authorized to send delegates to the next convention of the Social Democratic Party "to convey this resolution to said party and to invite the said party to appoint a similar committee ... any treaty of union evolved by the joint committee on union, including the question of party name, platform, and constitution [must] be submitted to a general vote of both parties." Nominations for candidates for the ensuing presidential campaign, according to the custom of the party since 1892, were made subject to such changes as might be necessary if union or coöperation resulted.

The leaders of the Social Democratic Party were more cautious than the mass of the delegates in regard to the negotiations for union. They agreed to the appointment of a committee of nine to meet with the committee of the Rochester group, but they recommended that the results of the conferences of the joint committee be submitted "to a referendum vote of each party separately," so that each party might veto the proposed union, even though a majority of the members might vote in favor of it. The leaders also insisted upon the retention of the name "Social Democratic Party" for the new organization. These recommendations were rejected after "a prolonged and heated debate" by a two to one vote. The committee of nine was then appointed and a presidential ticket nominated, consisting of Eugene V. Debs for President and Job Harriman for Vice-President — each of these men representing one of the parties to the proposed union.

The "joint conference committee" met in New York City late in March, 1900, and remained in session two days. The questions of candidates and platforms were settled with little discussion, but the matters of party name and headquarters gave rise to serious differences. A compromise finally provided for the submission of the choice of a name to the vote of the combined membership of both parties. Apparently the union was considered as practically complete at the time of adjournment, but within a week differences arose which seemed to threaten the entire agreement. The national executive committee of the Social Democratic Party charged the representatives of the Rochester group "with breach of faith," and called upon the members of their party "to repudiate the treaty of union." After the vote had been canvassed, these same leaders declared that the union had been rejected by their members and that their party would continue its separate existence.

Fortunately, a truce was arranged and maintained during the presidential campaign, and 97,730 votes were cast for the joint ticket — more than the Socialist Labor Party had ever won for its candidates in its most prosperous period. This unexpectedly large vote produced better results than prolonged negotiations had accomplished. A call for a convention of all socialist organizations at Indianapolis was responded to by all except the New York faction of the Socialist Labor Party. One hundred and twenty-four delegates attended, and the convention was "the largest and most representative national gathering of socialists ever held in this country up to that time." A new platform and constitution were adopted and the name Socialist Party was assumed. From July, 1901, the date of its formation, down to 1914, it remained a vigorous and growing organization, reaching a vote of over 900,000 for its presidential candidate in 1912.

SELECTED REFERENCES

1. Hillquit: *History of Socialism in the United States*, part II, Introduction, and chaps. I–V.
2. Commons: *History of Labor in the United States*, vol. II, part VI, chaps. II–IV, VI.
3. Hunter: *Violence and the Labor Movement*, chap. IV.
4. Lloyd: *Henry Demarest Lloyd*, vol. I, chap. V.
5. Buchanan: *The Story of a Labor Agitator*, pp. 373–426.
6. Russell: *These Shifting Scenes*, chap. VI.
7. Hill: *Decisive Battles of the Law*, pp. 240–68.
8. Gary: "The Chicago Anarchists of 1886," in the *Century Magazine*, vol. XLV, pp. 803–37.
9. Ely: *The Labor Movement in America*, chaps. VIII–XII.
10. Schlüter: *Lincoln, Labor and Slavery*.
11. *Daniel De Leon — The Man and His Work*. A Symposium published by the Socialist Labor Party in 1920.

CHAPTER IV

THE LABOR MOVEMENT

As in the case of socialism, labor organization in the United States did not make a permanent beginning till after the Civil War. There was scattered activity early in the nineteenth century in a few of the larger centers of population, but economic and social conditions were still too undeveloped to make any real progress possible.

The first period in American industrial history extended to the decade of the twenties — industrial independence and development lagged nearly half a century behind political independence. The occasional awakenings of the working-classes before 1827 did not take the form of concerted action by those engaged in different occupations, but appeared as mere fitful contests in separate trades. There was no labor movement, although traces of what was later to develop into such a movement may, perhaps, be found.

We have already referred to the relations of Robert Owen to the agitations of the period beginning about 1825. These agitations did not center about the organization of labor, for that was but one of the minor issues in a time which has never been surpassed in our history for the number of problems under consideration and the amount of discussion which they produced. The moral and humanitarian awakening of the period provided a nourishing atmosphere; Owen's propaganda directed attention to the needs of the workers and to plans for satisfying those needs. Finally, the extension of the suffrage furnished the instrument by which the desired improvements could be secured. At the same time the problems and organizations were quite different from those with which we are familiar at present. They were more political than economic or industrial. The United States was still a new country and the existence of cheap land prevented the formation of definite class lines between employers and employees.

EARLY LABOR AND SOCIAL REFORM

"The first coördinated movement of several trades in the United States occurred in Philadelphia in 1827 when, as a result of a strike of building trades workmen for a ten-hour day, there was formed the first effective city central organization of wage-earners in the world — the Mechanics' Union of Trade Associations. This in turn gave birth to the first labor party in the world — the Working-Men's Party, which led to the first industrial union, at least in this country — the New England Association of Farmers, Mechanics, and other Working-men. For several years this movement was not only the expression of labor's unrest, but was also an important political force with which the old established parties were obliged to reckon and to which they were obliged to make concessions." [1]

Early in 1827 the carpenters in Philadelphia demanded the ten-hour day and struck. They had been working from "sun to sun," which meant in winter a comparatively short day, but also much unemployment, since the bulk of the building was done in the late spring, summer, and early fall, when days were long, and the men required to work from twelve to fifteen hours.

Out of the ten-hour agitation grew the first union of all organized workmen in any city. During the latter half of 1827, there was formed the Mechanics' Union of Trade Associations. At one time it had in its membership fifteen trade societies, but the number diminished, and soon after

[1] Commons: *History of Labor in the United States*, vol. I, p. 169.

November, 1829, it seems to have ceased to exist. Its programme and the existing political situation in Philadelphia early drew it into politics, and, as it advanced politically, it retrograded as an industrial organization.

The old Federalist Party, which had disappeared from national politics, was still active in Philadelphia, while the Democratic Party was split into two parts — one made up of the members who supported Adams, and the other of the supporters of Jackson. After the election of Jackson to the Presidency in 1828, the Adams wing was weak and frequently fused with the Federalist Party.

When the Working-Men's Party was formed in July, 1828, the Federalist Party controlled the city, and the Jackson party the county. At the elections that year the Jackson party carried the city as well as the county. The eight candidates, who were exclusively on the working-men's ticket, received from 229 to 539 votes in the city and about 425 votes in the county. The candidates of each of the other parties, who were also on the working-men's ticket, ran from 300 to 600 votes ahead of their colleagues, but none of the candidates of the Federalist Party were elected by the aid of the working-men. All of the twenty-one working-men's candidates on the Jackson ticket were elected. The new labor party was, naturally, encouraged by its demonstration of political strength.

The election returns of 1829 showed that the working-men had secured the balance of power. In the city all the candidates of the working-men, who were on either of the other tickets, were elected. Of the fifty-four labor candidates put up in the city and county, twenty, who were also candidates of one of the other parties, were elected. The total vote in both city and county increased from 1000 to 2400.

In 1830 the new party elected a much smaller number of

candidates and lost the balance of power, and the following year was the last in which it nominated a ticket. Its failure was due to the workers' inability to play the game of politics as efficiently as the old party leaders.

Two years after the labor movement in Philadelphia began, a similar agitation over the ten-hour day developed in New York City. There the working-men had the ten-hour day, and consequently the struggle was essentially to retain it. It started with a meeting of mechanics, but passed over the city federation stage, and plunged immediately into politics. The distinguishing characteristics of the New York movement were its radical character and the violence of its internal dissensions. Robert Dale Owen and Frances Wright were active in its deliberations and organization, and it also received support from other parts of the State. In the city the movement was composed of "mechanics and other working-men," but, in the remainder of the State, farmers were included. The causes were the same as in Philadelphia; the old parties had not properly represented the interests of the working-classes and the remedy was believed to be the formation of a labor party.

In the election of 1829 in New York City the working-men were successful with one of their candidates for the Assembly — Ebenezer Ford, a carpenter. Another candidate, endorsed by one of the other parties, was also elected to the State Senate. In addition, two other candidates ran only about twenty-five votes behind Ford, and, with one exception, their entire ticket received over 6000 out of a total of about 21,000 votes. The working-men were, therefore, much encouraged, and believed that they had paved the way to future victory.

Early in 1830 organization began in many of the towns of the State of New York. "Committees of correspondence" were appointed, as had been done during the Revolutionary days, to further coöperation between the different communities. Local successes in the spring elections encouraged the idea of a State convention and the nomination of an independent ticket. Such a gathering was held in August with seventy-eight delegates from thirteen counties in attendance. Candidates for governor and lieutenant governor were nominated. Two weeks before the election, these candidates withdrew and the working-men were left without any regularly named nominees. About 3000 votes were cast for the representatives of a small faction of laborers. The New York Working-Men's Party, unlike the Philadelphia party, was primarily broken up by internal dissensions, and only secondarily by external opposition. It was really in its State-wide activity a revolt of Democrats against the element then in control of the Democratic Party — the "Albany Regency." The labor situation in New York City had been the occasion and had given a stimulus or immediate cause.

From Philadelphia and New York, the unrest spread to other cities and States, and was felt all along the Atlantic coast, and westward to Missouri. Evidence exists of organization in all the New England States, except New Hampshire, and in Delaware, New Jersey, and Ohio. The most important activity, outside of Philadelphia and New York, was in New England, and it continued during the years 1831 to 1834.

The New England agitation was not conducted by a working-men's party like those already described, but by a new type of labor organization, the New England Association of Farmers, Mechanics, and other Working-men, which undertook to unite producers of all classes in an effort to improve their conditions. It was designed to be a great industrial union, not unlike the later Knights of Labor. It grew out of the agitation for the ten-hour day, since all workers in New England were required to work from "daylight to dark." The other chief grievance was "the low estimation in which useful labor is held by many whose station in life enables them to give the tone to public opinion." The Association soon found the establishment of the ten-hour day by direct action impracticable, and turned its attention to other questions, most of them of a political character. This development resulted in their entry into State politics in 1833 with a candidate for governor, and with a candidate for Congress, in addition, in 1834. Its chief activities, however, were confined to the preparation of memorials to be presented to the legislatures of the New England States.

The working-men's parties from 1827 to 1834 failed, as have all succeeding efforts in the United States on the part of labor to enter politics. Yet in spite of their immediate and apparent failures, they forced their measures upon public attention and the specific abuses, of which they complained, were eventually removed. They were factors in pushing forward many measures which conservatives now accept as in the line of progress. As Carlton points out, the vitality of the movement for tax-supported schools was derived, not from the humanitarian leaders, but from the growing class of wage-earners.[1]

EARLY TRADE UNIONS

With the collapse of the working-men's parties during the early thirties, there were left only isolated trade societies, some of which had existed for more than a quarter of a century. Formerly they had been organized to protect their members against sickness and distress, but now they began to develop into trade unions. The shift from

[1] Commons: *History of Labor in the United States*, vol. I, pp. 169-332. Carlton: *The History and Problems of Organized Labor*, pp. 46-48.

mutual insurance to trade protection antedated by a few years the wave of industrial prosperity which came about 1835.

The next type of organization to be developed was the *city central union*, which resulted from the growth of cities. New York became after 1820 the metropolis of the country, and there, in 1833, was formed the General Trades' Union of the City of New York and Vicinity. Before the year was over, three other cities, Baltimore, Philadelphia, and Washington, had similar organizations. In 1834, one was formed in Boston, and, in 1835 and 1836, eight other city unions were established. By 1836 there were thirteen, at least, in the country. These unions specifically declared against political action and adhered strictly to industrial methods.

The New York General Trades' Union was particularly aggressive, sending aid and encouragement to strikers as far away as Boston and Philadelphia. Because of its aggressiveness, a case in court was made against it, charging its leaders with conspiracy, and twenty were arrested and convicted. As a protest against this action, a mass meeting, with 27,000 in attendance, was held, which demanded the repeal of the conspiracy laws and the reform of the judicial system.

A natural development from city unions was the formation of one on a national scale. The National Trades' Union was organized in August, 1834, and lasted till May, 1837. It resulted from an invitation sent out by the city union of New York, which brought together thirty delegates from Boston, New York, Brooklyn, Poughkeepsie, Newark, and Philadelphia. The convention created simply a national medium for conducting agitation without any effective control over local unions. It provided for the usual officers, and for a financial committee, composed of one delegate from each union represented, "to compute" the expenses, which were to be paid by each union contributing its proportion.

The convention of 1835 met in New York in October and forty-one delegates were present — twenty-six from New York, five from New Jersey, five from Pennsylvania, and five from Maryland. Three unofficial delegates from Boston were also in attendance. No important changes were made at this meeting in the structure, purpose, or power of the organization. The office of treasurer was created, and, to the new official, the financial committee was to turn over the funds collected from the local unions, in the manner provided at the first convention. A "Committee of General Correspondence" was also appointed to keep up a "semblance of existence" between sessions.

The third convention met in Philadelphia in October, 1836, and thirty-five delegates were present from New York, Albany, Newark, Pittsburgh, Reading, Philadelphia, Baltimore, Washington, and Cincinnati. This last convention went much beyond the preceding sessions in solidifying the working-men of the country, and in giving to the organization an individuality distinct from its component parts. A national fund was created, and the acts of the Union were to be binding, rather than merely advisory. Representation was also to be based partly upon the comparative memberships in local unions. What might have resulted from these changes can never be known, as the National Trades' Union disappeared during the panic of 1837.

NATIONAL TRADE UNIONS

An outgrowth of the general national organization of trades was the beginning of national trade unions. Following the 1835 convention of the National Trades' Union, the cordwainers (shoemakers) remained and laid the foundation for a national organization of their trade.

Forty-five delegates were present from five States. In the next two years, four other national trade unions were formed by the printers, the comb-makers, the carpenters, and the handloom weavers. The panic of 1837 checked the movement.

After 1840 there was a revival of coöperative and social reform philosophy, manifested in such communities as Brook Farm. The working-men were influenced by all the activities of these years. The fifties, however, witnessed a change. The confusion resulting from the large number of reforms and their conflicting claims was passing. Rising prices demanded immediate and concrete results, and the workmen "broke away from the benevolent and coöperative side-shows of the preceding ten years."

But for the interruption of the slavery conflict and the Civil War, the modern, after-the-war period of the labor movement might have been dated ten to twenty years earlier. Already in the fifties trade-unionism was taking on its modern form and policies. Shorter hours and higher pay were supplemented as issues by the minimum wage, the closed shop, the restriction of apprentices, and the secrecy of proceedings. The main weapon was the strike to establish wage standards and to maintain them.

The oldest national trade union now in existence is the International Typographical Union, which goes back for its preliminary organization to 1850. In 1853, the Stonecutters' Association was formed, followed in 1854 by the National Trade Associations of Hat Finishers of the United States of America. The Iron Molders' Union of North America first appeared in 1859.[1] The Civil War, of course, practically disrupted these organizations, and they were reorganized after the close of that struggle. Con-

[1] Commons: *History of Labor in the United States*, vol. i, pp. 335–80, 424–71, 575–623; Groat: *The Study of Organized Labor in America*, pp. 33–35.

sequently, labor organization in the United States in its modern form does not actually date back of the Civil War. The earlier organizations cited above are merely preliminary in their character, and of interest historically. The modern labor problem can hardly be said to have existed in the United States until after the Civil War. The conditions of a new country made it seem feasible for any workman to hope to become an employer and capitalist. As the door of industrial independence slowly closed, the loose associations of laborers began to merge into positive organizations with definite common purposes and increasing unity.

The years during the Civil War, and immediately following, witnessed persistent efforts for a larger organization which would unite all elements of labor into a single unit. "The National Labor Union was the successor in the sixties of the National Trades' Union of the thirties, and the predecessor of the Knights of Labor and the American Federation of Labor." It was formed at Baltimore in 1866 and held seven annual conventions. It was made up of delegates from local, State, and national trade associations, the membership of which at its highest point was said to have been 640,000. The growth of the organization proved to be of a mushroom character and after 1870 it declined rapidly. Professor Ely diagnosed its "fatal malady" as politics.

A National Reform Party was formed in 1872 and nominated candidates for President and Vice-President, who withdrew too late to allow new candidates to replace them. Besides the establishment of this short-lived party, the National Labor Union gave a strong impulse to the agitation for the eight-hour day and for the creation of bureaus of labor statistics.

Reference has already been made to the relation of the

National Labor Union to the European International and to socialist undertakings in the United States. The development of labor organization and of socialism as distinct movements had not begun. In every country the earlier efforts were more or less confused — in some cases the labor movement preceded, as it did in the United States, and again the reverse was true, as in a number of European countries. The specialization of organizations followed at a distance the developing complexity of industrialism. Starting more or less together, labor and socialism have become the right and left wings — the conservative and radical groups in the general working-class movement.

THE KNIGHTS OF LABOR

The first important, and, relatively permanent, organization to unite labor upon a broader basis than that of the national trade union, was the Knights of Labor, which began among some garment-cutters in Philadelphia in 1869 under the leadership of Uriah S. Stephens. In 1871, the name, the Noble Order of the Knights of Labor, was assumed. The membership was first limited to tailors, but soon others were admitted as associate members, or as "sojourners," as they were called, and after a period of training they were allowed to organize new societies in their own trades. The local unions were known as "assemblies," the parent assembly as Assembly No. 1, while the others were numbered serially in the order of their establishment. Before the end of 1873, eighty assemblies had been formed in various trades, and, by the close of 1876, there were over one hundred local assemblies.

With the expansion of the order outside of Philadelphia and into neighboring States, the need for a permanent central organization began to be felt. Accordingly, on Christmas Day, 1873, District Assembly No. 1 was founded. As in the case of the locals, district assemblies were designated numerically, and the parent local with other early locals became District Assembly No. 1. October, 1874, District Assembly No. 2 was founded at Camden, New Jersey, and in August, 1875, District Assembly No. 3 at Pittsburgh. This established the Knights of Labor in the industrial section of the United States and gave it a recognized place among wage-earners.

It was expected from the beginning that eventually a national organization would be formed. Meanwhile District Assembly No. 1 of Philadelphia was tacitly regarded as head of the order. District Assembly No. 3 of Pittsburgh became in time the representative in the West, and later, meeting with unusual success in the formation of new locals and districts, it began to consider itself, not only equal to, but even superior to, the original assembly at Philadelphia. Because of this rivalry the first attempts to establish a national organization proceeded simultaneously from the two independent centers, each of which claimed leadership.

Finally, the two rivals came to an agreement and a call for a convention to meet at Reading, January 1, 1878, was issued "for the purpose of forming a Central Assembly — and also for the purpose of creating a Central Resistance Fund, Bureau of Statistics, Providing Revenue for the Work of Organization, establishment of an Official Register. . . . Also the subject of making the name public." This convention, representing eleven district assemblies, located in seven States and including fifteen trades, formed a General Assembly and adopted a constitution which, with minor changes, lasted throughout the continuance of the order. Stephens was chosen grand master workman, as he had been of the first local and district assemblies.

The constitution provided for a highly centralized form of organization. Just as the district assembly had absolute jurisdiction over subordinate bodies, so the general assembly was given "full and final jurisdiction," and was made "the highest tribunal." It could also tax the members for its maintenance.

Any person over eighteen years of age "working for wages, or who at any time worked for wages," could become a member, but "no person who either sells, or makes his living by the sale of, intoxicating drink," could be admitted, and "no lawyer, doctor, or banker" could join the order.

One special feature of the Knights of Labor in its early years was its secret organization. Its name was designated by five asterisks, and this caused it to be referred to as the society of the "Five Stars." The disadvantages of secrecy became apparent in the middle of the seventies, when the criminal activities of the Molly Maguires in Pennsylvania threw suspicion upon secret labor organizations in general. The Catholic Church, especially in the region in which the Molly Maguires operated, joined the employers and the public in opposing secrecy. At the same time complaints were made in some sections that secrecy was hindering the work of organizing new local and district assemblies. As a result of all these complaints and criticism, the general assembly in 1881, by a vote of 28 to 6, decided to do away with the secret policy.

In 1879 Stephens retired and, through his recommendation, Terence V. Powderly became grand master workman and remained in office by annual elections until 1893. He was an active member of the Machinists' and Blacksmiths' Union during the early seventies. He joined the Knights of Labor in 1874 and soon brought his union into the order. He became master workman of his district assembly, and he was elected Mayor of Scranton in 1878, and again in 1882 and 1884.

"The stamp of the sixties was unmistakably visible on Powderly throughout his entire career as the foremost labor leader in the country. Unlike Gompers, who came to supplant him before the public mind at a later date, he was foreign to the spirit of wage-consciousness. He was more closely akin to William H. Sylvis, who advocated trade-union action as a mere preparation for coöperation. Herein, perhaps, lies the explanation of Powderly's sensitiveness to public opinion, as against Gomper's reliance solely on wage-earners." [1]

After his retirement, Powderly was admitted to the bar, identified himself with the Republican Party, and stumped for McKinley in 1896. From 1897 to 1902 he was Commissioner General of Immigration, and from 1907 to his death in 1917 he was Chief of the Division of Information in the Bureau of Immigration and Naturalization at Washington. His career as head of the Knights of Labor for fifteen years and his later activities marked him as a safe and sane leader of the working-people. He was one of the very few real leaders that the labor movement in this country has produced out of its own ranks. He failed to retain his leadership permanently, but his ability and integrity were respected even by his critics and opponents.

SUCCESSES OF THE KNIGHTS OF LABOR

The Knights of Labor took no aggressive action as a national organization until 1880. After that year its principal activity consisted in the conduct of strikes. Many of these strikes were unsuccessful, because the organization operated mainly among the unskilled and inexperienced in la-

[1] Commons: *History of Labor in the United States*, vol. II, 347.

bor controversies, and because its centralized character was not well adapted to a strike of the members of a single trade. The strike policy was not carried out without considerable opposition from within the order. This opposition came mainly from the non-wage-earning, or reform element, which desired the organization to engage in greenbackism, socialism, land reform, or coöperation. Powderly himself seems to have been opposed to the policy of exclusive attention to strikes, but he was obliged to acknowledge that that policy was responsible for the growth of the Knights.

Frequent railway strikes were a feature of the labor movement during the years 1884 to 1886. Some early successes of the Knights of Labor in the conduct of these struggles served as a powerful advertisement of the organization. The result was that strikes were declared and the strikers joined the Knights after they had struck. The almost unavoidable outcome of such a method was a second strike after a short interval in order to protect the existence of the new union. A strike on the Wabash Railway in August, 1885, was of this character. A lockout of the members of the Knights of Labor, under the guise of a reduction of forces compelled the general executive board to issue an order which would have caused a general strike affecting Jay Gould's Southwestern railway system. Gould would not risk a strike at that time and, accordingly, an agreement was made by him which satisfactorily settled the trouble. The effect of this victory was to give an exaggerated idea of the power of the Knights, both to the working-men and to the general public.

Estimates of membership ranged all the way from 500,-000 to 5,000,000. When Powderly spoke, the newspapers commented favorably, and gave considerable space to what he said. The "New York Sun" detailed a reporter "to get up a story of the strength and purposes" of the organization, and the story was copied widely by newspapers and magazines, thus giving prominence to its activities. In this account the writer declared that five men controlled the chief interests of 500,000 men and could at any time take the means of livelihood from 2,500,000 people. These men composed the executive board of the order of the Knights of Labor. The powers of the Federal Government were described as "petty authority" compared with that of these five officials.

Before long the Knights of Labor were able to benefit by this widespread publicity. It led in the agitation for prohibiting the immigration of alien contract laborers. The use of such laborers to defeat strikes brought the question rapidly to the front. Especially, to an organization with a large membership among the unskilled, it was a serious matter. The passage of a law by Congress in February, 1885, forbidding the importation of laborers under contract, was due almost entirely to the work of the Knights.

The outcome of the Gould strike of 1885, the exaggeration of the power of the Knights by the press and the public, and their success at Washington provided the setting for the great labor upheaval of 1886. This upheaval marked the appearance of a new class in the labor movement — that of the unskilled. They felt that they had found a champion who could curb the most powerful capitalists in the country. Their accumulated feelings of bitterness and resentment now caused a rush to organize under the leadership of the Knights. The rapid pace at which the order grew, the wave of strikes, particularly sympathetic strikes, the use of the boycott, the violence of the movement — 1886 was the year of the Chicago anarchist outbreak — all were evidences of the rise of a new class — the unskilled worker. The outburst bore the aspect of a social war. A frenzied hatred of capital was shown in every important strike. Many of the leaders of the Knights realized the danger created by the attitude of the rank and file, but they were powerless to restrain them.

Under such conditions disaster was almost inevitable. A second strike upon the Gould railway system, growing out of the settlement of the first strike, broke out March 1, 1886. It quickly spread to other lines, and affected over five thousand miles in Missouri, Arkansas, Indian Territory, and Nebraska. The leader, District Master Workman Martin Irons, regarded a strike as a crusade against capital rather than a more or less drastic means of obtaining better labor conditions. Hence all compromise was absolutely excluded from his conduct of the strike. Negotiations were carried on by Gould and Powderly for arbitration, but they failed and, after two months of sporadic violence, the strike came to an end. It made a profound impression upon the public mind and a Congressional committee was appointed to invesitgate it.

DECLINE OF KNIGHTS OF LABOR

This failure, with other complications due to the rapid development and enormous power of the Knights of Labor, was the beginning of its decline. It had reached its highest point, and its subsidence was as rapid as its rise had been. By the end of 1887 the disintegration had reached an advanced stage.

One of the causes of such a rapid decline is to be found in the fact that most of the strikes during the second half of 1886 ended disastrously to labor. Another explanation is to be traced to the employers, who organized strong associations, and began a policy of discrimination and lockouts, directed mainly against the Knights. This action of the employers, coupled with the incompetence of the leaders of the laborers, had a great deal to do with the turning of the tide against labor in the first half of 1887.

The change during 1887 was most marked in the large cities where the movement had manifested most clearly the character of an uprising of the unskilled. After 1887 the Knights of Labor became "an organization predominantly of country people, of mechanics, small merchants, and farmers, an element more or less purely American and decidedly middle-class in its philosophy." This change seems to account for the subsequent close affiliation between the order and the "Farmers' Alliance," as well as its support of the Populist Party.

Still another cause for the decline of the Knights may be found in the apparent superiority of the trade-union form of organization over the mixed or industrial union as revealed by the experiences of 1886 and 1887. The tendency on the part of the more skilled and better organized trades in the order to separate from the mixed district assemblies, and to create national trade organizations, was consequently strengthened. The struggle between the two kinds went on both outside and inside the order. The defeats of the Knights in 1886 and 1887 led to the withdrawal of skilled workers just as successes in earlier years had attracted them. The inherent difficulty of uniting the skilled and the unskilled in one great organization was a fundamental cause of the breakdown of the Knights of Labor.

The solidarity of the interests of laborers as a whole seems visionary and illusive when compared with the substantial benefits that skilled workers can command for themselves. The superiority of the industrial organization over its trade-union rival is still to be determined.

The membership of the Knights of Labor fell from 700,-000 in 1886 to 100,000 in 1890. After 1887, when the bulk of the unskilled had left the order, and it had lost its hold upon the large cities, the struggle with the trade unions became merely a contest between two rival bodies. As the Knights of Labor declined, the Federation of Organized Trades and Labor Unions, now known as the American Federation of Labor, grew in strength.

At the general assembly in November, 1893, James R. Sovereign, a farmer editor of Iowa, succeeded in defeating Powderly as grand master workman through a temporary alliance with Socialist delegates. The membership had fallen to 75,000 and the organization had ceased to be one primarily of wage-earners. It had shifted toward politics and the farmers. Powderly himself had exerted considerable influence in the various movements that led up to the formation of the Populist Party in 1891.

After 1897 little was heard of the Knights of Labor and it existed only as "a bushwhacking annoyance on the heels of its successor."

Groat, in his "Study of Organized Labor in America," summarizes the causes for the failure of the Knights of Labor as follows: (1) "The failure of expensive sympathetic strikes in which the order became involved in spite of its professed disapproval of such acts in its later years. (2) Activity in political affairs. This was, of course, the result of experience and there was an abundance of precedent in favor of political action. It did not bring strength. (3) The presence of the two distinct forms of organization, the mixed labor assembly and the national trade assembly. These proved to be factors that undermined rather than built up the strength of the order. (4) The over-centralization of power in the hands of the general officers. The promoters of the first assembly guarded very jealously their leadership. They were the source of authority. This relation generated restlessness and suspicion in the place of strength."

The Knights of Labor was not the only general organization beyond the lines of single trades formed during these years. The idea of and effort toward a larger consolidation were characteristic of the period and naturally grew out of the development of large-scale industry. Over against the corporation must be established a larger unit, if labor was not to be reduced to a state of hopeless submission.

The mixed or industrial union had a brief period of success from 1884 to 1886, followed by a rapid decline. While it was prospering, the trade-unionists accepted it, but as soon as it failed to produce results, they turned to the narrower but more effective method. In fact, even while the Knights of Labor were growing in power, the trade-unionists were never really friendly to the mass method. They realized its dangers, and that their interests and those of the unskilled were not identical. The industrial union comprehends a broader social vision, but the trade union keeps a firmer hold upon the realities of business and industry.

From time to time attempts were made to form a federation among the national trade unions. In 1873 an effort was made to reorganize the National Labor Union, and, in 1876, a similar undertaking at Pittsburgh resolved itself into a struggle between the Socialists and Greenbackers. Business depression during the seventies, and the consequent disintegration of trade unions, prevented successful results from these efforts. Nothing was accomplished until the return of prosperity.

The Federation of Organized Trades

The successful initiative came from a disaffected group of the Knights of Labor, who called a conference at Terre Haute, Indiana, in August, 1881, to establish a rival order. This meeting formed a temporary organization, and issued a call to all trades and labor unions in the United States and Canada to meet at Pittsburgh in November, 1881. The object was, chiefly, a national federation to look after the legislative interests of trade-unionists, and only secondarily to spread the principles of trade-unionism. The British Trades Union Congress was the model followed by the leaders in this enterprise.

The Pittsburgh convention had an attendance of one hundred seven delegates, representing eight national and international unions, eleven city trades councils, forty-two local trade unions, three district assemblies, and forty-six local assemblies of the Knights of Labor. Sixty-eight delegates, including mainly Knights of Labor, came from Pittsburgh and vicinity. The large representation of the latter organization was partly due to the fear of the formation of a rival to their order.

Some division of opinion occurred over the selection of a presiding officer. A majority of the committee on organization recommended Samuel Gompers, while a minority urged the election of Richard Powers, of Chicago. The contest was between the East and the West, and between the Socialists and their opponents. Mr. Gompers was described as the leader of the Socialist element and as "one of the smartest men present." Serious controversy was prevented by the withdrawal of the rival candidates, and the election of John Jarrett, of the Amalgamated Iron and Steel Workers. Gompers and Powers were made vice-presidents.

A permanent organization was effected under the name of the Federation of Organized Trades and Labor Unions of the United States and Canada. No president was provided for, but a legislative committee of five, including a secretary, were to constitute the only permanent officials.

The second convention met in Cleveland in November, 1882, with only nineteen delegates present. The reduction in numbers was due to the absence of representatives of the Knights of Labor and of the Amalgamated Iron and Steel Workers. Eight national and international trade unions and ten trades' councils were represented. The legislative committee, in its report, complained of poor support, which had prevented any real accomplishment. The annual budget amounted to only $445.31.

In August, 1883, the third convention met in New York with twenty-seven delegates in attendance. A discussion took place in regard to the steps to be taken to make the Federation representative of the whole labor movement. A resolution for the appointment of a special committee, "to confer with the Knights of Labor and other kindred labor organizations with a view to a thorough unification and consolidation of the working-people throughout the country," was amended so as to omit the name of the Knights of Labor. There were several instances of veiled or half-concealed hostility to the latter organization. The legislative committee was enlarged to nine, and a committee was also appointed to attend the next national conventions of the two great political parties, and to demand, in the name of "the organized workmen of the United States," the inclusion in their platforms of the eight-hour law, the incorporation of national trade organizations, and the establishment of a national bureau of labor statistics.

During 1884 the failure of the Federation as a legislative organization became apparent. The annual budget never exceeded $700, and, except in 1881, none of its conventions represented more than one quarter of the trade-union membership. The efforts to get consideration from the Republicans and Democrats met with no success.

When it became evident to the leaders that the organization could not continue if it confined itself to efforts to advance labor legislation only, it was determined to try to in-

fuse new life into it by the inauguration of a national movement for the eight-hour day. This decision was taken at a
convention held in Chicago in October, 1884, at which
twenty-five delegates were present. The entire membership at that time seems to have been less than 50,000. A
general strike, set for May 1, 1886, was an ambitious programme for so small an organization. Even by the unions
affiliated with the Federation the proposal was coolly received. The success of the plan depended upon the assistance of the Knights of Labor, and, upon the eve of the
eight-hour strike, the general officers adopted an attitude
of hostility. On the other hand, the strike idea found a
ready response among the rank and file of the unskilled
workers, who were then joining the order in large numbers.

As might have been expected from such an undertaking,
the results were comparatively unimportant. Many of
those who won shorter hours at the beginning lost their
gains soon after. Bradstreet's, in January, 1887, reported
the movement to have been "a conspicuous failure."

Nevertheless, the Knights and the Federation emerged
"with unequal prestige." Because of its greater prominence "the press and the public charged the Knights with
the responsibility for the crimes laid at the doors of organized labor, notably the Haymarket bomb, and praised the
trade unions by way of contrast." Such a view was wholly
inaccurate, but it developed naturally from the fear
aroused by the spectacle of the solidarity of labor, as illustrated by the Knights in the year of their greatest gains.[1]

During 1886 the combined membership of labor organizations came near 1,000,000 — a number not reached
again until 1900. Of this total the Knights had 700,000,
and the trade unions 250,000; the former were largely unskilled, while the latter were chiefly skilled workers. The

[1] Commons: *History of Labor in the United States*, vol. ii, p. 386.

leaders of the Knights realized the importance of the control of the skilled before the unskilled and semi-skilled could achieve success. Their constant effort to absorb the trade unions produced bitter conflicts between the groups in 1886 and 1887. The struggle was an internal one within the working-class — a clash between the principle of the solidarity of labor and that of trade separation.

A local contest in New York between a district assembly and the cigar-makers brought to a climax the intermittent struggle that had been going on for a number of years. This contest also gave Samuel Gompers, who belonged to the cigar-makers, an opportunity to come to the front. He had first obtained prominence in 1881 at the time of the formation of the Federation, but not till this conflict with the Knights did he get a real chance to demonstrate his capacity for leadership.

As a result of the action of the cigar-makers, of whom Gompers was the leader, a call for a general trade-union conference to meet at Philadelphia in May, 1886, was issued. For the first time in the eighties "the combined trade-union movement of the entire country" came together for common action. What the Federation failed to do with its legislative programme, the menace of the Knights accomplished.

A proposed treaty of peace with the last-named organization was drawn up and a committee appointed to conduct negotiations. The treaty was rejected by a special general assembly held the same month, but a conciliatory address was issued at that time to the trade-unionists. Negotiations continued during the summer and early fall. The regular annual general assembly of the Knights met in October, 1886. It represented the organization at its highest point of power. Over six hundred delegates were present, the majority of whom were attending a convention for the first time. The proceedings were dictated by the "union-haters" and an open declaration of war was made.

The American Federation of Labor

The conference of trade-union officials and the annual convention of the Federation met together at Columbus, Ohio, in December, 1886. The result of the combined meetings was the formation of the American Federation of Labor — the name of the existing organization which has continued down to the present time. The new association was not to be merely for the purpose of obtaining legislation, but was to have important economic functions. The place of the former legislative committee was to be taken by a president, two vice-presidents, a secretary, and a treasurer, together forming an executive council with the following duties: (1) "to watch legislation"; (2) "to organize new local and national trade unions"; (3) "while recognizing the 'right of each trade to manage its own affairs,' to secure the unification of all labor organizations"; (4) "to pass upon boycotts instituted by the affiliated organizations"; (5) "in cases of strikes and lockouts, to issue after an investigation general appeals for voluntary financial contributions in aid of the organization involved." The new Federation was to obtain its revenue from charter fees and from a per capita tax of one-half cent per month for each member in good standing. The president was given a salary of one thousand dollars a year.[1]

Another effort to negotiate a settlement with the Knights failed, and thereupon the Federation in turn declared war. As time went on, the Knights rapidly declined, and too late a more conciliatory attitude on their part developed. The trade unions, however, feeling their advantage, were not in

[1] Commons: *History of Labor in the United States*, vol. ii, p. 411.

a mood for concessions. Gompers, who had been elected president in 1886, expressed the hope that the Knights would in "the near future return to the fold."

In 1888 the convention of the Federation decided in favor of another general effort for the eight-hour day; the date set was May 1, 1890. The chief advocates were the carpenters. The Executive Council immediately inaugurated an aggressive campaign, and for the first time employed salaried organizers. Two pamphlets were printed and widely distributed. Mass meetings were held on holidays in the larger cities, and Labor Day, 1889, witnessed no less than four hundred and twenty such meetings. Apparently, though, the campaign attracted much less attention than that of 1886.

The convention of 1889 materially modified the plan to be followed. The idea of a general strike was given up, and the executive council was authorized to select one union at a time to take action for the eight-hour day. After one union had won, another was to be chosen, and so on till all organized laborers had gained the eight-hour day. To assist, a strike benefit fund was to be collected by a special assessment of two cents per week for each member for five weeks, levied by the executive council for each union which attempted to carry out the plan.

The carpenters were selected to lead the movement which was to start May 1, 1890. After they had won, the United Mine Workers were to follow. The special assessment was levied, and, though many of the unions failed to pay their full share, it netted a considerable sum. In addition organizers were sent out to help the carpenters. The choice was a fortunate one and a large measure of success was achieved. According to their secretary, they won the eight-hour day in one hundred and thirty-seven cities and a nine-hour day in many other places.

The selection of the mine workers was as unfortunate as the other choice had been fortunate. The miners were not ready to strike and wisely refused to do so. Besides the efforts of the carpenters no general eight-hour movement developed, but during these years many local strikes for shorter hours were taking place. Notable progress was undoubtedly made in the building trades.

At this time the Federation was almost entirely an economic organization. The only instance when it was officially represented before a Congressional committee was in 1888 when President Gompers appeared as its spokesman. In 1890 a motion to maintain permanent representation in Washington during the sessions of Congress was defeated, and instead instructions were given, in 1891, to the executive council to send copies of all resolutions approved to every member of Congress.

Such political self-complacency, however, came to an end in 1892. The Homestead and other strikes of that year, depression in trade, and the use of injunctions and court prosecutions were powerful aids to the socialist and radical leaders inside the Federation, who wished to convert it from an exclusively economic organization into a political body and to have it enter independent politics.

The Political Programme of 1893

The beginning of a change of policy was apparent in the resolutions adopted by the convention of 1892, endorsing two of the planks of the Populist Party platform — the initiative and referendum and Government ownership of the telegraph and telephone. The convention of the following year is "memorable," because it submitted to the consideration of affiliated unions a "political programme." As stated in the preamble, the programme was suggested by the action of British trade unions, which had recently entered independent politics, "as auxiliary to their economic action." The eleven planks demanded: compulsory education; the initiative; a legal eight-hour work-day; governmental inspection of mines and workshops; abolition of the sweating system; employers' liability laws; abolition of the contract system upon public work; municipal ownership of electric light, gas, street railway, and water systems; the nationalization of telegraphs, telephones, railroads, and mines; "the collective ownership by the people of all means of production and distribution"; and the referendum upon all legislation.[1]

The platform was presented by Thomas J. Morgan, a Socialist from Chicago, and a delegate of the International Machinists' Union; it received "a more than passive support" from President Gompers. Only one real test vote occurred in this convention. It took place upon a motion to strike out the recommendation to the unions to give "favorable consideration" to the programme. The motion was carried by a vote of 1253 to 1182. Without the recommendation of favorable consideration, the submission of the programme was voted by 2244 to 67. Several other resolutions of a political character were also adopted at the same time. It should be remarked that this was the time of the Populist movement of the early nineties.

After the close of the convention, unions began to endorse the political programme, and for some time no opposition appeared. Then conservative leaders like Gompers demanded that the plank in favor of collective ownership of the means of production and distribution should be stricken out.

During 1894 the separate trade unions were active in politics, although the Federation refrained from partisan activity, and confined itself to agitation and lobbying for

[1] Commons: *History of Labor in the United States*, vol. II, pp. 509, 510.

favored measures. A large number of trade-unionists were candidates of the Populist Party, but only a very few were elected.

President Gompers referred to these failures in his address to the annual convention, as an argument against the adoption of the programme by the Federation. The first attack was made upon the preamble, and by a vote of 1345 to 861, it was stricken out. The real fight, however, was over plank 10, endorsing collective ownership. A substitute was adopted calling for the abolition of monopoly in landowning, and the putting in its place of a title based upon occupancy and use only. Some of the delegates regarded this action as a vote for the single tax, but most of them probably thought of it favorably upon the principle of "anything to beat socialism." None of the other planks were materially altered. A motion to adopt the amended platform was voted down by 735 votes to 1173 votes. In revenge the defeated Socialists combined with the supporters of John McBride, of the mine workers, and elected him president in place of Gompers, thus defeating the latter for the only time from 1886 down to the present time.

After the adjournment of the convention, a dispute arose as to whether the amended programme had been adopted, since each plank separately had been approved. President McBride declared that it had been, but the convention of 1895 voted that the action constituted a rejection. Afterwards it declared that the platform embodied the "legislative demands" of the Federation. For several years it was printed in the "American Federationist" under the heading "Legislative Platform."

In the convention of 1895 the Socialists urged the organization of an independent labor party, but in place of such action, by a vote of 1460 to 158, it was declared "the duty of union working-men to use their franchise so as to protect and advance the class interests of the men and women of labor and their children."

Once more in 1896 the Federation was almost drawn into partisan politics. Three successive conventions had voted for the free coinage of silver, and, when in that year the Democrats nominated Bryan, many prominent trade-union leaders publicly declared themselves for him. Even President Gompers was charged in 1897 with acting in connection with Democratic headquarters in favor of Bryan. This accusation was made in spite of the fact that he had officially warned all affiliated unions to keep out of partisan politics.

THE FARMER-LABOR PARTY

Since 1896 the demand for independent political action has been largely confined to the Socialists. Very recently a new effort to form a National Labor Party has been made after an interval of more than twenty years. The unsettled political conditions and social unrest make this new activity significant and worthy of serious consideration.

In November, 1918, an Independent Labor Party was launched by the Chicago Federation of Labor. A platform was adopted to be submitted to the Illinois State Federation and to the American Federation of Labor in the hope of forming a labor party for the country as a whole with local organizations in every State and city. In April, 1919, the new party polled over 54,467 votes for its candidate for Mayor in the Chicago municipal election.

Later in the same month six hundred delegates assembled at the State Capital and formed the Labor Party of Illinois. In November, 1919, twelve hundred delegates met in Chicago to form the Labor Party of the United States. Thirty-seven States and forty labor organizations were represented and fraternal delegates were present from the Nonpartisan League, the Committee of Forty-Eight, and a couple of other non-labor associations. The convention formulated a platform of twenty-nine articles. Plans were also made for the nomination of candidates for President and Vice-President in 1920.

Another convention was held in Chicago in July, 1920, and the Farmer-Labor Party organized after vain efforts upon the part of various groups of "liberals" to form a more moderate party and to get the labor men to amalgamate with such an organization. Parley P. Christensen, of Utah, and Max Hayes, of Ohio, were nominated for President and Vice-President. The party was controlled by the leaders of a small labor group who have been conspicuous as insurgents against the present leadership of the Amercan Federation of Labor. The candidate for Vice-President was the Socialist candidate for president of that body against Gompers ten years before. The addition of "Farmer" to the name did not alter the character as a class party with a platform making no appeal to the American people as a whole.

Christensen and Hayes received approximately 200,000 votes, as compared with 900,000 for Debs and 200,000 for the Prohibition candidate. The States of Washington, Illinois, South Dakota, New York, Indiana, Pennsylvania, Montana, Michigan, and Iowa contributed over 10,000 votes each, Washington, Illinois, and South Dakota leading with 77,246, 49,630, and 34,707 respectively.[1]

The American Federation of Labor had become by 1900 "the sovereign organization in the trade-union world." Its success, as compared with the failure of the Knights of Labor, has been due chiefly to two main reasons

---

[1] *The Survey*, vol. XLI, pp. 264, 265; vol. XLII, pp. 83, 84, 247, 782; vol. XLIII, p. 229. Information obtained from printed matter issued by the Committee of Forty-Eight.

In the first place, it has been exclusively a trade organization, preserving the trade unions as units. Each union retains industrial autonomy and its distinctive character, while the common interests of all trades are attended to by the central organization. A federal union is thus constituted, the different trade unions occupying a position similar to that of the States in our governmental structure. Centralization and local self-government are consequently both provided for and neither is sacrificed within its own peculiar field. The mistakes of the Knights of Labor were avoided in the plan of organization of the Federation.

Secondly, the Federation recognized the dangers involved in the participation in politics. The history of American labor organization is strewn with the wrecks of such efforts. From the early labor parties of 1827 to 1831, through the National Labor Union of 1866 to 1872 to the Knights of Labor, the result has always been the same. Political activity has proved to be a fatal malady. On the other hand, the Federation has kept out even when the provocation to enter has been great. It alone has waxed strong and has succeeded where so many have failed. Its objects and attainments have been in a narrower field, and very probably its success has been chiefly due to its restraint. Its social vision may be criticized, but it has kept close to fundamentals. Hence its continued growth and permanence.

RAILROAD BROTHERHOODS

The four great brotherhoods of railroad employees have never been affiliated with the American Federation of Labor, although the relations of the two groups have usually been friendly. These brotherhoods, more than any other American trade unions, resemble the British unions formed in the fifties, which abandoned militancy in support of a highly developed beneficiary policy. The emphasis upon the insurance feature was due to the difficulty of obtaining protection for men engaged in train service from ordinary insurance companies. Because of their beneficiary policy, they kept aloof during the seventies from the unions engaged in strikes, and did not affiliate with the Knights of Labor or the Federation. The same policy was continued even after they began to make wage demands. Hence their aloofness which has lasted to the present time.[1]

The engineers were the first group of railroad men to organize. A preliminary association was formed in 1855, but a permanent brotherhood was not established until 1863. By that year the need for mutual protection was keenly felt throughout the country. Accordingly, at a convention, held in Detroit in May, 1863, an organization known as the "Brotherhood of the Footboard" was formed. The fundamental idea was the attainment of a "high standard of ability as engineers and of character as men," such as was demanded by the nature of the occupation, and which would entitle them to a liberal compensation.

At first firemen and machinists were admitted by some divisions, but in 1864 they were excluded and the name changed to "Brotherhood of Locomotive Engineers." William D. Robinson, who is regarded as the father of the organization, was chosen the first chief grand engineer. By 1865 there were twenty thousand members and the New England, Middle, and Western States were represented. In 1870 the headquarters were established at Cleveland, where the Brotherhood has one of the finest office buildings in the city, erected at a cost of $1,250,000.

P. M. Arthur was chosen chief in 1874 and remained in office until his death in 1903. His conduct of affairs was conservative and successful and won the respect of the em-

[1] Commons: *History of Labor in the United States*, vol. ii, pp. 309, 310.

ployers and of the general public. The "New York Sun," in an editorial in 1899, declared that, when Arthur entered the office of a railroad president, he was "treated with as much respect and consideration as if he were one of the largest stockholders or some other person of like distinction . . . the labor unions had better seek out the Peter M. Arthurs in their ranks, and then they may come to enjoy the sympathy of the public and the respect of the 'Sun.'"

Three general funds are maintained: (1) the current expense fund; (2) the charity fund; and (3) a contingent or strike fund which consisted in 1900 of about $100,000.

The insurance features are provided for under a separate organization and are conducted as a strict mutual insurance business. The cost is said to be much less than it would be possible for men in so dangerous a calling to obtain from ordinary insurance companies. The annual assessments per $1000 from 1894 to 1900 averaged $16.55, based on a membership of between 16,000 and 26,000, and with outstanding insurance amounting to from $30,000,000 to $53,000,000. The claims paid during the seven years totaled $4,551,327.89. Since its organization it has paid out nearly $40,000,000 in insurance.

The Brotherhood of Locomotive Engineers has refused to federate with other labor organizations or to allow its members to retain membership in any other labor organization. It has always been insistent upon raising the standard of men admitted; in one year — the fifth in the history of the organization — 172 men were expelled for intoxication.

The Order of Railway Conductors of America was formed in the spring of 1868 by a small group of Illinois Central conductors as the Conductors' Union. Shortly after, a second union was organized by conductors upon the Chicago, Burlington and Quincy Railroad, and in July the two divisions united to form the Conductors' Brotherhood. Two additional organizations were formed in August and September, and in October the officials of the Chicago, Burlington and Quincy Railroad ordered their men to leave the Brotherhood or the service of the railroad.

The result was a call to all conductors in the United States and Canada to send delegates to a convention to be held at Columbus, Ohio, December 15, 1868. This convention revised the constitution and established a benefit department. Annual meetings were held up to 1891, when biennial sessions were instituted. The present name — the Order of Railway Conductors of America — was adopted in January, 1879. Its headquarters are at Cedar Rapids, Iowa, and it includes conductors in the United States, Canada, and Mexico. In 1900 its total membership was 24,500.

In addition to the general funds there is a protective fund of $100,000 from which expenditures are made by a two-thirds vote of the members. The rules require an elaborate and conservative procedure in all negotiations with employers concerning conditions of employment and relating to grievances. The general policy is to obtain written agreements as to wages, hours, and conditions. The principle of arbitration is warmly supported and no decision of arbitrators has ever been violated.

The mutual benefit department is distinct, as to the management of its funds, from the general order. The insurance business is conducted upon the mutual plan. Regular monthly assessments to the annual amount of $16 per $1000 of insurance are collected, and, when necessary, additional assessments may be levied. Nearly $22,000,000 has been paid in benefits. In addition most of the local divisions pay sick and disability benefits.

Eleven firemen from the old Erie Road organized the

Brotherhood of Locomotive Firemen in New York in December, 1873. In the two following years thirty-one lodges were formed, and at the third convention, held in September, 1876, fifty-three lodges were represented. Up to 1877 it was largely an insurance and fraternal organization, but in that year it participated in the great railroad strike. The disfavor with which members of the Brotherhood were generally regarded after the historic strikes of 1877 retarded its growth.

Since 1885, however, the Locomotive Firemen have had a successful organization. In 1894 it adopted a declaration deploring strikes and insisting upon its members standing by agreements made with employers. The Brotherhood has also coöperated with other organizations of railway men to secure united action upon the part of legislative committees in order to strengthen their position with State and national legislatures.

One of the chief purposes of the Brotherhood has been to improve the character and condition of its members. The beneficiary department is compulsory for all members who are eligible to participate in its benefits. There is a protective fund for which each member is assessed seventy-five cents per quarter as long as it remains under $100,000. Striking employees are paid twenty-five dollars per month, but no member receives pay for longer than three months.

The virtual leader up to 1880 was W. N. Sayer, grand secretary and treasurer, who was removed from office by the grand master because of excessive use of intoxicating liquor. Eugene V. Debs was appointed as his successor and occupied the position until 1892. At the time of his election he was opposed to strikes, and at his suggestion a general anti-strike policy was adopted. This action reduced the opposition of the railroad officials and increased the prosperity of the organization. Debs resigned as secretary and treasurer in 1892, but edited the official magazine until 1894.

During the great railroad strike of 1894, the Brotherhood suffered greatly. It had no official connection with the American Railway Union, but many of its members were drawn into the struggle and its membership declined. Undoubtedly, the fact that its former secretary and treasurer was the leader of the railroad men in the strike was responsible for the outcome. It did not recover until 1898.

The membership in 1900 was 36,084, and it had paid insurance benefits to the amount of $5,474,911.67 since 1881, when beneficiary work began. The Brotherhood also maintains an employment bureau through which coöperative effort is provided for finding employment for members. The headquarters are in Cleveland.

The Brotherhood of Railroad Trainmen is the largest organization of railroad employees in the country. It was formed in New York in 1883, and includes men in train and yard service. Its headquarters are at Cleveland, and its growth has been quite steady from the beginning. At first the sole purpose was to act as a mutual benefit association for the killed and injured among its members. It provides death and disability insurance at little more than the cost of operation. Approximately $42,000,000 has been paid out for these purposes. Like the other railroad organizations, it has gained better wages, shorter hours, and improved working conditions for its members. Protective legislation has been obtained and representatives are maintained at Washington and at State capitals. The total membership in 1900 was 43,500.

At the present time there are a number of other railroad organizations, but none of them compare with the older brotherhoods in influence or in number of members. Many of the minor associations are affiliated with the American

Federation of Labor, but the four great orders maintain their independence.

Strikes have been a constant feature of American labor history, but certain great conflicts stand out from among the lesser ones as great mountain peaks tower above the surrounding summits. Carroll D. Wright aptly described these outstanding struggles as "Historic Strikes" in his "Industrial Evolution of the United States," and as "Great Modern Battles" in "The Battles of Labor." He enumerates the great railroad strikes of 1877, the Southwestern strike upon the Gould railroads in 1886, the Homestead strike of 1892, the Pullman strike of 1894, and the great coal strike of 1902. These great contests are significant as manifestations of the activity of labor and of the growth of social democracy. They indicate the developing power of the working-classes under modern industrial conditions, and they constitute the nearest approach to revolutionary movements that we have experienced down to the present time in the United States. The situation in Europe and recent experiences in our own country lend added interest to these historic contests.

It is also interesting to note that they correspond to certain social and political movements in each period: the Greenback Labor Party of the later seventies, the Union Labor Party of 1886, and the Populist Party of the early nineties, to mention only three of the coincident developments. In view of recent events we may well give serious thought to the constantly rising waves of labor and social unrest. We cannot safely ignore the repeated warnings going back to 1877. We ought to pass constructive measures for dealing with industrial disputes, and not expect "industrial peace by miracle" as we seem to have done down to the present.

Just as some League of Nations, however weak in 1914,

might have prevented the great World War, so some method of arbitration would have saved us the inconveniences and interruptions of the recent coal strikes.

SELECTED REFERENCES

1. Commons: *History of Labor in the United States.*
   Vol. i. Introduction.
      Part ii, chaps. i–vi
      Part iii, chaps. i, ii, iv–vi } Before the Civil War.
      Part iv, chap. vii
   Vol. ii. Part v, chaps. i–iv (The National Labor Union).
      Part vi, chaps. i, viii–x (Knights of Labor).
      Part vi, chaps. vii, pp. 318–31 } American Federation
      Part vi, chap. x, pp. 395–413 }   of Labor.
      Part vi, chap. xiii, pp. 471–88,
        495–514
2. Groat: *The Study of Organized Labor in America,* chaps. ii, v, vi, vii, viii.
3. *American Federation of Labor: History, Encyclopedia Reference Book,* pp. 5–46, 341, 431, 432, 444–46, 458, 477.
4. Hoxie: *Trade Unionism in the United States,* chaps. iv, v, new edition 1923.
5. Carlton: *The History and Problems of Organized Labor,* chaps. iii–v.
6. *The Industrial Commission* (1900), vol. xvii, pp. 821–47.
7. Kirk: *The Knights of Labor and the American Federation of Labor,* in Hollander and Barnett: *Studies in American Trade Unionism,* pp. 353–80.
8. Ely: *The Labor Movement in America,* chap. iii, and Appendix.
9. Wright: *The Industrial Evolution of the United States,* chaps. xxv, xxvi.
10. Carlton: *Organized Labor in American History.*
11. Beard: *A Short History of the American Labor Movement.*
12. Orth: *The Armies of Labor,* chaps. i–viii.
13. Watkins: *An Introduction to the Study of Labor Problems.*
14. Perlman: *A History of Trade Unionism in the United States.*
15. Carroll: *Labor and Politics.*
16. Douglas: *The Worker in Modern Economic Society.*
17. Henry: *Woman and the Labor Movement.*

CHAPTER V

HENRY GEORGE AND THE SINGLE TAX

ANOTHER influence toward social democracy in the United States dates from the publication of "Progress and Poverty" by Henry George in 1879, and the agitation for the single tax which grew out of this book and the propaganda carried on by its author. "Henry Georgeism has played in this country the rôle of Marxism and socialism in Europe." In general terms, it may be described as "a sort of agrarian socialism — the product of conditions peculiar to the undeveloped capitalism of the West and — a distinctly American contribution to economic thought." [1] During the years of his activity, George was conspicuous as a radical and labor leader and his influence extended to foreign countries. His effectiveness as a writer and public speaker made him a forceful figure and a vital factor during a formative period.

"Few movements of any sort bear such a striking relation to the life and work of a single individual as the single-tax movement bears to the life and work of Henry George. Scarcely anything in the history of social reform movements is more remarkable than the spectacle of this unknown California printer setting foot in New York City, poor in pocket, equipped solely with a book and the consciousness of a message, to become the founder of a new world-wide crusade against world-old evils. Like the founder of a new religion, Henry George believed that he had been called to be a prophet to his age. The task to which he set himself was to be the bearer of an economic

[1] Macy: *Socialism in America*, p. 63.

revelation, to point the way to social salvation, to show the 'great primary wrong' which causes a shadow to accompany our advancing civilization. He sent forth his gospel with unwavering faith that his message would find friends who would take 'the cross of a new crusade.' " [1]

His main proposal was "to tax out of land the value which is due to social effort; to deduct the value of the land itself as distinct from improvements on land, but to leave the cultivation and other use of land to private effort."

A survey of his doctrines makes clear that he was anticipated in all the essential ideas of his economic philosophy, but the reaching of such a conclusion does not imply that he was not original in his statement of his views. His pamphlet, "Our Land and Land Policy," published in 1871, indicates that, at that time, he had some knowledge of Malthus, Ricardo, and Mill, but not till later, while writing "Progress and Poverty," did he undertake thorough study of the economists. Unquestionably, he worked out his theory of the distribution of wealth by bold and fresh thinking upon economic problems, as he saw their development under new world conditions. "George saw the small people of the great rich West oppressed by the railroad octopus and the benefits of the fairly democratic Homestead Act nullified by land speculators." Furthermore, no book would have initiated such a movement without the personal propaganda to which he was engaged down to his death in 1897.

Henry George was born in Philadelphia in 1839. He left school before he was fourteen years old, and, after working at home for a time, he sailed as foremast boy on a voyage to Australia and India. He returned from his journey around the world after an absence of over a year, and began to learn the printer's trade. Eighteen months later, he

[1] Young: *The Single Tax Movement in the United States*, **p. 1.**

obtained an opportunity to work his passage to California, where he arrived in May, 1858.

LIFE IN CALIFORNIA

In California he drifted from one occupation to another and from place to place for a number of years. Most of his time, however, was spent in San Francisco, and he also finished his apprenticeship as a printer. His trade, as well as his own inclination to reading and study, led him to write for the press. His career as a newspaper man began in 1865 and, in 1868, he published an article in the "Overland Monthly," then edited by Bret Harte. In 1869 he wrote a letter to the "New York Tribune," attacking two great corporations in California — the Central Pacific Railroad and the Wells, Fargo Express. Another letter, written a few months later to the same paper, on the "Chinese on the Pacific Coast," brought him a letter of commendation from John Stuart Mill.

This experience in California as a working-man, struggling to support himself and family, and his observation of economic and social conditions, where great fortunes were acquired through the rapid increase in land values, directed his attention to the land problem. In 1871 he published a pamphlet with the title, "Our Land and Land Policy," in which he presented for the first time his views that "the pursuance of a wrong policy in regard to land" was the fundamental cause of poverty and social injustice. This book of forty-eight pages described the reckless prodigality of the existing land policy and its tendency to concentrate ownership in the hands of the few. It contained the arguments, later developed in "Progress and Poverty," showing that the landowners received the lion's share of the benefits of economic progress, and that the placing of the chief weight of taxation upon land would solve most of our social problems.

From 1871 to 1875, George was editor of a small daily paper in San Francisco, and he participated vigorously in the discussions of the land question — then the subject of much local controversy in the State. During these four years he developed and elaborated his arguments from the cruder form which they took in "Our Land and Land Policy" to the finished shape in which they appeared in "Progress and Poverty." His doctrines, therefore, were worked out in actual contact with practical problems; they were not the theories of a closet philosopher. The particular land situation existing in California in the period following the discovery of gold gave rise to an agitation the immediate aim of which went little beyond the breaking-up of the immense landholdings that had developed. Many supported George for the accomplishment of the immediate object, but relatively few were willing to accept the single land tax which he advocated.

After four years a change in the ownership of the paper compelled George to give up his editorship, and in 1876 he was appointed State Inspector of Gas Meters. He held this position for another four years, and it gave him leisure to write "Progress and Poverty." During this period he was active in politics, becoming prominent as a Democratic orator during the Hayes-Tilden campaign, and incidentally acquiring valuable training as a public speaker. In 1878 he was a Democratic candidate for the convention to revise the State Constitution. Since one of the important causes of the revision was the dissatisfaction with the existing tax laws, he was anxious for an opportunity to urge his own views of tax reform in the convention. The Democrats, however, were defeated and he lost the chance. The constitution, as finally adopted, seems not to have contained any direct results of his propaganda.

During the same year the first society to further his

views was organized by a number of his San Francisco friends under the name of "The Land Reform League of California." As a result of the activity of the new association, George delivered his first formal propaganda lecture, March 26, 1878. His subject was "Why Work is Scarce, Wages Low, and Labor Restless."

In September, 1877, he began "Progress and Poverty," and completed it in March, 1879. The times were favorable for such an inquiry. A period of hard times had followed the crisis of 1873. The contrast between the prosperity of the few and the poverty of the many called attention to the unconsidered problems of the new industrial development. Such an examination of the fundamentals of economic life as George had undertaken could not fail to awaken interest under the conditions existing during the later seventies in the United States.

The manuscript of "Progress and Poverty" was rejected by the Eastern publishers to which the author submitted it, and he could get no one to print it, except an old partner in San Francisco who had gone into the printing business.

In the fall of 1879, "Progress and Poverty" appeared as an author's edition of five hundred copies. The book attracted little attention in California beyond George's own group of friends. After the sale had nearly paid for the initial expense of making the plates, the author undertook to secure a publisher who would print it, and at length Appleton and Company agreed to issue it. By the time of George's arrival in New York in August, 1880, it was slowly beginning to gain recognition. His removal from California to the East was to enable him to begin the wider spreading of his economic gospel — a work which was to occupy him till his death in 1897.

REMOVAL TO NEW YORK CITY

Most of the reviews in 1880 regarded "Progress and Poverty" as a book of unusual character and recognized the power and appeal of its literary style. The agitation of the land question in Ireland was at its height, and early in 1881 George published a small book upon "The Irish Land Question." In the fall of 1881 he sailed for the British Isles where he was eager to present his own solution of the land question and to study Irish conditions.

His book had been very favorably received in England and several editions had been sold. His influence there reached all classes of people and it reacted upon his reputation in the United States. In October, 1882, he returned and received a remarkable reception. The Central Labor Union welcomed him at Cooper Institute, and a banquet in his honor at Delmonico's was characterized by the "New York Times" as "a distinguished assembly."

Henry Ward Beecher declared in an address that he came from a desire to join in honoring a man who had contributed some service besides material wealth to the community. He was in a fair way of becoming a literary light and was invited to speak before wealthy and fashionable audiences.

But such a book as "Progress and Poverty" could hardly be expected to escape attack from the orthodox economists. Professor W. G. Sumner, of Yale University, led the assault in articles published in June and November, 1881. In May, 1883, General Francis A. Walker, himself a critic of the conservative economists, delivered a series of lectures at Harvard University which were chiefly devoted to a reply to Henry George. These lectures, published under the title of "Land and Its Rent," were the first substantial criticism which George's work received from the economists.

Gradually the criticism began to take on a different tone, and instead of references to Henry George, "the distinguished author," he was spoken of as Henry George, "the social agitator." This change appeared in the reviews of "Social Problems," originally written by George as a series of articles for "Frank Leslie's Illustrated Newspaper." The different attitude was partly due to a change of tone on the part of George, who was not content with being merely a literary celebrity, but a propagandist making a proposal which he was intensely desirous of seeing actually tested and tried.

In spite of criticism and attack his views were seriously received by many people. The circulation of his books, reinforced by his speeches, had gained for him a wide hearing. As President Hadley remarked in the "New York Independent," "his books are sold and read in America and England as no other books are sold and read; the sales are numbered by the hundred thousand, the readers by the million."

The First Campaign for Mayor

By 1883, George found himself regarded as the apostle of a new social creed and the first phase of his career as a social reformer was completed. The second period in his life-work began with his campaign for the mayoralty of New York City in 1886. The author of a remarkable book, whose theories were regarded as of little more than academic interest, became the leader of dissatisfied workingmen and the champion of the masses. The year 1886 was one of labor and social unrest and was characterized by the rise of the unskilled worker to economic and political consciousness. The railroad strikes, conducted by the

Knights of Labor, and the outbreak of the Chicago anarchists were merely significant incidents. Henry George, a working-man himself, appealed with special force to working-men. As an editor he had been a champion of the workers, and his theory of the causes of poverty seemed a sympathetic one to men who were constantly struggling with the facts of poverty. Consequently, he suddenly found himself a political leader as well as the prophet of a new social order.

The Central Labor Union of New York City, which nominated Henry George for Mayor, grew out of a mass meeting held by the trade-unionists in the winter of 1881 to 1882 to express sympathy with the Irish people in their contest with the landlords. But interest in the land question was not the immediate cause of his nomination. The Central Labor Union determined to enter politics because of dissatisfaction with the administration of justice and the attitude of the courts on labor questions. George was nominated because it was thought that he "best represented the protest against unjust social conditions and the best means of remedying them."

When Henry George was asked whether he would accept the nomination, he made the unusual condition that he would become a candidate if thirty thousand signatures were obtained to a petition for that purpose. This difficult stipulation was promptly met and the campaign began late in September. The platform attacked monopolies and political corruption and urged as reform measures George's land tax and ballot reform.

Henry George was not primarily an office-seeker; he went into politics to advertise his theories and to promote their discussion. His candidacy secured an immense amount of publicity throughout the country. Entirely apart from his election, and whether or not he possessed administrative ability, there was general agreement that his campaign was of very considerable political and social significance. It could not fail to have great influence upon public opinion in a year of unrest and agitation.

The real contest was between Abram S. Hewitt, the Democratic nominee, and Henry George; Theodore Roosevelt, the Republican candidate, did not take a conspicuous part in the campaign. Hewitt defined the issues of the struggle in his letter of acceptance, in which he charged George with undertaking to array class against class, and declared that his aim was "to substitute the ideas of anarchists, nihilists, communists, socialists, and mere theorists for the democratic principle of individual liberty." He regarded the election of George as "the greatest possible calamity that could menace" the prosperity and future of the city. Thus the campaign was stressed as one between George's radicalism and Hewitt's conservatism.

With such a challenge, the contest was bound to be a spectacular one. George was then in his prime and a powerful and impressive speaker. He made over one hundred speeches during the campaign — on one occasion as many as eleven in one evening. Hewitt declined to meet his opponent in public debate, but the candidates exchanged a number of open letters which formed an unusual feature of the campaign. The newspapers opposed George and described him as dangerous and socialistic.

The official result was: Hewitt, 90,552; George, 68,110; Roosevelt, 60,435. The large vote for George represented much more than the widespread endorsement of his theories. It was a sign of political discontent, and it indicated the strength of the disaffected masses who saw in him a leader and friend. We must remember also that this election came only two years after the first defeat of the Republicans in a presidential campaign since the Civil War.

The bulk of the vote cast for George, however, came from the trade-unionists and represented the rise of the working-classes to political consciousness and power. Only a leader was needed to weld this new force into a real factor in American politics. Conditions in New York City and George's leadership gave it a temporary strength which almost carried him to victory. George believed that he had really been elected, and there is some reason for the opinion that the vote counted did not represent the vote actually cast.

Naturally, Henry George and his supporters believed that they had won a great victory, since the new labor party's vote was nearly a third of the total vote, and greater than that for the Republican candidate. A "congratulation meeting," held soon after the election in November, adopted a resolution calling for the organization throughout the United States of associations to carry on "the work of propagating truth by means of lectures, discussions, and dissemination of literature," and to prepare the way for political action. The ultimate aim was to be the organization of a national party. The meeting adjourned with cheers for "Henry George, our next Governor," and for "Henry George, the next President." Furthermore, the press frequently referred to him as a possible labor candidate for the Presidency.

ORIGIN OF USE OF TERM "SINGLE TAX"

The year 1887 was an eventful one in the career of Henry George. It was marked by the origin of the use of the term "single tax" to describe the movement begun by him; by the controversy with the authorities of the Catholic Church because of the adherence of Father Edward McGlynn to the doctrines of "Progress and Poverty"; by the founding of the Anti-Poverty Society; by George's candidacy for Secretary of State of New York;

by his quarrel with the Socialists; and by the defeat and break-up of the United Labor Party.

These events gave the new movement much greater solidarity. The heterogeneous following of 1886 was converted into a well-defined group, smaller in numbers, but active and energetic. The single-tax movement of to-day very largely dates back to 1887; the permanent character of the propaganda was determined during that year.

Before 1887 it was usual to describe the agitation as "the Henry George movement," "Georgeism," or "Henry George men." After political activity began, the need of a name came to be felt very strongly. A number of suggestions were made, but none proved satisfactory until Thomas G. Shearman proposed the term "single tax," which Henry George used in a notable passage in "Progress and Poverty." By the fall of 1887 it had become the common designation for the reform movement originated by Henry George, and since 1887 it has been customary to refer to it as the "Single-Tax movement."

During 1887, Father McGlynn, a Catholic priest of New York City, became very conspicuous in the movement, almost for a time dividing leadership with the founder himself. His interest had originally been attracted by George's discussion of the Irish land question. During the campaign of 1886 his support of the doctrines of "Progress and Poverty" got him into trouble with the authorities of the Church, and he was first suspended from his charge, and later excommunicated.

While the controversy was in progress, a group of single-taxers organized the Anti-Poverty Society in New York City, and Father McGlynn was chosen president and Henry George vice-president. The aim of the new organization was declared to be "an active warfare against the conditions that, in spite of the advance in the powers of production, condemn so many to degrading poverty, and foster vice, crime, and greed." Beginning with the first of May, 1887, public meetings were held every Sunday evening with addresses by McGlynn and George, with music and hymns, and with a great deal of religious fervor. The members talked of taking the "cross of a new crusade" and of "spreading the gospel." They used the methods employed by churches, such as engaging in personal work and circulating tracts. Thus the new organization gave a religious enthusiasm to the economic agitation begun by Henry George. The religious tone was emphasized by the protest aroused by the excommunication of McGlynn by the Church authorities. In June a parade of from 30,000 to 40,000 working-men was held in New York City to protest against the Church action.

The cumulative effect of all these activities was, of course, to stir up a wide public interest in the single-tax movement. The press ridiculed the spirit and methods, especially of the Anti-Poverty Society, but, as Henry George himself declared, "the anti-poverty cause" was gaining and the "pro-property folks" were scared.

OTHER POLITICAL CAMPAIGNS

Almost inevitably Henry George was drawn into the arena of State politics. The United Labor Party planned to enter the State campaign in New York in 1887 as preliminary to the presidential contest of the following year. There had been substantial agreement among the supporters of George during the city campaign of 1886, but preparations for 1887 brought out differences between the single-taxers and the Socialists. The latter had accepted the single-tax programme of 1886 because they had regarded it as aimed against capital, but early in 1887 they began to insist that the real question was not a land tax, but the abolition of all private property in the instruments of production. They contested the continued leadership of Henry George and made persistent efforts to force socialistic doctrines upon him.

The controversy came up for settlement in the State Convention of the United Labor Party in August. George declared his opposition to socialism, and the Socialist delegates were refused admission, on the technical ground that the United Labor Party required its members to sever their connection with other political parties — a condition that the Socialists would not accept. They resented their exclusion and organized a Progressive Labor Party in opposition to the United Labor Party. They denounced George, his platform and personal political machine, and accused him of pandering to the prejudices of the capitalist class.

After the expulsion of the Socialists, the convention adopted a platform similar to that of 1886, and nominated a full list of candidates with Henry George at the head of the ticket as candidate for Secretary of State. An active campaign was waged for two months before the election. George, McGlynn, and others stumped the State; more than a million tracts on the land question were distributed; and supporters arranged meetings and organized clubs in all parts of the State.

At the close of the campaign the prospects for a large vote were thought to be good, but the hopes of the leaders were doomed to disappointment. George received 72,781 votes — only a few thousand more votes than he had received the year before in New York City. A little over one half of his vote was in New York City and 15,000 of the remainder in Brooklyn.

There were a number of reasons for the result in the State election. The loss of Socialist support, together with their open hostility, alienated a considerable number. Much more important was the opposition of the Catholic Church due to George's defense of McGlynn and his attacks upon those responsible for the treatment of the excommunicated priest. Furthermore, the campaign for Secretary of State was necessarily far less spectacular than that for Mayor. It had more significance for national party politics and there was less probability of independent voting than in a municipal campaign. The single tax as an economic formula for social reform was much less generally attractive as a campaign issue than a protest against municipal corruption and a manifestation of discontent among working-men because of inequality before the law. Under these circumstances the outcome of 1887 was by no means the utter defeat which many considered it.

Nevertheless, hopes of immediate success through independent political action were shattered and the single-tax leaders were confronted with the problem of determining the policy to be followed. Henry George precipitated the controversy in December, 1887, by declaring his conviction that it was the duty of single-taxers to support the Democratic Party if it should make tariff reform the issue of the coming presidential campaign. President Cleveland's tariff message had just indicated such a possibility. George's position was acceptable to most of the leaders and to a majority of the rank and file of the single-taxers, but it was opposed by McGlynn and a few of the labor leaders who favored independent political action.

George and his supporters took an active part in the campaign for the reëlection of Cleveland. They formed free-trade clubs and made many speeches in behalf of the Democrats. McGlynn and his following finally came out for the Republican candidate, when effective independent political action proved impossible.

The defeat of Cleveland in 1888 was the third political disappointment for the single-taxers in as many years. Evidently the time was not ripe for any wide acceptance of their views. As a political guide Henry George had been found lacking in the choice of issues and of methods of work. He was a preacher and prophet rather than a practical political leader.

NATIONAL PROPAGANDA FOR SINGLE TAX

After the close of the campaign in 1888, two alternatives presented themselves: one was to concentrate effort upon a single State and secure the adoption of the plan with the expectation that the demonstration of its successful working in one State would insure its rapid spread throughout the country; the other plan was to devote work to the circulation of national and State petitions for the purpose of arousing public interest and influencing legislation. The latter method had been tried out in several places during 1888. The two proposals were not mutually exclusive, but single-tax opinion soon came to favor the petition way as the main line of work. The petition asked Congress to appoint a commission to investigate and report upon the single tax as an exclusive method of raising revenue.

Work upon the petition began in December, 1888, and by March, 1892, it was ready for presentation to Congress with 115,503 signatures. It did not induce Congress to authorize the desired inquiry, but in spite of this failure it had proved to be an effective means of propaganda. When the collection of signatures began, there were less than twenty active organizations in the whole country, while by the end of 1889 the number had increased to 131. Of these New York had 22, Ohio 14, Pennsylvania 13, Massachusetts 12, New Jersey 9, Indiana 6, California, Colorado, Illinois, and Iowa 5 each. There were 12 in the

South and 23 were scattering. Through the various activities of Henry George and his followers the single-tax movement had become in ten years a national one.

In September, 1890, a national conference was held in New York City with five hundred delegates in attendance from more than thirty States. The Single-Tax League of the United States was formed with a national committee composed of one member from each State. A platform was adopted which remains the authoritative statement of principles and purposes. One of the incidents of the meeting was the welcome given to Henry George upon his return from a trip around the world.

The organization of 1890 proved to be mainly a paper organization. A second conference met at Chicago in 1893, but the attendance was smaller and all efforts to establish a national organization were given up for many years. Another national meeting was not undertaken till 1907.

The Second Campaign for Mayor

Again in 1897 George became a candidate for Mayor of New York. The election was the first held after the formation of the Greater New York City. There were three other candidates: the Tammany nominee, Judge Robert A. Van Wyck; the Republican machine candidate, General Benjamin F. Tracy; and Seth Low, the nominee of the Citizens' Union, an organization formed as a protest against the bad politics represented by the two old parties.

George entered the campaign as the representative of Democrats who opposed Tammany and who had supported Bryan in 1896. George himself had supported Bryan and was bitterly disappointed by his defeat. He did not believe in the free coinage of silver, but he preferred it "to the principle of privilege which the monopolistic powers gathered around the gold, or so-called 'sound money' candidate.''

As in the earlier campaign of 1886, George saw an opportunity to advance the single-tax cause, and he became a candidate in spite of the opinion of his medical advisers that his active participation in the campaign would probably cost him his life. A few years before he had suffered a stroke of aphasia. His great exertions in propagating his doctrines had worn out his strength and were undoubtedly responsible for his breakdown.

He entered the campaign with all his usual energy and enthusiasm, making sometimes from three to five speeches a day. He justified his candidacy as a reformer in addition to Low by the statement that Low was "an aristocratic reformer," while he was "a democratic reformer." Low would "help the people"; he would "help the people to help themselves."

His tragic death came five days before election. On Thursday evening, October 28th, he spoke four times, and early the next morning a stroke of apoplexy came and he died without regaining consciousness. His oldest son, Henry George, Jr., was named in his place and received 20,000 votes. How many votes George might have received can never be known. The Tammany candidate received 228,000; Low received 148,000; and the Republican candidate 101,000.

The death of Henry George in 1897 marks the end of a remarkable career. Whatever may be thought of the soundness of his doctrines, there can be no doubt as to his earnestness and devotion. Rarely has it been given to any man to inaugurate and lead a reform movement so completely as he did. He worked out his theories from his observations in California; he marshaled them in "Progress and Poverty"; and he gave nearly twenty years to the spread of his views. Never once did he waver in his belief that he had discovered and explained the fundamental cause of human misery.

The key to his place and influence is to be found in his statement justifying his entrance into his last campaign; he was a democratic reformer. He was the one leader who has risen from the ranks of the laboring-class in the United States who has had principles wrought out from his own experience, and who as a speaker and writer could present them in an attractive and effective form. He is unique in this respect in our history down to the present time.

Powderly, Gompers, and Bryan have been influential leaders of the rank and file, but they have originated no comprehensive programme and they have undertaken to work out no fundamental remedy. Like Karl Marx, George originated a movement and left disciples who have continued to hand on the torch of his inspiration to succeeding generations. The absolute truth of his principles has nothing to do with the greatness of his achievement as a prophet and preacher.

His place in the development of social democracy in the United States is secure, for he insisted upon the importance of the study of poverty long before the condition-of-the-people question had come within the range of view of political parties. This contribution to social democracy ranks with that of the third parties of the eighties and nineties and the social workers in more recent years. These forces have socialized our politics and our democracy.

The Single Tax since 1897

Since 1897 the single-tax propaganda has been carried on by George's immediate supporters and their successors. In 1907 a third national conference was held in New York City with delegates from California, Florida, Ohio, Illinois,

Alabama, Maryland, Connecticut, Pennsylvania, Massachusetts, Washington, the District of Columbia, and Canada. The American Single-Tax League was organized, but like its predecessors it ceased to exist after a year or two.

Early in 1909, Joseph Fels, the manufacturer of Fels-Naptha soap, promised to contribute twenty-five thousand dollars a year for five years for the promotion of the single tax in the United States. He also offered a like sum for the support of similar work in Great Britain, and varying amounts for use in Germany, Denmark, Hungary, Australia, and Canada. He stipulated that in each case single-taxers should raise equal amounts. Actually he did not hold them rigidly to this requirement. He entrusted the administration of the fund in the United States to a commission with headquarters in Cincinnati.

The aim of Fels and the commission was "to put the single tax into effect somewhere in the United States within five years." It was proposed to center efforts in a number of States where prospects seemed favorable. In general the commission offered to become the central supervisory agency for the American movement, and it had the support of the great body of single-taxers in the country.

Fels died early in 1914, but Mrs. Fels carried on the work down to the end of 1916, when it was transferred to a newly formed national Single-Tax League of the United States.

The United States, the birthplace of the single tax, does not stand first in the record of its achievements. Western Canada, Australia, England, as a result of the Lloyd-George budget of 1909, and Germany before 1914, show greater results. Of course, the taxation of the unearned increment of land values does not represent the acceptance of the principle of the single tax, and its adoption is not entirely due to Henry George and his followers and successors.

Furthermore, the movement has not gained any con-siderable number of adherents in the United States. According to an estimate by the editor of the "Single-Tax Review" in 1916, there were then between 25,000 and 50,000 "convinced single-taxers who are in the possession of the full vision." Another authority doubts whether the number of believers has increased much since George's death in 1897. As a rule single-taxers are members of the middle class, and among them are writers, educators, members of the medical and legal professions, social workers, and clergymen. An exceptionally able and influential personnel chiefly accounts for the importance of the movement. Henry George's designation, "democratic reformer," hardly applies to the more recent membership of the movement.

In the introduction to the twenty-fifth anniversary edition of "Progress and Poverty," in 1905, Henry George, Jr., stated that more than two million copies of that book had been printed to date and, including other books written by his father, about five million copies had been distributed. Such widespread publicity, supplemented by constant activity as a speaker at home and abroad, was a challenge that could not be ignored. Economic thought has been broader and deeper since 1880; opinion upon social problems has profoundly changed; and it has become plain that "no true civilization can avoid the duty of finding a means to 'extirpate poverty' and 'to lighten the burdens of those compelled to toil.'"

"The nineteenth century cannot show a handful of American authors writing upon economic subjects whose style, in clearness, strength, and spiritual understanding, surpassed the style of Henry George." [1]

[1] *The Literary Review*, February 12, 1921.

SELECTED REFERENCES

1. Young: *The Single-Tax Movement in the United States.*
2. George: *The Life of Henry George,* vols. IX and X of *Complete Works of Henry George,* published by Doubleday, Page & Co.
3. Fels: *Joseph Fels: His Life and Work,* chaps. X–XIII.
4. Carver: *Essays in Social Justice,* chap. XI.
5. Johnson: "The Case Against the Single Tax," in the *Atlantic Monthly,* vol. XCIII, pp. 27–37 (January, 1914).
6. *The Single-Tax Year-Book* (1917).
7. Fillebrown: *The Principles of Natural Taxation.*
8. Post: *Taxation of Land Values.*
9. Bullock: *Selected Articles on the Single Tax.* Debater's Handbook Series.
10. Commons: *History of Labor in the United States,* vol. II, chap. XII.

CHAPTER VI

NATIONALISM

ANOTHER factor in the development of social democracy in the United States was "Nationalism," originating in the novel "Looking Backward," published by Edward Bellamy in 1888. Public opinion had been aroused at that time by the recent discovery of the first "trusts," and the book consequently had a great sale for a few years. According to accounts, it sold for a time at the rate of a thousand copies a day, and a total of 350,000 copies were sold in two years. Undoubtedly, it was the book of the hour. The temporary success of the movement, originated by the story, lasted only a few years, and its sudden eclipse has almost blotted out the remembrance of a very interesting episode in the history of social thought in the country. The publication of a novel at just the right psychological time created a short-lived social movement of considerable importance.

EDWARD BELLAMY AND "LOOKING BACKWARD"

Edward Bellamy, a novelist by profession, who found himself suddenly the leader of a social reform movement, was about forty years old at the time of the publication of "Looking Backward." He was born in Massachusetts, educated at Union College, studied for a year in Germany, read law and was admitted to the bar in 1871. From 1871 to 1876 he was engaged in journalism in New York and Massachusetts, but after 1876 he devoted himself to writing fiction. Before 1888 he had published a number of novels and short stories. "Ingenuity, sometimes a little strained," and "fanciful idealism rather than careful realism," characterized his earlier writings, and "Looking Backward" belonged in the same class.

By far the larger part of the book is occupied with conversations, in which a citizen of Boston in the year 2000 A.D. explains the highly novel social and political situation. The narrator of the story, a young Bostonian, wealthy and cultivated, was afflicted with insomnia and had had an underground sleeping-room constructed in his house. Put to sleep by a "magnetic" physician on the 30th of May, 1887, he did not awaken until the year 2000. The house had probably been burnt down the same night, the subterranean chamber hermetically sealed, and the vital processes are supposed to have been suspended.

His awakening resulted from an excavation for a cellar made by a physician who happened to be living on the site of the destroyed property. An ingenious explanation is given of his resuscitation, the setting and characters are described, and then the author plunges directly into an account of the new economic and social conditions.

Such a question as the labor question was not known in the year 2000. "The solution came as the result of a process of industrial evolution which could not have terminated otherwise. All that society had to do was to recognize and coöperate with that evolution, when its tendency had become unmistakable." This tendency was toward the concentration of capital in fewer and fewer hands. At first the "outcry" against it was "furious," but at last it was recognized as a process which when completed would "open a golden future to humanity."

Beginning during the last decade of the nineteenth century, the evolution resulted in the "final consolidation of the entire capital of the nation" early in the next century. "The industry and commerce of the country, ceasing to be conducted by a set of irresponsible corporations and syndicates of private persons, at their caprice and for their profit, were entrusted to a single syndicate representing the people, to be conducted in the common interest for the common profit. The nation, that is to say, organized as the one great business corporation in which all other corporations were absorbed: it became the one capitalist in the place of all other capitalists, the sole employer, the final monopoly."

The change had taken place without violence, since the great combinations had given object lessons as to the practicability of the plan. No effort is made to explain how private and corporate property became public property, but the inference is that the National Government confiscated it, as no one owned anything but a small amount of personal property under the new conditions.

Under the new social order every man and woman was enrolled in the industrial army. This universal industrial service rested upon the accepted idea that every citizen ought "to contribute his quota of industrial or intellectual work to the maintenance of the Nation." The period of service was twenty-four years, beginning at the close of the course of education at twenty-one, and terminating at forty-five. After forty-five, while discharged from labor, the citizen still remained liable for special calls in case of emergencies. Every new recruit belonged for three years to the class of unskilled or common laborers. After this term he was free to choose the kind of work with hand or brain which he preferred to do. It was the business of the administration to equalize the attractions of the different trades by making the hours vary according to their arduousness. The principle was that "no man's work ought to be, on the whole, harder for him than any other man's for him, the workers themselves to be the judges."

The President of the United States was the head of the industrial army of the Nation. He must have passed through all the grades from common laborer up. Professional men, who did not belong to the industrial army proper, could vote for President, but were not eligible themselves. The various trades were grouped into ten great departments, each of which had a chief and these chiefs formed the council of the President. Excellence as a worker qualified a private for the rank of officer; officers were ranked in an ascending scale as lieutenants, captains or foremen, colonels or superintendents, and generals of the guilds or departments. Each officer made appointments to the grade below from the candidates having the best record. The generals, however, were chosen from among the superintendents by vote of the members of the guild who had served their time and had been discharged. The President was chosen in the same way from heads of departments and served five years. Congress had but little to do beyond passing upon the reports of the President and the heads of departments at the end of their terms of office. There were no parties or politicians under this ideal scheme of social organization.

In this Utopia, money was unknown. Buying and selling were processes entirely antiquated. The nation was the sole producer and all persons were in its employment. Credit-cards were issued to all persons, which were presented to the national distributing shops when there was need of anything. Mr. Bellamy does not anywhere state the amount of the yearly allowance, but he does say that *it is the same for all.* Consequently, cripples, idiots, and children received the same share as able-bodied workers, a certain amount of *effort* only being required, not of performance. Such was the force of public opinion that no one able to work refused to exert himself. Equality of payment was thus the rule and the notion of charity was therefore dismissed. The membership of individuals in the nation as citizens entitled them to support.

The author of "Looking Backward" ingeniously described the social scheme which had replaced the existing order. The various features differed in their probability. In general they consisted in removing the objectionable characteristics of the present social order, and replacing them in a more or less arbitrary and mechanical way by others, which are described as ideal in their workings. Thus, the then comparatively recent concentration of capital in the form of "trusts" was made the basis for a fundamental transformation of industry. The actual steps in the process of change are passed over. The military organizations of France and England were used to provide the plan for the new industrial army. It is described as working successfully and as having solved the labor problem. In the same manner, equality of compensation is used and public opinion declared to have provided against any kind of slacking on the part of the worker. The problem of poverty is also done away with in the same summary fashion by basing payment upon effort rather than upon accomplishment. Just how the effort of the idiot, for instance, is to be measured is passed over without comment.

Bellamy's social dream imagined a nation in the highest degree centralized, a society in which no differences of natural or acquired ability were distinguished in the reward of services, in which private property was limited to a few personal belongings, in which there was no money, no buying or selling, no taxes, in which the Government had full control of the citizen for twenty-four years, and in which the Government is the one employer of labor, the one producer, distributor, and publisher. In other words, a scheme where "Prussianism" would dominate every part of human life.

THE AUTHOR BECOMES REFORMER

Apparently Mr. Bellamy undertook the writing of "Looking Backward" with no purpose of attempting any serious contribution to social reform. It was "a mere literary fantasy — a fairy tale of felicity." While working out the details he made use of the idea of an industrial army like the great military forces of France and Germany. Gradually he perceived the possibilities of the military system as a model or pattern for a national industrial service. He became convinced that he had stumbled upon the "corner-stone of the new social order." The result was a complete recasting of the form and purpose of the book. "Instead of a mere fairy tale of social perfection, it became the vehicle of a definite scheme of industrial reorganization."

The author soon came to believe that "the mantle of a genuine prophet had fallen upon him." The literary aspect of his work was subordinated to its character as an argument for a scheme of social reform. Viewed in this way "Looking Backward" cannot be regarded as particularly convincing. Furthermore, Bellamy's response to criticisms did not inspire respect for his grasp upon economic and social facts. To a suggestion that seventy-five centuries hence would be a more probable date for such a transformation than the year 2000, Bellamy replied that "the dawn of the new era" was "already at hand" and "the full day" would "swiftly follow." This assertion he based upon a reference to the swiftness with which the independence of the United States and the unity of Germany and Italy had finally been achieved. He seems to have entirely overlooked the long duration of, and the enormous cost of the preparatory work which led up to, the successful conclusion. In an address made in 1889, he declared that "Plutocracy or Nationalism is the choice which, within ten years, the people of the United States will have virtually decided upon." After thirty years the decision is still in doubt.

NATIONALIST CLUBS

"Looking Backward" described the change from the old to the new social order as brought about by the "National Party," which arose early in the twentieth century. A considerable number of Bostonians, who had read the story with the conviction that it expressed the true social gospel, came to believe that associations to spread the ideas set forth in the book should be formed as forerunners of the coming National Party. Accordingly, the "Boston Bellamy Club" was organized in September, 1888, and became the first "Nationalist Club" in the following December. The constitution of the club described its object to be "the nationalization of industry, and thereby the promotion of the brotherhood of humanity. The economic tendency of the age being favorable to this end, this club seeks to promote its practical adoption by familiarizing the people with the beneficent idea underlying it, and by encouraging national and local measures tending in this direction."

By December, 1889, the pioneer club had grown from about thirty to two hundred active members and a large number of associate members. Two other clubs of an aggregate membership of about two hundred were also in existence and others were forming in many places in Massachusetts. In another year it was estimated that there would be five thousand enrolled Nationalists in Boston and the suburbs.

The growth of the movement as a whole is indicated by the fact that there were over fifty organized clubs in fourteen States. California led in the number of clubs with seventeen in the State. There were estimated to be over six thousand "organized adherents" of Nationalism and probably five hundred thousand "believers." "Looking Backward" was in its two hundred and ten thousandth and selling at the rate of over ten thousand a week. Since May, 1889, sixty-nine thousand copies of the monthly magazine, "The Nationalist," had been circulated, and there was the need of printing a sixth edition of the May number.

In December, 1889, the anniversary of the Boston club was celebrated by a great meeting in Tremont Temple, which was addressed by Edward Bellamy. The next day a conference was held between the visiting delegates and the local members. There were present representatives from California, Washington, Brooklyn, and New York City. Attention having been called to the expense that the Boston club was under, a delegate expressed the opinion that each club should send to that club one dollar a year from each member. A resolution was accordingly passed recommending the formation of a Nationalist propaganda fund for the purpose of organization and for disseminating information. It was also suggested that for the time being the sum should be paid to the Boston club to aid it in the work of organizing the Nationalists of the country.

By the middle of 1890, information had been received of the organization of one hundred and twenty-seven clubs located in twenty-seven States. It had been determined to wait until a majority of the States had organized before forming a National League of Nationalist Clubs, but as there were virtually two thirds of that number such an organization could not long be delayed.

The movement was attracting prominent members and leading officers of the Farmers' Alliance, the Knights of Labor, Woman's Suffrage, and the trade unions. Some capitalists, such as the president of the Chicago and Alton Railroad and the general manager of the Boston and Maine Railroad, openly advocated Nationalism. There was reason for the belief that before five years had passed the telegraphs and railroads would be nationalized and one important step of Nationalism accomplished. The movement was, in the opinion of its advocates, likely to result in a merger of the many existing reform organizations.

California had in June, 1890, fifty-five clubs of which thirty-three were in Los Angeles. The clubs had joined hands with the organized workers and with the Farmers' Alliance. Over fifty thousand pamphlets were distributed and ten thousand copies of "Looking Backward" sold in the city.

Besides the California clubs there were organizations in the various States as follows: Colorado 2, Connecticut 3, Illinois 2, Indiana 1, Iowa 3, Kansas 2, Maryland 1, Massachusetts 9, Michigan 6, Minnesota 4, Missouri 2, Nebraska 1, New Hampshire 1, New Jersey 2, New York 13, North Dakota 2, Ohio 3, Oregon 2, Pennsylvania 4, Rhode Island 1, South Dakota 1, Tennessee 1, Washington 1, Wisconsin 1, and District of Columbia 1.

In October, 1890, there were over one hundred and fifty clubs scattered through twenty-seven States. California was still far in the lead with sixty-four, New York was second with twenty-one, and Massachusetts third with eleven.

NATIONALISM IN POLITICS

Nationalism seems to have reached a climax as an independent movement late in 1890. Thereafter it merged more and more in the various reform movements which finally resulted in the Populist Party in 1891.

Early in 1891 Rhode Island put a Nationalist ticket in the field in the State election. In California and Michigan Congressional candidates were nominated, and in "several localities" there were candidates for the State legislature. The votes of these nominees were very small, ranging from four hundred in Rhode Island to one thousand in California. Nationalism never achieved any political strength either in the States or in the nation. At the most it was a permeating force. It developed at a time of social and industrial unrest and its influence cannot be estimated as a distinct factor.

The Nationalists were "invited by name" to attend the conference at Cincinnati in May, 1891, at which the Populist Party was organized. Eight members of the National Committee of the new party were members of Nationalist clubs and active workers in the cause; five Nationalists were upon the committee on resolutions. Nationalists from nine States assembled at Cincinnati endorsed the formation of the new party and pledged themselves to render their best efforts to advance it.

Plans were made in Massachusetts by the local members of the national committee of the new party for a conference of the various reform bodies in the State. A large number of persons formerly interested in the Butler Party, the Greenback Party, the Industrial Alliance, Christian Socialists, and Knights of Labor were anxious to form a State organization. Later a People's or Populist Party was formed — which was described as "so strongly nationalistic in many of its propositions as to have secured the support" of the official organ, "The New Nation," edited by Bellamy, "as being the best party for Nationalists to vote for." The Massachusetts party went further in the line of Nationalism than in any other State. Eight planks out of fourteen had a Nationalistic flavor. The West did not reach such high ground.

After the Omaha Convention of the new party, in July, 1891, when presidential candidates were nominated, "The New Nation" declared that the platform was unchanged from earlier platforms as to substance, but "the Nationalist planks were intensified and emphasized." The chief burst of enthusiasm during the convention attended the reading of the platform, and no plank elicited "such tumults of applause as the most Nationalistic proposition of all — that of Government ownership and operation of railroads."

At Omaha a meeting of Nationalists was held during the convention. "A feature of the meeting, aside from the reports from many States as to the growth of Nationalism, was the suggestions made by speakers as to the most practical methods of reaching the public. Among these was the work of the clubs in pushing public ownership in the municipalities." It was decided to appoint a national committee for propaganda work. Members were chosen or suggested from Alabama, Arkansas, California, Colorado, Connecticut, the District of Columbia, Florida, Illinois, Indiana, Kansas, Louisiana, Maine, Massachusetts, Michigan, Minnesota, Mississippi, Missouri, Montana, Nebraska, New Jersey, New York, North Carolina, North Dakota, Ohio, Oregon, Pennsylvania, Rhode Island, South Dakota, Tennessee, Texas, Virginia, Washington, West Virginia, Wyoming, and Wisconsin — thirty-four States and the District of Columbia.

The committee of correspondence appointed at Omaha arranged for a meeting of Nationalists at Chicago, August 30, 1893. All Nationalists who visited Chicago were invited to register and were asked to plan their visits to the

World's Fair so as to be in the city at the time of the meeting. It was proposed to complete the organization of the committee and to plan work for the ensuing year.

As arranged the committee met and Eltmeed Pomeroy, of New Jersey, was made chairman. The report of the secretary showed that committee members had been chosen in twenty-seven States. Mrs. Anna L. Diggs, of Kansas, Herbert Burrows, of the London Social Democratic Federation, William Clarke, of the Fabian Society, and J. W. Sullivan, of New York, made addresses. The secretary was empowered to call another meeting within one year, the time and place being left to his discretion.

Apparently no later meeting was ever held. The Omaha and Chicago sessions represented the nearest approach to national organization achieved by the Nationalists. As already indicated, they merged with the other reform groups of the period in the formation of the Populist Party. Bellamy in "The New Nation" supported the new party. After the November elections of 1892, an editorial in the paper stated that the party "by its demands for the nationalization of the telegraph, telephone, and railroads, and the exclusive issue of money by the National Government deserved and received the enthusiastic support of Nationalists . . . we trust and believe that the leaven of Nationalism which has thus far proved the preponderating influence in the new party, will continue to exert an increasing power and that in the near future it will adopt not merely the immediate programme, but the ultimate ideal of Nationalism, coming out boldly and fully for the complete plan of national industrial coöperation with the economic equality of all citizens as the corner-stone of the finished structure." [1]

[1] Information from *The Nationalist,* May, December, 1889, January, June, October, 1890, and from *The New Nation,* February 14, March 14,

INFLUENCE OF NATIONALISM

The membership in the Nationalist clubs was largely literary, and they appealed to persons who had some philanthropic interests. "Bright young journalists and warm-hearted women" were most active, while there was a conspicuous absence of business and professional men. Undoubtedly, like all new reform organizations, it attracted a considerable number of the class of persons who are usually described as "cranks."

A monthly magazine, "The Nationalist," was published from May, 1889, to April, 1891, and from February, 1891, to January, 1894, Bellamy edited a weekly known as "The New Nation." The period of the issue of these publications covers the limits of the active life of Nationalism.

Their greatest practical influence, however, was exercised in their advocacy of municipal ownership of gas, electric light, and water plants, of street railroads by local communities, and of the ownership of the telegraph and railway systems by the National Government. Like the English Fabians, whose programme they followed, they may be described as "gas and water" socialists. Whatever actual accomplishments stand to their credit are to be found in this narrow field. Their propaganda may have slightly aided during a few years in the extension of municipal ownership of public utilities. The nationalization of the railroads and the telegraph remains still for the future — the Nationalists contributed almost nothing in this field. Their programme was too far in advance of public sentiment in the early nineties.

The press treated Nationalism as merely a Boston

April 11, May 2, 30, June 6, November 14, December 5, 1891, February 13, March 5, July 9, 16, 23, November 19, 26, 1892, May 27, July 22, and September 16, 1893.

"fad"; the labor organs derided it "as the sentimental nostrum of people who are out of all vital touch with working-men"; and the followers of Henry George would have nothing to do with it.[1] Its prominence was due to the wide reading of the novel and to the friendship of literary people for its author. Such a basis could hardly be expected to form a foundation for a substantial social movement. Much more thoroughly organized efforts, resting upon long-continued economic studies, have failed as yet, under more favorable conditions, to develop a strong socialist movement in the United States. Certainly a vague enthusiasm for a different social order, generated by an ingenuous literary Utopia, could have only a passing influence.

SELECTED REFERENCES

1. Bellamy: *Looking Backward.*
2. Bellamy: *Equality.*
3. *The Nationalist*, May, 1889, to April, 1891.
4. *The New Nation*, January 31, 1891, to February 3, 1894.
5. Gilman: *Socialism and the American Spirit*, chap. VI.
6. Gilman: "Nationalism in the United States," in the *Quarterly Journal of Economics*, vol. IV, pp. 50–76 (October, 1889).
7. Leacock: *The Unsolved Riddle of Social Justice*, pp. 101–23.
8. Hertzler: *The History of Utopian Thought*, chap. VI.

[1] Henry George described *Looking Backward* as a "castle in the air with the clouds for its foundation."

CHAPTER VII

THIRD PARTIES [1]

THE usual view of third or minor parties in the United States has ignored their real significance. An individualist political philosophy has led most people to think of them simply in relation to the great parties. The chief contrast has been a matter of size. The Republican and Democratic parties are coextensive in their organization with the Nation; while third parties are not necessarily organized nationally and do not contest every election. Then, again, the utopian character of their demands, as they appear to the practical American, has aroused his sense of humor. His amusement has not always allowed him to see the real nature of the organization beneath the apparent absurdity.

The caricatures of Kansas Populists, as presented by the cartoonists of the metropolitan press, are typical of the way in which third parties have been regarded by the majority of Americans. According to this view a man of good sense connects himself with one of the regular parties in preference to throwing away his vote upon a third-party candidate. To such a person, representing as he does the more or less prevalent popular view, a third party is made up largely of reformers, cranks, and discredited leaders of the older parties. All others ought to find a place in one of the two great parties.

A broader view of these minor parties regards them as a means of agitation and education. Especially is this true

---

[1] A part of this chapter is taken from the writer's *Third Party Movements,* published by the State Historical Society of Iowa in 1916.

in the case of an organization such as the Prohibition Party, which may not only enable the citizen to perform more efficiently his political duties, but may also educate him to take a higher view of his responsibilities. Moreover, such an opinion concerning third parties develops an attitude which regards them as an expression of social discontent — as a means of indicating objection to the existing economic régime.

The great influences favoring democracy in this country have come from the West: the experiences of the pioneers on the frontier developed individual enterprise and a sense of personal independence. The margin of free land on the frontier provided an outlet for the more adventurous; and so the West has been the seat of democratic ideas. The Greenback, Granger, Free Silver, and Populist parties were the expression of repeated efforts on the part of the democratic citizens of the West to assert themselves against the prevailing characteristics of the industrial and social development since the Civil War. Often shortsighted and visionary in their specific remedies, these leaders of the people were fundamentally sound in their opposition to the growing influence of wealth. Their instincts opened their eyes to features in contemporary developments that were not discovered for many years by the people in the older parts of the country. It is only necessary to read the platforms of the minor organizations to find the origin of many of the planks that are later prominent in the proposals of the Democratic and Republican parties. For the most part these short-lived parties represent forward movements in the development of government of the people, for the people, and by the people, rather than the outbursts of fanatical reformers based upon the imaginings of poorly balanced minds.

Looked at from the social point of view, the chief function of third parties has been to bring new issues before the people; they force new policies upon the older parties, and after accomplishing their work they pass away. One reason for their brief lives is undoubtedly due to the fact that reform is a good issue with which to arouse enthusiasm, but after the first impulse to activity is over the enthusiasm declines. A more important reason for the failure of such movements seems to be the "innate political conservatism of the bulk of the American people ... [who] prefer ... to bring forward the new issues and to work out the desired reforms in the established parties rather than to attempt to displace them with new organizations."

Permeation of the old parties by the influence of third-party organizations formed to advocate some urgent reform has been the American method of dealing with political and economic reforms. The larger the number of votes cast for a third party, the greater the probability that its issue will be adopted by one or both of the great parties rather than that its manifest strength will help it to displace or take a place alongside the established parties. So regularly has this occurred since the Civil War that a recent writer has declared that "it is a truism of political history that minority parties ultimately write the platforms for all parties. In time, the causes which they have the temerity to espouse are taken up by the established organizations when direct appeal to the latter may have proven fruitless."

Certain minor characteristics of third parties may be noticed at the outset. All of them take a broad view of the Federal Constitution. Thus, General James B. Weaver declared that "every good Greenbacker spells the word 'Nation' with the biggest kind of an N." This attitude results from the fact that they are urging policies that the older parties refuse to espouse on constitutional grounds.

Back of constitutional limitations there are economic and social forces which are more or less consciously working for recognition. The Constitution must either break or bend. Happily, the genius of Alexander Hamilton and the wisdom of John Marshall developed the doctrine of "implied powers" so that the Granger demand for Government regulation of railroads could be satisfied by constitutional interpretation without serious strain to the Constitution.

Again, every third party aspires to become one of the ruling parties, so that, in addition to its chief issue, it extends its platform to include other issues in order to absorb the strength behind such issues. This course is almost always followed, in spite of the fact that there are grave doubts as to whether more is not lost than gained through the danger of factions arising from contending interests. To the leaders of minor parties fusion often seems the open door to real political power; but fusion has probably been more often fatal to such parties than any other cause. Either the larger party will swallow up the smaller, or the natural antagonism that seems to develop between parties most closely related appears and a fierce quarrel ensues, which is equally fatal to the smaller body.

The real value, then, of third parties is that they stir the waters and prevent stagnation. What an agitator is among individuals, the third party is in relation to the older party organizations. These parties may go on as a result of the momentum acquired from past services. "Parties can and do exist for a considerable time without any peculiar doctrines; nothing is much more common than to see a party looking for a principle, seeking what we call an 'issue.' Both parties do this in fact, but the minority party is more eager than the one having the advantage of office and authority." If this does not happen, then a new party soon comes into existence. "If the principles they present are looked on with favor by a large portion of the people, these principles will be taken up by one or the other of the older parties or proved by a short time to be undesirable." Balance of power is the lever in the hands of the third party by which its principles may reach accomplishment, although in time its organization almost certainly ceases to exist.

So regularly has this course of events occurred since the Civil War that it may almost be regarded as a fixed order of American political life. Party machinery has become so complex and requires so much technical skill in its manipulation that there seems less and less chance of its overthrow or seizure by inexperienced workers. It almost seems as though the Republican and Democratic parties must go on indefinitely; and yet we know that they must inevitably adjust themselves to the new social and economic problems that continually become urgent. Social and economic problems are, indeed, the real forces behind the third parties, without which they would be of minor importance, but with which they are factors that cannot be ignored or neglected. Already they have been seen to exercise such influence upon the two great parties that there is more in common between sections of the different parties than between divisions of the same party. The progressive Republican has much more in common with a progressive Democrat than he has with the conservative members of his own party. Hence the significance of President Wilson's reference in his inaugural address to all "forward-looking" men.

There are few tasks more difficult than that of tracing the history of minor parties — which must be judged rather by their effects upon other bodies than by direct study of their own activity. How these minor parties have influenced the Republican and Democratic parties is an important but hitherto neglected phase of the history of political parties in the United States. What Bryce has called the "Fatalism of the Multitude," and what Von Holst has described as the "Worship of the Constitution," have blinded the people of the United States in their interpretation of very important and influential phenomena — the manifestation of social and economic forces that are only beginning to be understood.[1]

LIBERAL REPUBLICANS

The term "third party" has usually been applied to the series of minor parties formed since the Civil War in opposition to the two great parties — the Republican and Democratic. In 1872 the so-called "Liberal Republicans" joined with the Democrats in an effort to prevent President Grant's election for a second term — the beginning of a succession of opposition movements that have exerted a noteworthy influence upon our politics.

The Liberal wing of the Republican Party began in Missouri immediately after the Civil War, the particular object of its activity being a more liberal treatment of the suffrage privileges of former Confederates. The movement met with a sympathetic reception in other States where dissatisfaction with President Grant's administration had begun to take shape. Finally, in May, 1872, a national convention met in Cincinnati, at which well-known Republicans from Ohio, Illinois, Michigan, Wisconsin, Missouri, Massachusetts, Connecticut, New York, and Pennsylvania were present. Horace Greeley was nominated for the Presidency and his nomination was accepted by the

[1] The best discussions of third parties are to be found in Fess's *The History of Political Theory and Party Organization in the United States*, pp. 241–68; Ostrogorski's *Democracy and the Party System in the United States*, pp. 294–320; Ray's *An Introduction to Political Parties and Practical Politics*, pp. 40–73.

Democrats. The election resulted in Grant's success, the Republicans carrying all but six or seven States, and receiving a popular majority of 750,000.

The usual accounts describe the Liberal Republican movement as begun, developed, and ended in 1872. As a matter of fact, as has been stated, it began much earlier in Missouri. Again, the failure of 1872 did not complete the influence of the Liberals, for it persisted in Ohio, Connecticut, Massachusetts, and New York during 1873, 1874, and 1875. The presidential election of 1876 gave them another chance to exert their power upon a national scale. The nomination of two men of the character and reputation of Mr. Hayes and Mr. Tilden, together with the approaching retirement of General Grant, removed the most urgent object of their opposition and they did not make separate nominations.

In 1880 they protested against the proposed third term for General Grant, demanding "from a party without a master the nomination of a candidate without a stain." They were satisfied with the nomination of Mr. Garfield.

Finally, the candidacy of Mr. Blaine in 1884 brought out perhaps the most effective protest of the independents. They labored throughout the campaign to defeat him and to elect Mr. Cleveland. They were successful in their work.

The independent became a recognized factor in our political life, helping to shape party policies and exercising a wholesome influence upon public life — a result due very largely to the Liberal and independent activity from 1872 to 1884. Their great service was to break down the Chinese wall of partisanship which surrounded the larger parties in the seventies — a work that was destructive rather than constructive. For real constructive work one must look to the third or minor parties that grew contemporaneously with the independents, but largely separate from them.

Granger Parties

The first of the so-called "third parties" to exercise any considerable influence and to attract public attention throughout the country was a "farmers' movement" in the Central and Northwestern States in the years from 1873 to 1875. Under the names of "Independent," "Reform," or "Anti-Monopoly" parties, the farmers organized for political action in eleven States. In some places victories were secured by fusion with the Democrats, while in others independence was maintained. Three States secured the election of Independents to the United States Senate.

These independent or granger parties grew out of an economic condition existing in Illinois, Iowa, Wisconsin, and Minnesota, which were the greatest wheat-producing and corn-producing States, and which had attracted a large immigration from Europe with the result that the area under cultivation was extended and the crops increased beyond the capacity of home consumption. Accordingly, it became necessary to send large quantities of grain to Eastern markets. The development of railroad facilities did not keep pace with the increased production, so that grain accumulated and the railroads were unable to handle it. An increase in freight rates caused great dissatisfaction among the farmers, who held that the railroads were extortionate and made grain production unprofitable.

At the same time there developed in these States a great number of farmers' clubs and organizations, known as the "Patrons of Husbandry," or more popularly as "granges." The grange was non-political in character, but that did not prevent it from taking a position upon public questions.

Its advocacy of Government regulation of railroad rates was natural under the circumstances, and it undoubtedly prepared the way for the formation of the so-called granger parties with railroad regulation by the States as a principal demand. In this way developed what has come to be known as the "Granger movement."

It was during the years 1873 and 1874 that the greatest successes were achieved. In a few States there was activity in 1875. The eleven States in which granger parties were organized were Indiana, Illinois, Michigan, Wisconsin, Minnesota, Iowa, Missouri, Kansas, Nebraska, California, and Oregon. The "granger laws," that provided for State railroad commissions to regulate railroad charges, were the principal achievement of these parties. They raised the question of the public control of transportation by the States and the acceptance of the principle by the Supreme Court made it a part of the law of the land. The "Granger movement" began "that radical but tedious revolution of American ideas which is slowly bringing industry under the political power of democracy."

Greenbackers

With the subsidence of the farmers' movement for the regulation of railroads, there came into prominence an agitation in regard to the use of greenbacks. The crisis of 1873, with the prolonged business depression lasting till 1878, produced the usual unrest and discontent. The lack of currency seemed to inexperienced observers to make necessary a larger issue of money, and they naturally turned to the familiar greenbacks as the simplest way out of the difficulty. They had been the best money the West had ever known, since before the Civil War the circulating medium there was mainly composed of the bills of wild-cat banks.

After the failure of the so-called "Inflation Bill" of 1874, and the passage of the Resumption Act in the following year, providing for a return to specie payments January 1, 1879, the supporters of greenbacks realized that an independent party must be formed. Consequently, in May, 1876, a national convention met in Indianapolis, and formed a national independent party, adopted a platform and nominated Peter Cooper for President. A preliminary organization had been formed in November, 1874, but the convention of 1876 was its first appearance in the national sphere. As was to be expected the election results in actual votes were insignificant — about 80,000 out of a total of over 8,000,000.

In 1878, at a meeting held in Toledo, Ohio, an alliance was arranged between the Independent or Greenback Party and a Labor Reform Party that had been active in the industrial States of the East since 1870. Delegates attended from twenty-eight States and the result was an organization to be known as the "National Party," although it was popularly referred to as the "Greenback Labor Party." The Congressional and State elections in the autumn registered over a million votes for the new party, and showed it to be the strongest "third party" in the country up to that time. The successes naturally raised high hopes for the presidential election of 1880. The chief support of the movement came from the States of the Central West.

As in the case of other independent parties, the Greenbackers manifested their greatest strength in local and State elections; their success in national politics never indicated more than a third as much strength as was shown in 1878. The national convention of the party in 1880 selected General James B. Weaver, of Iowa, as the party's candidate for the Presidency; and he carried on an active campaign, traveling from Arkansas to the northeastern corner of Maine and from the east side of Lake Michigan to Mobile.

The campaign of 1880 was the first in which a third party took an aggressive part. The candidate, General Weaver, was an experienced and able speaker. He carried on the kind of canvass that people have come to be familiar with more recently in connection with Mr. Bryan and Mr. Roosevelt. Indeed, there is good ground for saying that General Weaver was the first candidate for the Presidency to make his appeal directly to the voter and to undertake to cover the country personally. In General Weaver the radical, progressive sentiment, the so-called "third party," according to our traditional method of describing such enterprises, found its first real leader. His place in the movement for economic and industrial reform looms larger as we are able to understand it better and to see it in its proper perspective.

In spite of the gain made in 1880 as compared with 1876, from 80,000 to 300,000 popular votes, it was evident that the expectations aroused by the successes of 1878 were not to be realized immediately. The more conservative and practical of the independents drifted back into their former party relations, leaving only the more radical elements. The results were shown in the election of 1882, when, as a Republican paper in Iowa declared, there was a "landslide, a tidal wave, an earthslip, or whatever you like to call it." There were several reasons for the overwhelming Democratic victories of that year, but without doubt one reason was the fusion of many independents with the Democrats. As in 1874, the passing of the apparent power of the independents is to be explained by their absorption into the Democratic Party with the result that that party became temporarily the majority party.

The Democratic victories of 1882 proved to be preliminary to success in the presidential election of 1884. The Greenbackers nominated General Benjamin F. Butler, of Massachusetts, but he received only 175,000 votes, a falling-off of 125,000 from 1880. The Independent Republican opposition to Blaine, to which we have already referred, was an important factor, but in a certain sense the first Democratic national victory since the Civil War was the culmination of the "Greenback movement." As has happened frequently in the history of third parties, real gains are recorded in the votes cast for, or taken away from the two great parties. Repeatedly, opposition to the Republican Party has shown itself by support of its traditional opponent. Sometimes a third party has figured in the situation.

Populists

The years between 1884 and 1888 witnessed an attempt to organize the radical elements of the country under labor leadership, but without very much success. The Greenback Party gradually disappeared, leaving the field clear for the organization of a new "farmers' movement." Like the earlier granger agitation, it grew out of economic conditions in the West and South, particularly during the years immediately preceding 1890. Farming was again unprofitable, and the reasons most apparent seemed to point to the conditions of the currency. Free coinage of silver took the place of a demand for more paper money as the chief feature of the programme of the Populists. A free-silver agitation began in the West and South which was carried on with a religious fervor. It was aided by the formation of new farmers' organizations known as "Alliances" which had a remarkable growth during the last years of the decade of 1880 to 1890. Though at first non-political in character like the granges, the alliances soon drifted into political activity, and in 1890 they took a hand in the Congressional and State elections with startling effects. In the South they elected three Governors, one United States Senator, and thirty Congressmen, and in addition controlled a majority in five State legislatures. In the West they elected two United States Senators, eight Congressmen, and had a majority in two State legislatures.

Again in this election, as in 1874 and 1882, the Republicans were overwhelmed "by a tidal wave of popular anger." They lost control of the House of Representatives, a membership of 166 being reduced to 88, while the Democrats increased from 159 to 236. The most influential issue was certainly the McKinley Tariff Act, so far as the country at large was concerned; but in the Middle West particularly the "political revolution" was just as surely determined by the activity of the farmers. As in 1874 and 1882, the strength of the "third party" was registered in the votes taken away from the Republicans, and given partly to independent candidates and partly to the Democrats. Economic and social factors had again overwhelmed leaders who persisted in ignoring them while they occupied themselves with the disposal of offices and legislation for business to the apparent injury of the farmer and average man.

Again in 1892 General Weaver was the candidate of the new Populist Party which had been formed in 1891. He carried on a vigorous campaign, canvassing the country in the same way in which he had done in 1880. By September 17th he and the vice-presidential candidate, General James G. Field, of Virginia, had visited fifteen States, and they continued their campaign until November. At the general election the Populist candidates received over a million popular votes and twenty-two electoral votes. For the only time between 1860 and 1912, a third-party candidate had won a place in the electoral college. Of the million popular votes, over 800,000 were cast in the Western and Southern States.

Between 1892 and 1896 conditions were favorable for the continued growth of the new party. Business depression followed the crisis of 1893, while the repeal of the silver purchase clause of the Sherman Act antagonized the great numbers of people in the West and South who had come to believe that free coinage of silver would be a panacea for all their ills. Industrial unrest due to business depression and unemployment produced such outbreaks as the great railroad strike of 1894 and the marching of the Coxey or Industrial armies. At no time in the history of the United States has there been a period when social unrest has been so threatening. Only the firm attitude of President Cleveland saved the country from worse disorder.

By 1896 it was apparent that the Democratic Party would adopt free silver in order to absorb the strength of the Populists. Mr. Bryan's "Cross of Gold" speech at the Democratic National Convention in Chicago completed the work of committing one of the great parties to the free coinage of silver. The Republicans were compelled to take the other side. Mr. Bryan became the candidate of both Democrats and Populists with Mr. McKinley as the Republican standard-bearer. Since 1896 the issues formerly urged by third parties have been fought out within the two great parties, except in the campaign of 1912.

The Election of 1896

The strength of these issues was shown in the campaign and election of 1896. Mr. Bryan carried his canvass directly to the people, making "the most remarkable tour in all the annals of political 'stumping.'" During fourteen weeks he made four hundred speeches in twenty-nine States and traveled eighteen thousand miles. Altogether he probably addressed several million voters.

Mr. McKinley, though remaining at his home in Canton, Ohio, carried on "an oratorical campaign . . . which in its own kind has . . . never been paralleled." Almost every day he was visited by delegations that expected an address. In the busiest part of the canvass it was estimated that as many as thirty thousand persons visited him in a single day. From June to November he made three hundred speeches to more than seven hundred and fifty thousand persons from about thirty States. Never before had candidates made an appeal directly to as many of the voters; a new standard for political campaigns had been set.

Careful observers of the progress of the campaign have expressed the opinion that, if the election had been held in August, Bryan's election would have been almost certain. Even the Republican National Committee had no confidence in the success of its efforts until October. Only the "vigorous, exhaustive, and systematic work" under Mr. Hanna's management made possible the final outcome. Even then Mr. Bryan lost by a popular vote of only about 500,000 in a total of nearly 14,000,000 votes.

The significance of the election of 1896 in the history of social politics in the United States is independent of the economic soundness of its chief issue as a remedy to meet existing evils. It marked a new epoch in our political life in which the lines began to be drawn between the rich and poor. It represented the culmination of agitations that had their beginnings in the early seventies and which were aimed at the eradication of special privileges that had been growing worse for a quarter of a century. A part of the unrest was a blind protest against conditions regardless of consequences, but persons of social vision believed that behind the superficial aspects they saw "the first great protest of the American people against monopoly . . . the first great struggle of the masses . . . against the privileged classes."

AFTER 1896

The larger part of the Populists became Democrats after 1896. The Democratic Party had adopted the issues for which they contended. The million votes cast for Weaver in 1892 had opened the eyes of the great party leaders to the strength of the new party. It would be only a question of time when one of them would accept their demands in order to gain their support. The Democrats took this step in 1896, and Mr. Bryan became the head of the combined parties, General Weaver taking an important place in the group of leaders. Recently Mr. Bryan said that, had he been elected in 1896, he had decided to make General Weaver a member of his Cabinet.

The influence of the Populists was not confined to the Democrats. The Republicans, impressed by the strength of the opposition in 1896, realized the importance of meeting the issues raised by them. The succession of Mr. Roosevelt to the Presidency in 1901 gave an opportunity in the national sphere that had not been possible under Mr. Bryan. The conjuncture of a man and an occasion made Roosevelt the protagonist for nearly eight years of a veritable revolution in national party policies. So completely did he dominate the stage that it was hardly an exaggeration to call his administration, as one writer did, the "Epoch of Roosevelt." His administration might well be described, as Von Holst characterized that of Andrew Jackson, as the "Reign" of Roosevelt.

SELECTED REFERENCES

1. Ray: *An Introduction to Political Parties and Practical Politics,* pp. 40–73.
2. Woodburn: *Political Parties and Party Problems,* chaps. VIII–X.
3. Haynes: *Third Party Movements,* chaps. VI, VIII–XI, XIV, XV–XVIII.
4. Buck: *The Granger Movement.*
5. Buck: *The Agrarian Crusade.*
6. McVey: "The Populist Movement," in *Economic Studies,* vol. I, no. 3.
7. Beard: *Contemporary American History,* chaps. IV, VI, VII.
8. Paxson: *The New Nation,* chaps. XI, XIII, XIV.
9. Paxson: *Recent History of the United States,* chaps. XVII, XVIII, XIX, XXII.
10. Arnett: *The Populist Movement in Georgia,* in *Columbia University Studies in History, Economics and Public Law,* vol. CIV. no. 1.

CHAPTER VIII

THE PROGRESSIVE MOVEMENT [1]

PRESIDENT ROOSEVELT's success in the sphere of national politics was largely due to the preliminary work which had been done in the different States — work similar to that done by La Follette in Wisconsin.

LA FOLLETTE

Robert M. La Follette was "the first among the Republican political leaders to comprehend the character of the irrepressible conflict within the party, between public interests and the present-day organization of private business," according to the opinion of Senator Jonathan P. Dolliver expressed in a speech in Wisconsin a few weeks before his death in 1910. La Follette began his reform work in 1894. In 1896 and 1898 he lost the Republican nomination for Governor, after entering the conventions with enough delegates instructed and pledged to vote for him, because the delegates were lured away by money and promises of place by the party machine. His experience led him to study out some substitute for the convention and caucus by which nominations might be made directly by the people.

Finally, he won the nomination in 1900 and was elected that year and reëlected in 1902 and 1904. His chief reform measures, in addition to the direct primary, were laws by which the railroads were to be compelled to pay their proper share of taxes, and by which they were to be regulated by a commission in the interest of the people of

[1] A part of this chapter is taken from the writer's *Third Party Movements*, published by the State Historical Society of Iowa in 1916.

the State, rather than for the benefit of corporations and big business. All three of these laws he succeeded in placing upon the statute books in the face of bitter opposition during the years from 1903 to 1905. He was elected United States Senator in January, 1905, but did not take his seat until January, 1906, after his programme for Wisconsin had been completed. He was reëlected in 1910, 1916, and 1922.

When he entered the Senate, he was alone in that body as the representative of a new movement in the Republican Party which had "its beginning in a desire to take party control away from men who, as parts of the managing organization . . . maintained a close corporation in manipulation of party affairs and in distribution of rewards, and were too intimate with and subservient to railroad companies and other capitalistic combinations. It rapidly spread to agitation against the corporations themselves, chiefly railroads. . . . In short, it is a movement to emancipate the party from the domination of the established 'system,' and to make the party more directly responsive to the popular will."

At first La Follette was ignored by the older members of the Senate, but he forced them to recognize him by refusing to be suppressed. He broke traditions by speaking a score of times before the end of his first session as a Senator. His place in the Senate was made, however, by a speech on the Railroad Rate Bill of 1906 which revised the powers of the Interstate Commerce Commission. He knew the railroad problem thoroughly, having studied it for years; and when Senators "tried to haze him by emptying the chamber," he paused to say that he could not be indifferent to the want of interest in what he had to present, but that the public was interested, and if the question was not "rightly settled, seats now temporarily vacant may be permanently vacated by those who have the right to occupy them at this time."

In 1909 he was one of the small group of Republican Senators who refused to vote for the Payne-Aldrich Tariff Act, which was one of the chief causes for the formation of an insurgent faction in that party, and which finally resulted in the division of 1912.

In 1904, Governor La Follette and his supporters controlled the Republican State Committee in Wisconsin and dominated the State Convention. "Each faction had nearly one half of the delegates without dispute. There were contested seats of sufficient number to make the control of the convention depend upon the settlement of the contests." These contests were all settled in favor of La Follette, and his opponents, led by the two United States Senators, Spooner and Quarles, withdrew and named delegates to the Republican National convention. Contesting delegations, therefore, appeared at Chicago, and the National Committee by unanimous vote seated the Spooner-Quarles delegates, excluding La Follette and his associates.

In 1908, La Follette was in complete control in Wisconsin and the delegation from that State came to the national convention to present him as a candidate for President, and "had prepared in advance a strong platform, ably written, going into much greater detail as respects railroad regulation, trusts, and some other economic and political questions than the platform favored by the majority. This platform was brought before the convention as a minority report by Congressman Cooper, of Wisconsin, and several of its proposals were made the subjects of separate roll-calls in the convention. One of the demands thus voted on was that of publicity for campaign contributions; another was that calling for a physical valuation of railroad properties as a basis for the fixing of just rates;

and another was that for the direct election of United States Senators. A good many delegates from other States than Wisconsin recorded their votes for one or another of these propositions. Wisconsin was strongly represented in the convention, and the speeches made in presenting the name of Mr. La Follette for President were among the best of all those the convention heard."

A demonstration, lasting twenty-three minutes, following the speeches presenting Mr. La Follette as a candidate, was interpreted by an experienced Massachusetts Congressman as meaning "that the Western country wanted more hot stuff in the way of public regulation and corporate supervision than yet had been served to it; that the appetite had grown by what it had fed on, until a surprisingly large number of the onlookers . . . welcomed the La Follette idea. Another Congressman . . . from the West declared that this showed the hand of Chautauqua and that the East had overlooked the importance of the Chautauqua movement. For years La Follette and Champ Clark and Tillman and Dolliver and all the other glib-tongued speakers holding progressive views have been addressing Chautauqua audiences, telling them of new and popular reforms, until they have built up an amount of public sentiment which it is hard to gauge. La Follette had absolutely no means of doing anything with that convention . . . no tickets were distributed by him and no claquers were stationed in the galleries. He could create no artificial sentiment in his favor. But he has become a great hero of the Chautauqua circles and similar aggregations of earnest people in this great valley . . . the demonstration in behalf of La Follette, following the rejection with such emphasis of the three planks on which his followers asked a roll call, give[s] an extremely valuable hint" of the trend of public opinion.

Senator La Follette's programme and his accomplishments and those of his associates came to be known as the "Wisconsin Idea," and that State was pointed out as the ideal type of a progressive democratic commonwealth — it was regarded as embodying in a peculiarly successful way the purposes and objects of the Progressive movement.

THE PROGRESSIVES IN THE STATES

Other States where the foundations for the Progressive movement were laid locally were Michigan, Ohio, Oregon, Missouri, and Iowa. Hazen S. Pingree, of Detroit, Samuel M. Jones, of Toledo, Tom L. Johnson, of Cleveland, Joseph W. Folk, of Missouri, and Albert B. Cummins, of Iowa, were among the leaders in these States.

HAZEN S. PINGREE

One of the earliest of these local leaders was Hazen S. Pingree, of Detroit, who was elected Mayor of that city in 1889 and served four terms. His most noteworthy achievement was the so-called "Potato Patch Plan" which he inaugurated in 1894 and 1895 in order to aid the unemployed in those years. Vacant lots in the suburbs were used in parcels of a quarter or half acre each, upon which potatoes and garden truck were planted and cultivated by needy families under the supervision of a committee, funds being raised by subscriptions and the use of the land permitted by its owners. The first year 3000 applications were received, but only 945 families could be provided for, who produced from $12,000 to $14,000 worth of crops at an expense of $3600 to the committee, or about $3.45 per lot. The second year 1546 families cultivated 455 acres, producing crops of the value of over $27,000 at a cost of $4900. The plan was adopted in many cities, and in various forms has continued to be used down to the present time. It illustrated the application of business ability and inventiveness to an urgent social problem.

Another object to which Mayor Pingree gave considerable attention was the reduction of fares upon the street cars. After he had been in office nine or ten months, a strike of the employees of the local car lines occurred, giving rise to rioting in the streets and some destruction of property. The street-car company was very unpopular and public sympathy was with the strikers. The Mayor "harangued the strikers and told them in effect that they were right and that he endorsed their conduct." Under the circumstances the company surrendered and made terms with its employees. This result made him a hero in the eyes of the working-classes, but greatly embittered the capitalistic class against him. The great majority of the voters supported him and he overcame almost all opposition.

Mayor Pingree's warfare against the street-car company — "the octopus" as he called it — continued until the close of his career ten years later; in the course of the controversy he came into contact with Tom L. Johnson, of Cleveland, who was associated with the New York capitalists who purchased the interests of the company to which the Mayor was opposed. He fought the consolidation of the street railways in every possible way, but was finally defeated by the decision of the Supreme Court of the United States. An interesting account is given, in Johnson's "My Story," of the relations between the reform Mayor of Detroit and the future reform Mayor of Cleveland.

In 1896, Pingree was elected Governor of the State of Michigan by a vote of 304,431 as against 221,022 for his Democratic opponent, his vote exceeding that of

McKinley by 10,849. He undertook to hold both offices for a year, as his term as Mayor did not expire for twelve months. His reason for such action was to enable him to oppose the consolidation of all the street railways of the city. Proceedings were started to oust him as Mayor, and "the Supreme Court held that, since the law provides that the Mayor is subject to be removed by the Governor, both offices could not properly be held by the same person at the same time."

His two issues as Governor were primary election reform and railroad taxation, but he was unable to do much more than to urge them upon the attention of the legislature. He also "paid his respects" to the professional lobbyist, and "dealt somewhat" with the question of public franchises. He objected to the consideration of his nominations by the Senate in secret sessions and threatened "to break in and listen to the harsh things said about himself. . . . Nevertheless, in spite of all this friction nearly all his nominations were confirmed; at least he fared no worse in this respect than the average of governors." He was reëlected in 1898 by a plurality of 75,000. Altogether he was an interesting personality and a pioneer whose work is now largely forgotten. He anticipated in many ways the development of social policies of later years. Arousing great bitterness, he nevertheless possessed a strong hold upon the confidence of the people of Michigan.

"Golden Rule" Jones

Mayor Samuel M. Jones, of Toledo, Ohio, was elected first as a Republican in 1897 and reëlected three times as an Independent, receiving at his second election 16,752 votes to 4260 for his Republican opponent and 3155 for his Democratic opponent, notwithstanding the opposition of all the newspapers and both political machines. In his last campaign the newspapers adopted the plan of keeping absolutely silent about his candidacy, while the corporations were hostile and many of the churches opposed him because he had not closed the saloons. Somehow the simplicity and genuineness of the man drew to him a support that remained loyal until his death in office in 1904.

His sobriquet, "Golden Rule" Jones, suggests the fundamental character of his life and work. He was of Welsh ancestry, coming to America when three years old. As a young man he began work in the oil regions of Pennsylvania. About 1893 he invented an improvement in the apparatus of oil wells, and established a factory for its manufacture at Toledo, in which he posted the Golden Rule as a basis for the regulation of his business. A minimum wage, an eight-hour day, and welfare benefits were the concrete manifestations of his application of the Biblical rule to industrial problems. He recognized the fact that his patent enabled him to disregard the competitive rate of wages in his factory, and every year he distributed a dividend of five per cent upon the amount earned by each man who had worked for him six months. As his business prospered, he built a fine house on one of the beautiful residence streets, but when he had the housewarming, his workmen and their families were the guests. "It used to amuse Jones to reflect that his literal acceptance of the fundamental principle of Christianity should have been such a novel and unprecedented thing that it instantly marked him out from all the other Christians and made him famous in Christendom."

His political-municipal platform was thus announced by him: (1) equal opportunities for all and special privileges for none; (2) public ownership of all public utilities; (3) no grant of new or extension of existing franchises; and (4) the abolition of the private-contract system of doing city work. His great contribution to the betterment of municipal government was nonpartisanship in local affairs. He used to describe himself as "a man without a party"; but he was really and fundamentally a representative of that democratic spirit of which Lincoln was a type. He recognized instinctively that there is but one issue locally — that which is represented by the conflict of wealth and democracy. His career in Toledo was a part of the common war waged all over the country for the restoration of popular government.

Tom L. Johnson

Tom L. Johnson, of Cleveland, was another of the men who by local work made possible the success of the Progressive movement in the nation at large. Johnson had become a rich man through street railroads and iron manufacture before his election to Congress in 1890. He served for two terms in the House of Representatives, being defeated in 1894 for reëlection. Through his interest in the single tax and his acquaintance with Henry George, his views underwent a complete transformation and he became a "reformed business man" or "converted special privilege man." In 1901 he was elected Mayor of Cleveland and remained in office until his defeat in 1909.

His great fight in Cleveland was for a three-cent fare upon the street cars; as an expert in the business he maintained that there was profit in such a fare under proper business conditions. He waged a long fight for his doctrine and lived to see it successful in a way, though not exactly as he hoped. He gathered around him a remarkable group of men — Peter Witt, "a fiery young radical," who was originally an opponent and who was city clerk under all his administrations, and later street railway commissioner under one of his successors; Newton D. Baker, who was city solicitor from 1902 to 1912, Mayor of the city from 1912 to 1916, and Secretary of War from 1916 to 1920; Frederic C. Howe, who had been elected to the council as a Republican from one of the aristocratic wards, won over by Johnson, and renominated on the Democratic ticket (later Commissioner of Immigration at New York and an authority on municipal government); and the Reverend Harris R. Cooley, director of charities and corrections, who made a name for himself by his methods of handling dependents and criminals, and of whom Johnson used to say that instead of being a preacher he had become a minister.

Johnson made an unsuccessful attempt in 1903 to redeem the State as he had the city. He used his big French touring-car and held "immense meetings in a circus tent which was taken down and sent on ahead each night. In this way he was entirely independent of local committees, and they did not like that very well; it had been his wealth more than his democracy that had made him seem so logical as a candidate to some of the Democrats." His platform during this campaign demanded "a two-cent-a-mile railway fare and the taxation of railroad property at something like its value." Within two years of his defeat, his first proposal became law with but one dissenting vote.

The "Oregon Plan"

Another important contribution to the upbuilding of the Progressive movement came from the State of Oregon. No prominent single leader focused the work there, but a real democracy was skillfully led by men who did not struggle for office, choosing rather to devote themselves to quiet work of a fundamental kind. One man, William

S. U'Ren, has been described as the "father" of much of the democratic legislation. Apparently he is as near being the originator of it as any single individual.

Mr. U'Ren's early history is exceedingly suggestive for the study of the development of the Progressive movement. He was born in Wisconsin, in 1859; moved with his family to Nebraska, Colorado, and Wyoming; and finally, after a wandering life as a young man in search of health, reached Oregon in 1891. His father had been a reader of "Greeley's Paper," he himself had studied law in Denver, and about 1889 and 1890 had read "Progress and Poverty." A little later he ran across a pamphlet describing the initiative and referendum, and through it became a convert to direct legislation. Just at this time the Populist Party was gathering strength, and U'Ren joined its ranks. In 1896 he was elected to the State Assembly, taking part in a long, corrupt senatorial contest the following year, in which he became familiar with all the methods of the commercial politics of the period. In 1898 he was a candidate for the Senate, but was defeated.

Afterward he was not a candidate for office, but worked for an amendment to the State Constitution providing for the initiative and referendum. In 1902 he was finally successful in having the direct legislation amendment ratified by the people by a vote of eleven to one. Two years later a thoroughgoing primary law, which included the nomination and election of senatorial candidates, was presented to the people and adopted by a large majority.

The original feature of the Oregon primary election law was its unique provision for nominating and electing candidates for the United States Senate. Members of the legislature could be pledged to vote for the candidate who received the highest number of votes at the general election, regardless of party or individual preference. This pledge was known as "Statement No. 1." If the candidate for the legislature was unwilling to make such a pledge, he could sign "Statement No. 2," which declared the vote of the people merely a "recommendation." Obviously the candidate who refused to sign "Statement No. 1," would find himself distinctly at a disadvantage as against a competitor who had signed it. The effect of "Statement No. 1" was to make the legislature a mere registration body as is the electoral college. Virtually it was popular election of Senators without amendment of the Federal Constitution. As the "Oregon Plan" it played an important part in the contest for the adoption of the Seventeenth Amendment.

Joseph W. Folk

Joseph W. Folk's "Fight for Missouri" began with his attempts to punish political corruption in St. Louis as Circuit Attorney in 1900. His exposure and prosecution of municipal boodling and bribery led him on to uncover the relations of the city ring with big business and its affiliations in State and Nation. The punishment of the city boss and nearly all the members of the "boodle combine" did not destroy the ring, because behind the ring stood the big business man, and behind the big business man were his relations with other men and interests throughout the country. To make even a beginning of reform the sphere of activity must be State-wide; and so Folk became a candidate for Governor in 1904 and was elected as a Democrat, although the Republicans elected the presidential electors, the lower house of the legislature, and all the other State officers. The Democrats had been the ruling party in the State for many years, and their overthrow was largely due to the exposure of political corruption accomplished by Folk. This triumph of independent voting was made in spite of the difficulty of splitting tickets in Missouri. The simple issue was presented and the people responded by electing Folk in 1904 and the complete Republican ticket in 1908. In 1912 the State returned to its former Democracy. The negative work of exposure had not been followed by positive constructive legislation as in Wisconsin and Oregon.

William Allen White, of Kansas, described the Progressive movement as "one of the big self-evident things in our national life." The common characteristics of all the local and State activities just discussed may be grouped under two main divisions and classified as warfare against political bosses and as warfare against special privilege; and these two classes are practically one, because they have a common source and a common purpose. They constitute what Senator A. J. Beveridge so aptly described as "the invisible government." Lincoln Steffens, in his studies, "The Shame of the Cities" and "The Struggle for Self-Government," repeatedly makes the assertion: "Not the political ring, but big business — that is the crux of the situation. . . . The trail of the political leader and the trail of the commercial leader are parallels."

That the Progressive movement was nonpartisan is shown by the fact that the leaders came from both of the major parties. Doing public business in the open, dethroning bosses, giving the people a direct voice in public affairs, restoring popular government, and abolishing special privilege — these activities have no essential or fundamental political relations. Hence the breaking-up of the older parties into Progressives and Standpatters — the real divisions being based upon social and economic differences, while the nominal party lines are traditional and historical. Again we meet the fact of the growth of social politics in place of the older political separations.

The Split in the Republican Party

When President Roosevelt retired in 1909, the Republican Party had apparently been transformed along lines similar to those according to which Bryan's leadership had carried the Democrats in 1896. Both of the great parties had taken over the demands of the successive third parties.

The first serious division in the Republican Party came in the House of Representatives, and was directed against the arbitrary power of the Speaker which had grown up since the adoption of the "Reed Rules" in 1890. Joseph G. Cannon, of Illinois, had been Speaker since 1903 and had used his power to maintain the established system and in opposition to many Progressive measures. The beginning of the contest came in March, 1910, when about forty insurgents joined with the Democrats to overrule a formal decision of the Speaker. The struggle continued for four days and ended with a vote for the reorganization of the Committee on Rules.

By far the most dramatic and important struggle between the regular Republicans and the insurgents occurred in the Senate in the debate upon the Payne-Aldrich Tariff Bill. Upon the final vote ten Republicans voted against it. These were from Indiana, Iowa, Kansas, Minnesota, Nebraska, South Dakota, and Wisconsin. President Taft had used his influence to bring about the improvement of the bill, but the Progressive Republicans felt that he might have helped them in a more positive way.

The campaign of 1910 was dominated by the division within the ranks of the Republican Party. President Taft tried to mediate, but without success. As was to be expected under such circumstances, the elections resulted in a "landslide" for the Democrats. It was a distinct rebuke to the regular Republicans and indicated that the country supported the position of the Progressives.

A division arose among the Progressives as to the candidate who would be most likely to defeat the renomination of President Taft. Senator La Follette was first encouraged to announce himself, but later he was urged to withdraw in favor of Mr. Roosevelt as a leader more likely to defeat the President. Dissension resulted and became the basis for a bitter personal feud between Roosevelt and La Follette.

In February, 1912, a conference was held in Chicago, which was attended by seven Republican Governors and seventy leaders from twenty-four States. The seven Governors addressed a letter to Mr. Roosevelt in which they asked him "to declare whether, if the nomination was offered to him unsolicited and unsought, he would accept it." Two weeks later, Mr. Roosevelt replied that he would accept the nomination under the conditions suggested.

President Taft and Mr. Roosevelt waged a vigorous campaign against each other by means of public speeches during the interval before the meeting of the nominating convention in June. The bitterness of this unfortunate personal campaign was increased by the fact that ten States had provided by law for a presidential preference primary. So far as there was an opportunity for a popular expression, it plainly indicated Roosevelt as the choice. The partial character of the presidential primary left the decision to the convention.

The preliminary arrangements were in the hands of the National Committee, chosen four years before, which favored the renomination of President Taft. As soon as it became certain that the supporters of the President would control the convention, Mr. Roosevelt declared that he was "through" and advised his delegates not to act longer with "a fraudulent majority." Later Mr. Roosevelt announced his willingness to accept a Progressive nomination.

FORMATION OF THE PROGRESSIVE PARTY

At the close of the Republican Convention "the Roosevelt delegates . . . with their alternates and thousands of Roosevelt followers, held a meeting in Orchestra Hall" in Chicago. Resolutions were adopted, and Mr. Roosevelt made a long speech, in which he declared that the time had come for all Progressives to get together in one party. He expressed his willingness to be a candidate, but any other man nominated would receive his "heartiest support." A provisional committee was appointed to arrange for a new organization.

On July 8th a call was issued for a convention to meet in Chicago on August 5th to organize the new party. This call was signed by men representing forty States, including Governor Hiram Johnson, of California, Judge B. B. Lindsay, of Colorado, James R. Garfield, of Ohio, and Gifford Pinchot, of Pennsylvania.

"The National Progressive Convention met at Chicago August 5th. There were eighteen women delegates . . . prominent among whom was Miss Jane Addams, of Chicago." Ex-Senator Albert J. Beveridge, of Indiana, was temporary chairman and made an eloquent address which aroused the delegates "to a high pitch of enthusiasm. The convention, with ten thousand people in attendance, sang fervently the 'Battle Hymn of the Republic,' and 'Onward, Christian Soldiers,' and the demonstrations and spirit that was manifested led even hostile newspapers' correspondents to report that nothing like this convention had ever before been known in American politics; that it seemed more like a religious assembly imbued with a humanitarian spirit of enthusiasm and devotion."

On the second day of the convention, Mr. Roosevelt was received with great enthusiasm, and made his "Confession of Faith," which a New York newspaper strongly opposed to him described as "the best, the ablest, the most persuasive of all his public utterances."

On the third day a platform was adopted, candidates nominated, and the convention adjourned. Roosevelt and Johnson were nominated for President and Vice-President. The official name of the party was designated as the "Progressive Party." The distinctive feature of the platform was its programme of social and industrial justice, in which it was declared that "the supreme duty of the Nation is the conservation of human resources." This programme included "legislation regarding industrial health and accidents, child labor, wage standards, women's labor, hours and days of labor, convict labor, industrial education, and industrial research."

The significance of the convention was finely stated by Miss Addams in her brief address seconding the nomination of Mr. Roosevelt. "Measures of industrial amelioration," she said, "demands for social justice, long discussed by small groups in charity conferences and economic associations, have here been considered in a great National Convention and are at last thrust into the stern arena of political action. A great party has pledged itself to the protection of children, to the care of the aged, to the relief of overworked girls, to the safeguarding of burdened men. ... The new party has become the American exponent of a world-wide movement toward juster social conditions, a movement which America, lagging behind other great nations, has been unaccountably slow to embody in political action."

The campaign was an exceptional one, with a number of dramatic incidents. On October 14th an attempt was made

to assassinate Mr. Roosevelt in Milwaukee and he was seriously wounded. On October 30th Vice-President Sherman
died after a long illness. Senator La Follette repeatedly
made bitter personal attacks upon Mr. Roosevelt, and "he
was understood to be throwing his influence privately" for
Governor Wilson.

The result of the election was "a sweeping Democratic
victory . . . by pluralities in so many States as to give that
party's candidate the largest vote and the largest majority
in the electoral college ever given to a party candidate."
President Taft carried two States, Vermont and Utah; Mr.
Roosevelt carried five States, Pennsylvania, Michigan,
Minnesota, South Dakota, and Washington, and received
eleven of the thirteen electoral votes of California; Governor Wilson carried all the other States, and received four
hundred and thirty-five electoral votes to eight for President Taft and eighty-eight for Mr. Roosevelt. The popular
vote was as follows: Wilson, 6,290,818; Roosevelt, 4,123,-
206; Taft, 3,484,529; and Debs, 898,296. Governor Wilson
had "a popular plurality of more than 2,160,000 over his
nearest competitor," but there was a popular majority
against him of nearly 2,460,000. "The combined vote for
Taft and Roosevelt would make a majority of 1,316,927
against Wilson. . . . It is known that many Independents,
Anti-Bryan Democrats, and Republicans voted for Mr.
Wilson, and it is therefore obvious that very many former
Bryan Democrats must have voted for Roosevelt or for
Debs, or refrained from voting." [1]

SELECTED REFERENCES

1. DeWitt: *The Progressive Movement.*
2. Weyl: *The New Democracy.*
3. Lippmann: *A Preface to Politics.*

[1] For a more detailed account of the Progressive movement and party
see the writer's *Third Party Movements*, chaps. xxiv–xxx.

4. Lippmann: *Drift and Mastery*.
5. Croly: *Promise of American Life*.
6. Croly: *Progressive Democracy*.
7. La Follette: *Autobiography*.
8. Wilson: *The New Freedom*.
9. Roosevelt: *The New Nationalism*.
10. Haynes: *Third Party Movements*, chaps. XXIV–XXX.
11. Stanwood: *A History of the Presidency*, 1897–1916, chaps. I–IV.
12. Beard: *Contemporary American History*, chaps. X, XII, XIII.
13. Paxson: *The New Nation*, chaps. XVII, XIX, XX.
14. Paxson: *Recent History of the United States*, chaps. XXVIII, XXXI, XXXII, XXXVIII, XL.
15. *The American Year Book*, 1912, pp. 1–44.
16. *The New International Year Book*, 1912, pp. 542–89.
17. Lewis: *The Life of Theodore Roosevelt*, chaps. XXI–XXIV.
18. Howland: *Theodore Roosevelt and His Times*.
19. Bishop: *Theodore Roosevelt and His Time*, vol. II.
20. Charnwood: *Theodore Roosevelt*.

CHAPTER IX

THE SOCIALIST PARTY

FROM the time of its formation in 1901 to the entrance of the United States into the European War, the Socialist Party was the leading organization of its kind in the country. The development of its political strength is shown by the increase of the votes cast for its candidate for President from just under 100,000 in 1900 to over 400,000 in 1904, and to nearly 900,000 in 1912. A well-informed observer, not a Socialist, declared after the election of 1904, that if the Socialists increased in the same ratio during the next eight years as they had during the four years preceding 1904, they would elect a President of the United States.[1] Such an outcome seemed a real possibility after 1912.

EUGENE V. DEBS — EARLY LIFE

The recognized leader of the party during these years was Eugene V. Debs, to whom reference has already been made as one of the group of men responsible for its formation. In four presidential campaigns, 1900, 1904, 1908, and 1912, he was the candidate, and in 1916 he would have been nominated again had he not positively declined to be the standard-bearer. In 1920, although serving a sentence at Atlanta penitentiary for violation of the Espionage Act, he was renominated for the fifth time by his party.

Eugene V. Debs was born in Terre Haute, Indiana, in 1855, of parents who were both natives of Alsace and "passionately fond" of their home country, France. There were ten children, six of whom lived to adult age; four sisters, and one brother. He seems to have had a happy home

[1] Stelzle: *The Social Application of Religion*, p. 21.

life, although his parents were very poor. In May, 1870, at the age of fourteen, he began work in the railroad shops and later became a locomotive fireman. His mother's fears for his safety led him to give up the latter employment in 1874 for a place in a grocery store, where he remained five years until his election as city clerk, an office which he held for four years. His reputation was vouched for by his early employers during the 1912 campaign, after an intimate acquaintance of more than forty years. In 1907, the Mayor of Terre Haute, replying to an inquiry as to his standing in his home community, wrote that, "while the overwhelming majority of the people" were opposed to his social and economic theories, there was not probably a single man in the city who enjoyed "to a greater degree than Mr. Debs the affection, love, and profound respect of the entire community."

The entrance of Debs into the labor movement occurred in February, 1875, when a local lodge of the Brotherhood of Locomotive Firemen was organized at Terre Haute. He had already at that time helped to form unions for various classes of railroad workers. His first recognition as a leader came in 1878 when he was made associate editor of the "Firemen's Magazine." In 1880 he was appointed secretary and treasurer and editor and manager of the "Firemen's Magazine." He served in the first two offices until February, 1893, and in the latter two until September, 1894.

When Debs took charge of the Brotherhood of Locomotive Firemen, the order had only sixty lodges and a debt of six thousand dollars, but in a short time he had added two hundred and twenty-six lodges and had paid off the debt. At the time of his retirement he was receiving a salary of four thousand dollars per year. His first tender of his resignation was unanimously refused and he was unanimously re-elected. When he again resigned, and insisted upon its acceptance, he was unanimously voted two thousand dollars for a trip to Europe, as a mark of appreciation, but he declined the offer.

Debs believed that "organization should be broad enough to embrace all the workers," and he planned to devote himself to the building-up of such an organization. In June, 1893, with the assistance of a few others, he formed the American Railway Union at Chicago. This was one of the very first attempts in this country at industrial unionism, or the "one big Union," a form of organization which has come to be looked upon by many workers as the most effective method of dealing with industrial problems. Debs was made president of the new union; his salary dropped from four thousand dollars a year to seventy-five dollars a month; during the last two years of his service he drew no salary at all.

The first strike, called by the American Railway Union on the Great Northern Railroad, began April 13, 1894, and lasted eighteen days. J. J. Hill, the owner, was taken unawares and offered arbitration. Debs refused to change his terms, and, in spite of the intervention of the Governor, the strike was quickly won. The settlement of details was left to fourteen representative business men of the Twin Cities. The preliminaries took considerable time, but once in session these men, all of whom were capitalists and employers of labor, reached a conclusion in one hour for the employees, by which $146,000 more money would be distributed among the wage-earners engaged in the strike.

Debs returned to his home May 3, 1894, and was greeted by four thousand of his friends and neighbors. He addressed his fellow citizens in a public park near the Terre Haute House. In his opinion the contest had been successful because the men were united and, as a result of their unity, "they gained ninety-seven and one-half per cent of what they claimed as their rights." There was no rowdyism or lawlessness and there was not a single drop of human blood spilled. The American spirit of fair play was manifested by all involved in the struggle.

The American Railway Union officials, against the advice of Debs, decided to call a sympathetic strike to aid the workers of the Pullman Car Company, who, encouraged by the successful outcome upon the Great Northern Railroad, had struck in June, 1894. This controversy was so widespread that it involved the Federal Government because of the interference with the movement of mail trains. A special grand jury was impaneled in the United States District Court for Northern Illinois to consider evidence concerning the activities of the American Railway Union and the Pullman strike. With no further evidence than copies of telegrams sent from the headquarters of the American Railway Union and those received by the officials of the strikers, the grand jury returned indictments against four officers, including Debs as president. In ten minutes after the judge received the indictments, warrants were issued for the arrest of Debs and his co-officials.

The four men were arrested later for alleged violation of an injunction issued by the judges of the Federal Court. This injunction was in many respects one of the most remarkable ever issued by Federal judges, since by this instrument it became a crime to use persuasion on workingmen to join a strike. The men refused to give bail and were sent to Cook County jail, where they remained till July 23d. On that day a motion for the dismissal of the contempt proceedings, and a plea for a trial by jury, both met with denial. As a result Debs and his associates were sentenced to serve six months in jail for contempt of court.

The trial for conspiracy was interrupted by the illness of a juror and was never completed.

CONVERSION TO SOCIALISM

Debs's term in jail ended November 22, 1895. He entered jail a labor unionist, but came out a Socialist. On November 23, 1895, there appeared in "The Coming Nation," a Socialist journal, a letter by Debs in which he advocated the use of the ballot by working-men as a means of establishing "the Coöperative Commonwealth." The following year, 1896, he supported Bryan, but many years afterwards he declared that he was "a long way toward Socialism even at that time." January 1, 1897, he issued a circular letter to the members of the American Railway Union upon "Present Conditions and Future Duties." It closed with the following statement: "The issue is Socialism *versus* Capitalism. I am for Socialism because I am for humanity. We have been cursed with the reign of gold long enough. Money constitutes no proper basis of civilization. The time has come to regenerate society — we are on the eve of a universal change." The Social-Democratic Party was formed June 21, 1897, with Debs as its champion and leader. We have already pointed out that the Social-Democratic Party merged with other similar organizations to form the Socialist Party.

His conversion to socialism was described by Debs himself in 1902:

"The Chicago jail sentences were followed by six months at Woodstock, and it was here that Socialism gradually laid hold of me in its own irresistible fashion. Books and pamphlets and letters from Socialists came by every mail, and I began to read and think and dissect the anatomy of the system in which working-men, however organized, could be shattered and battered and splintered at a single stroke. The writings of Bellamy and Blatchford early appealed to me. The 'Coöperative Commonwealth' of Grönlund also impressed me, but the writings of Kautsky were so clear and conclusive that I readily grasped — not merely his argument, but also caught the spirit of his Socialist utterance — and I thank him and all who helped me out of darkness into light.

"It was at this time, when the first glimmerings of Socialism were beginning to penetrate, that Victor L. Berger came to Woodstock, as if a providential instrument, and delivered the first impassioned message of Socialism I had ever heard. As a souvenir of that visit there is in my library a volume of 'Capital,' by Karl Marx, inscribed with the compliments of Victor L. Berger, which I cherish as a token of priceless value.

"The American Railway Union was defeated but not conquered — overwhelmed but not destroyed. It lives and pulsates in the Socialist movement, and its defeat but blazed the way to economic freedom and hastened the dawn of human brotherhood."

Debs made his first political speech in 1878 in support of the Democratic Party, and soon after he was offered the nomination for Congress in a district where his acceptance would have been equivalent to an election. In 1885 he was chosen a member of the State Legislature. His acceptance was with the avowed purpose of obtaining, for the working-class in general and for railroad employees in particular, much-needed legislation. This office in addition to the city clerkship, already referred to, constitutes his entire experience in governmental work.

First Campaign for President

Comparatively little is recorded about the first campaign made by Debs for the Presidency in 1900. He was the candidate of the Social-Democratic Party, the name by which the Socialists were known immediately before the merger of groups which formed the Socialist Party in 1901. The large vote cast for Debs in 1900 was probably the chief influence in effecting the union at that time. McKinley and Bryan were the nominees of the Republicans and Democrats, and neither of them made a more energetic and intensive campaign than Debs, "who covered every state and Territory, not once but several times." His vote was 96,116.

This campaign made Debs a national figure. He showed himself a public speaker of great ability and "arresting sincerity." Consequently, it was natural that he should be the candidate of his party again in 1904.

The Reverend George D. Herron made the speech nominating him for President in May, 1904. He declared that no man in America "more surely and faithfully" incarnated "the heartache and the protest and the struggle of labor for its emancipation, or more surely" voiced "that struggle, than Eugene V. Debs." The nomination was unanimously accepted by the convention and, when Debs appeared to make his speech of acceptance, the chairman introduced him as "the Ferdinand Lassalle of the twentieth century."

In the campaign of that year he again carried the message of socialism into every State and Territory. For two months before the election he was traveling constantly, "sometimes delivering six to ten speeches a day. The intensiveness of his campaign was the marvel of political circumstances, and the sincerity with which he conducted it evoked the admiration of all who heard him." His vote jumped to 402,321 — an increase of over four hundred per cent.

Between 1904 and 1908, and for some time afterwards,

Debs was contributing editor to the "Appeal to Reason," a Socialist weekly, published at Girard, Kansas. Between his presidential campaigns he toured the country several times under the auspices of the labor movement. He was never too tired to respond to a pressing demand, and they were many, to stop off at a wayside town or village to address his comrades. Scores of times after filling strenuous speaking engagements he has sat up all night on trains so that he might stop off at some city or town along the route to visit a faithful follower whom he knew to be ill or in need."

CAMPAIGN OF 1908

In 1908 the Socialists planned the most intensive presidential campaign they had ever waged. As usual they were the first of the political parties to hold their national convention. Of a total of 198 votes cast, Debs received 159; the vote for him was then made unanimous. The opposition was based upon the ground that his health might be seriously impaired if he were to undergo again the strain of a national campaign.

Debs himself wrote Ben Hanford, the vice-presidential nominee in 1904 and 1908, that his throat and general health had improved considerably since he had had a chance to lead a more regular life and get a reasonable amount of rest. He preferred in the campaign to see what he could do with his pen and give his tongue a rest. He had never refused to do, as far as he could, anything the party had asked of him, and he never would. He had taken the nomination under protest, and had no desire to run for office, and a "positive prejudice against the very thought of holding office."

The campaign which Debs waged for sixty days before election was spectacular and filled with dramatic circumstances and was carried from one end of the country to the other. The National Executive Committee, early in July, decided to raise a fund to finance a "Red Special" campaign train to carry the candidate into every part of the United States. It consisted of a combined sleeper, observation, and dining-car, a baggage-car, and an engine. As it entered each State, local speakers and candidates were taken aboard to aid in the work in their States. There was a band of music on the train to arouse the people as it approached a city or town. The baggage-car was filled with Socialist publications of every kind, and these were freely circulated throughout the country. The "Red Special" cost twenty thousand dollars, which was contributed voluntarily by members and sympathizers.

The Socialist train left Chicago for the West August 31st. On his swing around the country Debs ran across hundreds of old American Railway Union men, and he went out of his way many times to visit their homes, and he was usually laden with gifts for the wife and children.

At Muscatine, Iowa, Debs addressed two thousand people. The "Kansas City Times" described his meeting in that city at which twenty-five hundred or three thousand persons paid an admission fee. He was referred to as "the greatest spell-binder of the party," who drew only three dollars a day for conducting his own campaign. The audience was composed largely of working-men, but many business men listened attentively to his statements. A large number of women were also present. On his way from Des Moines to Kansas City he had made ten speeches, some of them forty minutes in length, between six in the morning and six-thirty in the evening.

Several times it seemed likely that the "Red Special" would have to be abandoned for lack of finances, but appeals for funds were made and this contingency was avoided. On October 2, 1908, the train reached New York State. At Rochester five thousand people struggled for paid admission into Convention Hall, and four days before Debs spoke at the Hippodrome in New York City every seat was sold. Ten thousand people paid from fifteen to fifty cents for admission. No other political party could do the same thing. According to one of the newspapers, the Hippodrome was transformed into "a mountainous red-capped wave of revolution that whistled and screamed for Socialism when Eugene V. Debs appeared and answered the cry of humanity. For twenty-five minutes the full-lunged protest gave tongue to the protest against the 'System' in an unparalleled demonstration." In the opinion of his friends, Debs delivered one of the best speeches of his career at the Hippodrome meeting.

In some places efforts were made to prevent Debs from speaking. He was refused admission to the Stanford University Chapel, and in Philadelphia the police department raised barriers to his use of the Grand Opera House. The chairman of the local campaign committee adjusted the difficulty by having him speak in two smaller halls instead of the large one.

During the campaign the two major political parties had considerable controversy about the funds contributed by corporations and rich individuals to each other's campaign fund. Debs issued a statement concerning the funds raised by the Socialist Party:

"The Socialist Party has always published all receipts and expenditures in connection with its political campaigns, and this year will be no exception to the rule.

"The campaign fund of the Socialist Party is made up almost wholly of the nickels and dimes of the working-class, and all contributions are published in the official bulletin of the national party at the time they are made, and at the close of each campaign due report of all receipts and expenditures is made by the campaign committee and the national secretary, copies of which are furnished to the party press and the party membership. Not a dollar so far has been received by the Socialist Party from any corporation, and not a dollar ever received by it has been used except for the education of the working-class."

Despite the great meetings, the remarkable enthusiasm displayed, and the "Red Special," the Socialist vote showed but a slight increase over that of four years before — 420,973 as compared with 402,321. Debs had waged an educational campaign for socialism such as the country had never experienced before, but the gain in votes was small indeed for all the effort made.

CAMPAIGN OF 1912

The 1912 convention of the Socialist Party was held at Indianapolis. Since 1908 the Industrial Workers of the World, founded in 1905, had grown to be an organization which exerted a good deal of influence in industries employing large numbers of unskilled and poorly paid workers. Debs had been one of the leaders in its formation, but resigned in 1906. He had favored industrial unionism as against trade-unionism ever since the days of the American Railway Union. When the Chicago faction eliminated the political clause from its constitution in 1908, he termed the act "a monstrous blunder," but he continued to entertain a strong regard for the I.W.W. movement because of its positive attitude on economic and industrial questions.

Debs believed that if the I.W.W. had continued as it began, "a revolutionary industrial union, recognizing the need of political as well as industrial action, instead of being hamstrung by its own leaders and converted . . . into an anti-political machine," it would have become "the most formidable labor organization in America, if not the world." [1]

When the convention met at Indianapolis serious controversy was threatened because of the I.W.W. Conservative Socialists maintained that the organization was objectionable, because it advocated "sabotage" and "direct action" and discouraged political action. Many Socialists were members of both associations, and William D. Haywood, the most conspicuous leader of "the Reds," was a member of the National Executive Committee of the Socialist Party.

Concessions, however, were made on both sides. The principles of industrial unionism were endorsed without giving official support to any particular organization, and a section was added to the party constitution condemning violence and sabotage. Any member who advocated such practices or opposed political action was made liable to expulsion from the party. Accordingly Haywood was recalled from the National Executive Committee because of his opposition to political action, but the expulsion provision remained without enforcement. [2]

In spite of this division in the convention, when the time came to name a presidential candidate, there was no serious opposition to the nomination of Debs for the fourth consecutive time.

Both groups recognized that "Debs, more than any other man in the American labor movement, stood solidly and squarely for the complete overthrow of the capitalist system by both industrial and political methods, intelligently and peacefully applied, and in the final analysis that was the aim of both the I.W.W. and the Socialist Party."

The total vote in the convention for candidates for Presi-

---

[1] Brissenden: *The I.W.W.; A Study of American Syndicalism*, pp. 252, 253.
[2] *The American Labor Year Book*, 1916, pp. 91, 92.

dent was 165 for Debs, 56 for Emil Seidel, former Socialist Mayor of Milwaukee, and 54 for Charles Edward Russell, of New York. Mr. Seidel was made the nominee for Vice-President after the declination of Mr. Russell.[1]

Debs made his usual vigorous campaign. He polled 897,-011 votes, more than doubling his vote in 1908. Since the report of the national secretary in the early part of 1912 showed a party membership of only 125,823, a great many voters, who were not in active affiliation with the Socialist Party, were evidently in sympathy with its propaganda. A writer in the "Review of Reviews" for October, 1912, esti-mated that in the thirteen years of his career as presiden-tial candidate and lecturer, Debs had probably been seen and heard by nearly every one of those who would vote for him. This fact represented one of the strong factors in the increase of the Socialist vote during the four campaigns in which he was the standard-bearer. His following was pre-eminently a personal one.

The vote in 1912 established a record for the Socialist Party in a national election which has never since been equaled; it seemed, immediately after the close of this campaign, that the Socialists might become at least an effective minority party in the not distant future. The So-cialist Party in political strength stood where the Populist Party did in 1892. A moderate, opportunistic policy might have permeated the two major parties as did the Populist leaven of twenty years before. A union of moderate So-cialists with the Progressives might have brought about the reorganization of parties for which we have been waiting these many years, and which is indispensable if we are to meet constructively the economic and social problems of the times.

[1] Karsner: *Debs: His Authorized Life and Letters*, chaps. VI–VIII. The account of Debs and his campaigns is based largely upon this study.

CAMPAIGN OF 1916

The campaign of 1916 was late in opening, and when it did get under way it had to contend with the predominating interest of the public in subjects connected with the war and militarism. For reasons of economy the usual convention was done away with and nominations were made by referendum. After Debs and Russell had declined, Allen L. Benson, of New York, was named as the candidate for President and George A. Kirkpatrick, of New Jersey, as the nominee for Vice-President.

In commenting upon Benson's nomination "The New Republic" declared that the Socialists had done "more than select their ablest pamphleteer. They have declared against an increase of armaments, and for all practical purposes suppressed that small faction headed by Mr. Charles Edward Russell which has advocated preparedness. Mr. Benson ought to make an excellent campaign. He does not suffer from a Marxian technique. He talks the language of American radicalism, and his approach is more like that of the older muckrakers than of the hard intellectualists who constitute the priesthood of socialism. Mr. Benson will carry much conviction because he begins not with a few concepts about property and the class struggle, but with a rough-and-tumble experience of American business and politics. His nomination may be said to mark a stage in Socialist history, for his predecessor, Mr. Eugene V. Debs, belonged to an earlier American tradition, to the evangelist radicalism of the Middle West. He had a great heart, and those who knew him loved him. Mr. Benson is admired, and is likely to be feared." [1]

Senator F. M. Davenport, in his correspondence upon the "Pre-Nomination Campaign" printed in "The Out-

[1] *The New Republic*, vol. VI, p. 165.

look," expressed a similar opinion. He declared that people who did not believe in socialism might be glad to have the leadership of socialism in the United States "pass out of the merely emotional and agitator stage into the stage of responsible reasoning. A pamphleteer and thinker like Benson is a needed complement to a flaming evangelist and radical of the type of Debs." [1]

Benson spoke at sixty meetings and Kirkpatrick at sixty-one. Seven others toured the different sections of the country under the direction of the National Office. As usual the campaign funds were raised by contributions, by the sale of literature and by charging admission to political meetings. Five individuals contributed one hundred dollars each; all other contributions were for smaller sums.

The campaign was exceptional in the amount of literature distributed. A total of 22,039,500 leaflets was published and circulated. Leaflets written by the candidate for President were made a feature of the campaign. Ten were circulated in amounts from 1,260,000 copies for No. 1 to 3,000,000 for No. 10. The total cost of literature was $7923.90, while up to November 1, 1916, the total receipts were $5860.75, with stock still on hand. Supplies and novelties, including buttons, pencil clips, watch fobs, pennants, posters, and moving-picture films, were also provided for the campaign. The total cost was $2456.47 and the receipts $2706.94, with accounts outstanding and some stock on hand.

The vote for the Socialist Party in 1916 showed the first decided setback since its formation following the election of 1900. The total of 590,294 represented an absolute loss of 310,000 since 1912 and a relative loss of approximately forty-five per cent. The percentage of the Socialist vote of the total vote since 1900 is as follows:

[1] *The Outlook*, vol. cxii, p. 869.

Per cent

1900	.6
1904	2.9
1908	2.9
1912	5.9
1916	3.2

The relative strength of the Socialist Party as expressed by the vote for President, was approximately what it was in 1904. Comparing the presidential vote with the gubernatorial and senatorial votes for the same year, we find that these votes were only 14,000, or less than three per cent in excess of the presidential vote. That vote may, therefore, be regarded as a fair test of the strength of the Socialist Party.[1]

Probably the break in the party ranks in regard to the proper attitude toward the European War, and preparedness on the part of the United States, explain to a considerable extent the reduced vote. Furthermore, the substitution of a comparatively unknown writer for Debs undoubtedly contributed to the falling-off in votes. As a campaigner Debs has few equals, and in addition he is greatly beloved by the party members. Few who know him only through the newspapers realize how much he is admired by those who know him personally. He is not a great politician; he is really an evangelist, a wandering agitator who for years has gone up and down the country preaching the gospel of socialism. His opponents admit his ability, but those who follow him speak of his devotion, of his sacrifice, and of his love. They agree with James Whitcomb Riley's homely lines to Debs:

> "Go, search the earth from end to end,
> And where's a better all-round friend
> Than Eugene Debs? — a man that stands
> And jest holds out in his two hands
> As warm a heart as ever beat
> Betwixt here and the Mercy Seat!"

[1] *The American Labor Year Book*, 1917–18, pp. 335, 336.

Distribution of Political Strength

The increase of the political strength of the Socialist Party in the country at large is indicated by the growth of the vote cast for its candidates for President from 1900 to 1916. The distribution of the vote among the States can also be measured by the size of the vote cast in the different States for the same candidates. The distribution of the vote throws light upon the character of the movement and upon the possibilities of its growth in the future.

In 1908, fifteen States, in 1912, twenty-five States, and in 1916, eighteen States cast over 10,000 votes for the Socialist candidates. Of these States, four were Eastern in 1908, five in 1912, and four in 1916; five were Central in each election; and five were Western in 1908, eleven in 1912, and seven in 1916. Only one, Missouri, was Southern in 1908; West Virginia, Kentucky, and Texas were added in 1912, and Missouri and Texas remained in the group in 1916. No very definite conclusions can be drawn from this showing of the distribution of socialism among the States, although its small influence in the South is evident. In the Eastern and Central States it seems to be stationary, while in the West its growth is manifest.

A comparison of the relative strength by States, based upon the percentage of the Socialist vote of the total vote, gives more significant results. In 1912 six States exceeded ten per cent, twenty cast from five to ten per cent, nine from three to five per cent, nine from one to three per cent, and four less than one per cent. In 1916 there were two over ten per cent, seven between five and ten per cent, twelve between three and five per cent, nineteen from one to three per cent, and eight with less than one per cent.

American socialism has its chief strength, not in the manufacturing centers, but in the Western States where mining and farm tenantry prevail. In 1912 New York was the twenty-ninth in Socialist strength and in 1916 the twenty-fourth; Pennsylvania in 1912 was the nineteenth, in 1916, the eighteenth; New Jersey, the thirty-first and thirty-second; Connecticut, the twenty-fifth and twenty-eighth; Rhode Island, the thirty-seventh and twenty-ninth; Massachusetts, the thirty-sixth and thirty-first.

Contrasted with these manufacturing States of the East are Oklahoma and Nevada, which were respectively first and second in both 1912 and 1916; Montana was third in 1912 and eighth in 1916; Washington, fourth and sixth; Idaho, sixth and fifth; Arizona, ninth and seventh; Florida, eighth and third; Texas, twelfth and ninth. In 1912, Florida, Ohio, and Wisconsin were the only States east of the Mississippi which were in the first fifteen States, while in 1916 Wisconsin and Florida were the only ones. Thus, it is evident that the older industrial States are dropping into the rear of the Socialist procession, while the States of the West and South are taking their places near the head of the column.[1]

The election figures reveal the fact that the Socialist Party, at its point of greatest political strength before the disturbances growing out of the European War had affected it, was ceasing to be a party of wage-earners, and was appealing to farmers, middle-men, and small capitalists.

If the Socialist Party were the party of the wage-earners, it would be strong where the wage-earners are many, and weak where the wage-earners are few. But it is in the great industrial States of the Union, with cities and factories and dense masses of workmen, that the Socialists are the weakest. In New York State, after more than forty years of propaganda, the Socialist Party vote (1912) is only 4 per cent of the vote of the State. In other words, only one voter in every twenty-five votes the Social-

[1] *The American Labor Year Book*, 1917–18, p. 338.

ist ticket. In Massachusetts, a typically industrial State, only 2.6 per cent of the votes are Socialist; in Rhode Island, only 2.6 per cent; in New Jersey, only 3.7 per cent; in Maryland, only 1.7 per cent.

On the other hand, in certain agricultural States, where there are few wage-earners, and where farm-owners and tenants who wish to become farm-owners do not even know what wage-slavery is, the Socialist vote is comparatively strong. In Kansas, in Minnesota, in Texas, in several other preponderatingly agricultural States, the proportionate Socialist vote is much larger than in New York, Pennsylvania, New Jersey, and other industrial States. In the South, where there is hardly any industrial proletariat, the Socialist vote is growing. In Florida, 9.3 per cent of all the votes cast in 1912 were for Mr. Debs. The Socialist proportion of votes in Florida was considerably over twice as great as in New York and over three times as great as in Massachusetts.

But it is in the newest States in the West that the Socialist vote is the strongest of all. The State with the largest proportion of Socialist votes is not New York, Pennsylvania, Massachusetts, Illinois, Ohio, New Jersey, Michigan, or Connecticut — which are the eight greatest industrial States, comprising over 63 per cent of all wage-earners employed in manufacturing — but brand-new, corn-growing, hog-raising Oklahoma. In that State 16.6 per cent of all voters vote the Socialist ticket, or more than four times the proportion of New York and more than six times the proportion of Massachusetts. After Oklahoma the States which have the largest Socialist vote are the sparsely settled agricultural and mining States of the Far West. The only States which have 10 per cent or more of their votes Socialistic are the seven Western States, Oklahoma, Nevada, Montana, Arizona, Washington, California, and Idaho.

It almost seems as though the Socialist Party is weakest where it has been longest in the field, where its propaganda has been the most active, and where conditions seem ripest for the inevitable economic revolution. Thirty-six years ago, in 1878, when there were already twenty-four newspapers "directly or indirectly" supporting the Socialist party and the Socialists were piling up large votes in Cincinnati, Cleveland, Chicago, and St. Louis, Oklahoma was not even on the map, and the hope of the party seemed to lie in the industrial States of the East and Middle West. But the party growth did not keep pace with the industrial development of these States. Year by year an ever smaller proportion of the total Socialist vote was to be found in these great industrial commonwealths, and in several States an increased vote has been followed not only by a relative but by an absolute decline. In Massachusetts, where the decline has been greatest, the Socialist Party vote was 33,629 in 1902, and only 12,616 ten years later.

What we find everywhere is a deproletarization of the Socialist Party, and an opening of the party doors to all sorts of voters, proletarian, non-proletarian, and anti-proletarian. . . . To gather in the non-proletarian voter the Socialist Party platform is progressively watered so that the flaming red of a generation ago becomes a delicate pink. . . . How this development will work itself out, what are the ultimate chances of success of this new semi-progressive party, is a question of engaging interest. It is difficult to prophesy how it will modify its tactics and its leadership in an effort to gather in the vaguely radical vote.[1]

The election returns of 1914 supported the contention that the Socialist vote in the great industrial States is becoming relatively less important, while making greater progress in the agricultural and mining communities of the West. The total vote of 1914, as is usual in the years when only Congressional elections occur, "was less than in 1912, but the loss in the seven great Western States (Oklahoma, Nevada, Montana, Arizona, Washington, California, and Idaho) was only eight per cent, while the loss in the greatest industrial States (New York, Pennsylvania, Massachusetts, Illinois, Ohio, New Jersey, Michigan, and Connecticut) was forty per cent. In five of the Western States the Socialist vote in 1914 was actually higher, in several cases much higher, than in 1912, while in every one of the great industrial States the vote fell off, the decline in Pennsylvania, Illinois, and Michigan being over fifty per cent. In 1914, nineteen per cent of all Oklahoma electors

[1] *The New Republic*, vol. I, December 12, 1914, pp. 10, 11.

voted the Socialist ticket, while in Massachusetts the proportion of Socialist voters was only two per cent. To-day the State of Washington has as many Socialist Party voters as Massachusetts, Connecticut, and New Jersey combined, Montana has more than Michigan, and California more than New York."

Again, from 1904 to 1912, the total vote of the eight chief industrial States declined only from 48.3 to 44.2 per cent of the total vote of the Nation, while the Socialist vote of those States decreased from 49.93 to 42.07 per cent of the total Socialist vote. In addition there is no reason why a smaller proportion of all the voters in the industrial States should vote the Socialist ticket than in the Far Western States. Yet in the industrial States only 5.7 per cent of the voters were Socialist, while in the Western States 15.23 per cent voted for Debs.[1]

THE MILWAUKEE ELECTION, 1910

Significant as was the growth of the political strength of socialism in the Nation at large and in the States from 1900 to 1912, the most conspicuous gains have been made in city and local elections. The most noteworthy victory was won in Milwaukee in April, 1910, when Emil Seidel was elected Mayor by a vote of only five thousand less than the combined votes of his opponents. Twenty-one out of thirty-five members of the Council and all the minor city officers chosen were Socialists. It was not the first time that an American city had elected a Socialist Mayor, but it was the first time that such an event had occurred in one of the large cities of the country, and the first success won in so complete a manner.

Dissension in the ranks of both the old parties, the lead-

[1] *The New Republic*, vol. I, January 9, 1915, pp. 10, 11; January 16, 1915, pp. 10–12; January 23, 1915, p. 6.

ership of Victor L. Berger, one of the ablest Socialist speakers and writers, and a municipal programme that contained many items that were extemely popular and for which non-Socialists could vote, explain the victory. The customary American method of punishing the older parties resulted in a temporary success for the Socialists. The election was regarded everywhere at the time as a great triumph for socialism. Actually it was the normal result of American political methods, by which one party is frequently chastised by electing its opponents, and occasionally both are so treated. With only two parties of importance as a rule, an independent or third party must occasionally be supported.

The Socialists gave Milwaukee "about the best administration it ever had," and yet in 1912 they were defeated by a coalition of Republicans and Democrats. Again in 1914 the union of the older parties easily defeated Seidel, although the administration of their candidate had been less satisfactory than that of the Socialists.

Such an outcome demands an explanation which is found in the attitude of the Socialists toward their victory. They regarded it as a vindication and triumph for socialism. Really it was nothing of the kind, but merely a political reaction such as happens not infrequently in the country. Naturally they explained the defeats of 1912 and 1914 as due to the deliberate rejection by the people of the advantages of socialism. They ignored the facts of the situation. Their failure was a failure in imagination, in humor, and in knowledge of men. At a time when party ties were notably weakening, they insisted on stringent partisanship. Their emphasis upon class and sect was also equally unsuited to the times. Their continuous assumption of a virtual monopoly of righteousness and wisdom offended and alienated their friends.

Seidel had been in office seven months when Berger ran for Congress from the Milwaukee district and was elected. When his vote fell below that for Seidel, the Socialists showed disappointment and acrimony. Berger himself, in a signed statement, declared that "the vote went backward if compared with last spring; however, it did not go much backward as compared with the total vote cast. The fact is, nevertheless, that we have lost all the so-called sympathizers and protesters — also all the goody-goodies and church-club men. . . . It was a class victory — a victory of the working-class."

The spirit of this statement constantly animated the utterances and shaped the attitude of the Socialists. They were "hard, dogged, truculent, unintelligent, and, above all, sectarian." Furthermore, they opposed every important democratic measure, except home rule for cities, that their local supporters were interested in. The short ballot, a smaller city council, the vesting of the confirmation of appointments in a non-political civil service board, and measures to concentrate power and responsibility in the hands of the Mayor, were some of the proposals which they opposed. When some one asked Mr. Berger why they opposed these experiments in the simplification of government, he replied, with some vehemence, "But will all these things put one more sandwich in the dinner-pail of the working-man?"

Such an answer was typical of most of the Socialists. They frankly acknowledged the charge of sectarianism and rather gloried in it. One declared that he would prefer defeat rather than any victory which was not a straight class victory. Another said, "We have been persecuted for ages and generations; now we intend to conquer, and then we will persecute." [1]

[1] Nock: "Socialism in Milwaukee," in *The Outlook*, vol. cvii, pp. 608–12.

OTHER ELECTION SUCCESSES

The success in Milwaukee was the first considerable political victory won by the Socialists in the United States. Their gains in votes in the Nation and in the States had been noteworthy since 1900, but they had never had sufficient votes to give them actual political power. Their triumph in Milwaukee gave them an opportunity to show their ability in actual administration.

A year later the Socialists claimed successes in thirty-three States and in nearly two hundred municipalities. The officials elected included one Congressman, one State Senator, sixteen State Representatives, twenty-eight mayors, village presidents, and township chairmen, three city commissioners, one hundred and sixty-seven aldermen, councilors, village and township trustees. Sixty-one others were chosen for important executive, legislative, and departmental positions. Of the remainder, fifteen were assessors, sixty-two school officials, and sixty-five connected with the work of justice and the poor.

The State of Wisconsin furnished approximately twenty-two per cent of all the Socialists in office, while ten contiguous States grouped near the center of this region were responsible for fully seventy per cent. These States were Wisconsin, Illinois, Minnesota, Michigan, Missouri, Iowa, North Dakota, Kansas, Arkansas, and Nebraska. Five of the ten, Wisconsin, Illinois, Minnesota, Michigan, and Missouri, contributed fully one half of the total number of officials elected by the Socialists.

The bulk of these office-holders did not come from large cities. Of fifteen conspicuous cases, including Milwaukee, only three, besides that city, had more than ten thousand population, and ten had less than five thousand people. That did not mean that a majority of the Socialist officials came from agricultural and non-industrial communities. Actually a majority of the places were engaged in manufacturing, mining, or were transportation centers, but agricultural communities played a fairly considerable part.

The actual political power obtained by the party as a result of these election successes was exceedingly slight. Most of the victories might be regarded as "scattering." Only in Wisconsin, where thirteen Socialists sat in the legislature, did they acquire any effective power outside of particular municipalities. Even in the cities they were in a minority and in many cases were represented by single unimportant officers. In the few places like Milwaukee where they had a majority, they were handicapped by the opposition of the minority and by the limitations imposed by the city charter, the courts, and the State legislatures. About all they could do was to give an honest and efficient administration.

Any attempt to give a single, all-inclusive explanation of these Socialist successes is bound to fail. Certain fairly distinct types, however, can be discerned. There was "the victory of a broad, liberal, opportunistic, moderate type of socialism of comparatively slow and solid growth," which appeared in Wisconsin and the neighboring States, and of which Milwaukee was representative.

Another type consisted of "a more class-conscious socialism" which placed more emphasis on "ultimate Socialist ideas." It was to be found in mining camps and owed its existence to the mine-workers' unions. It occurred more frequently in the bituminous and Far-Western coal fields than in the anthracite regions. It resulted from the leadership of the old Eastern stock crowded West by the influx of eastern and southern Europeans into the anthracite sections.

A third type was developed by Socialist organization

and agitation in agricultural or semi-agricultural communities. These victories were quite generally distributed, but their "special habitat" seemed to be in the former strongholds of Populism. Usually the successes were only of a temporary character and disappeared in a year or two.[1]

Early in 1912 it was estimated that there were not less than 1141 Socialist office-holders in thirty-six States and 324 municipalities. As many as 642 Socialists were voted into office in the November elections of 1911, but of these only four represented areas larger than a county; one half were minor local officials. Only eight cities were captured, and none of them compared with Milwaukee in size; Schenectady, New York, with a population of 72,826, was the largest. Wisconsin remained the leading Socialist State, and it was the only one in which the Socialists had any considerable power outside of municipalities.

The new victories were in distinctly large and industrial communities, and, instead of being scattering, were massed in particular regions and particular municipalities. There was reason for believing that the real tendency was in the direction of an increase of middle-class membership and control in the party.

A careful study of the results of the elections gave the general impression that the country was "at last face to face with a vigorous and efficient Socialist movement" — a movement which was "Nation-wide," which was laying "the foundation for a permanent structure by building from the bottom of the political system," which was "recruiting its main strength in the important civic and industrial centers," and which was "growing at a rapidly accelerating rate." If the recent progress continued, a decade

[1] Hoxie: "The Rising Tide of Socialism," in the *Journal of Political Economy*, vol. xix, pp. 609–31.

would see it "seriously challenging the supremacy of one or both of the old political parties."

There was "a distinct tendency toward the establishment of a characteristic or predominant type of Socialist victory." This type was a composite of the successes in Milwaukee and such mining centers as Butte, Montana. Its leaders claimed adherence to the general theory of socialism, but it was really "moderate, opportunistic, and reformatory." [1]

The Socialists continued to win elections after 1912, but the outbreak of the European War in 1914 diverted public interest. Discussion and conflict as to the policy to be followed in view of their anti-war position interrupted their normal growth. Apparently 1912 marked the crest of the Socialist wave in local and State elections as it did in the national sphere. The decline in the Socialist vote in 1916 probably indicated the trend throughout the country. At the same time it should be remembered that minor parties receive a relatively larger share of the votes in local than in national elections.

In 1914 a second Socialist Congressman, Meyer London, was elected from a district in New York City, which was largely made up of Jews. He was reëlected in 1916, but defeated in 1918. Berger, the first Socialist ever elected to Congress, whose election was referred to in connection with the Socialist success in Milwaukee, was defeated for reëlection in 1912, 1914, and 1916, although his vote in the last year was larger than in 1910, when he was first elected. In 1918 he was elected for a second time, but was refused his seat because he was under indictment for disloyal acts at the time of his election. Since 1916 Milwaukee has elected and reëlected a Socialist Mayor. Wisconsin, con-

[1] Hoxie: "The Socialist Party in the November Elections," in the *Journal of Political Economy*, vol. xx, pp. 205–23.

sequently, continued to be the leading Socialist State —
the only one where the Socialists have any real political
power in the United States.

SOCIALIST PROSPECTS

A survey of the growth of the Socialist Party from 1900
to the outbreak of the European War confirms the opinion
expressed in an earlier chapter as to the lack of a really
vital Socialist movement in the United States. The popular vote of nearly a million in the presidential campaign of
1912, the Socialist success in Milwaukee in 1910, and the
election of two Socialists to Congress comprise their most
significant achievements up to date. Actually these accomplishments represent no really effective power in American political life. Compared with Socialist results in Europe, they seem of minor importance.

Commenting upon the Socialist Party Convention of
1908, Professor R. F. Hoxie, of the University of Chicago,
declared that there was a conflict for control between "a
comparatively small group of very intelligent, skillful, moderate, and constructive leaders, drawn to a large extent
from the middle class, and an unorganized, impulsive, comparatively unintelligent, sentimental, for the most part
negative, and in part revolutionary mass, drawn from all
classes and actually representing none."

The constructive group won a partial victory in the convention by eloquence and adroitness in handling issues,
and by strong professions of loyalty to the principle of
the revolutionary class struggle. As a matter of fact, however, the future of the party depended more upon the party
personnel than upon declarations of party policy.

In Professor Hoxie's opinion, the future of the organization was "threatened most seriously by a certain ignorant,
doctrinaire, ultra-revolutionary, semi-anarchistic element

represented by such men as Bill Haywood, and certain individuals connected with such sheets as the 'Appeal to Reason.'"

Haywood was forced to withdraw from the contest for leadership during the campaign of 1908, but the moderate group could not nominate "a man of their own stripe, but were forced to choose between popular idols." They could not find "a real working-class leader of suitable caliber." Debs and Hanford were chosen again, though it was clearly understood that Debs no longer had "mind nor character for leadership," and that neither of the candidates really represented "the dominant trend in party policy." [1]

These comments, made by a careful and thoughtful observer in 1908, help to explain the collapse of the party since 1912. Undoubtedly, the complications growing out of the European War have been primarily responsible for the result, but they have simply aggravated the existing situation. They have helped to throw the control of the party into the hands of the revolutionary element described by Professor Hoxie. The tendency represented by the European syndicalists and the American Industrial Workers of the World has swamped the more constructive influences that were struggling for control in 1908 and 1912.

Debs's leadership, although it has coincided with the great growth in the voting strength of the party, has contributed nothing of a constructive character. The very qualities by which he attaches his supporters through personal loyalty and devotion have made him a more dangerous obstacle to any constructive effort. The combination of such a leadership with the industrial and social conditions since 1900 has resulted quite naturally in the defeat of the constructive leadership in the Socialist Party.

[1] Hoxie: "The Convention of the Socialist Party," in the *Journal of Political Economy*, vol. xvi, pp. 442-50.

The collapse of the Progressive movement in the Republican Party since 1912 suggests that the Socialist decline has not been an isolated phenomenon. The existing situation at home and abroad seems to warrant the opinion that liberalism and radicalism must make a new start if they are to play a part in the changing world. Apparently the millennium is not quite so near as it seemed to be a few years ago to some enthusiasts.

SELECTED REFERENCES

1. Macy: *Socialism in the United States.*
2. Walling: *The Socialism of To-Day.*
3. Hillquit: *History of Socialism in the United States* (fifth edition), part II, chaps. IV, V.
4. Hughan: *American Socialism of the Present Day.*
5. Karsner: *Debs: His Authorized Life and Letters.*
6. Hoxie: "The Convention of the Socialist Party," in the *Journal of Political Economy*, vol. XVI, pp. 442–50.
7. Hoxie: "The Rising Tide of Socialism," in the *Journal of Political Economy*, vol. XIX, pp. 609–31.
8. Hoxie: "The Socialist Party in the November (1911) Elections," in the *Journal of Political Economy*, vol. XX, pp. 205–23.
9. *The American Labor Year Book*, 1916, pp. 89–159.
10. *The American Labor Year Book*, 1917–18, pp. 335–79.
11. Nock: "Socialism in Milwaukee," in *The Outlook*, vol. CVII, pp. 608–12.
12. *The New Republic*, vol. I, December 12, 1914, pp. 10, 11; January 9, 1915, pp. 10–11; January 16, 1915, pp. 10–12; January 23, 1915, p. 6.

CHAPTER X

THE INDUSTRIAL WORKERS OF THE WORLD

The roots of the I.W.W. reached out most vigorously and numerously in the western part of the United States and its greatest strength has been manifested in that part of the country. The way was prepared for it by Western organizations — the Western Federation of Miners being the chief forerunner. Two other organizations, having their chief strength in the East, played an important part during the decade before the formation of the I.W.W. These were the Socialist Labor Party and the Socialist Trade and Labor Alliance. The Socialist Trade and Labor Alliance was organized in 1895, the same year in which the organized syndicalist movement was born in France in the form of the Confédération Générale du Travail. The idea of the Alliance seems to have originated with Daniel De Leon, and it was patterned closely after the Knights of Labor.

Contrary to the common opinion, the main ideas of I.W.W.-ism were American, not French. Similar sentiments were developing in France during the nineties, but the I.W.W. is an indigenous product, a home-grown child of American labor conditions. It was only after 1908 that the revolutionary syndicalism of France had any direct influence on the revolutionary industrial unionist movement in the United States. Even then it was largely a matter of borrowing such phrases as "sabotage" and "direct action." The tactics back of these words had been practiced by American working-men years before the terms came into use. These principles were applied in the Rocky Mountains, under the leadership of Haywood and others, several years before the French Confederation of Labor was formed.[1]

The I.W.W. is "a union of unskilled workers in large part employed in agriculture and in the production of raw materials. . . ." Its membership consists largely of "migratory workers currently called hobo labor . . . very few of these migratory workers have lived long enough in any one place to establish legal residence and vote, and they are also womanless. Only about ten per cent have been married, and these have either lost their wives or deserted them. . . . 'They are floaters' in every social sense. . . . Half of the migratories are of American birth, the other half being largely made up of the newer immigration from southeastern Europe."

The conditions under which the American unskilled worker lives and works and is prepared for the drop down into the migratory class must be understood in connection with a study of the I.W.W. In 1910, of the 30,091,564 men listed by the United States Census as wage-earners, 10,400,-000 approximately were engaged in the kind of unskilled work from which the migratory is recruited. The combination of low wages, the unskilled, monotonous character of the work, and its great irregularity, tends to break the habit and desire for stable industry among these workers. They drift into migrating from one industrial center to another in search of work. They slide down the scale and join "the millions of unskilled or lost-skilled who float back and forth from Pennsylvania to Missouri and from the lumber camps to the Gulf States and California."

" It is a conventional economic truism that American industrialism is guaranteeing to some half of the forty millions of our industrial population a life of such limited happiness, of such restrictions on personal development, and

[1] Brissenden: *The I.W.W.: A Study of American Syndicalism*, pp. 46-54.

of such misery and desolation when sickness or accident comes, that we would be childish political scientists not to see that from such an environment little sacrificing nation-love, little of ethics, little of gratitude could come.

"The casual migratory laborers are the finished product of an economic environment which seems cruelly efficient in turning out human beings modeled after all the standards which society abhors. The history of the migratory workers shows that starting with the long hours and dreary winters of the farms they ran away from, or the sour-smelling bunk-house in a coal village, through their character-debasing experience with the drifting 'hire and fire' life in the industries, on to the vicious social and economic life of the winter unemployed, their training predetermined but one outcome, and the environment produced its type. The I.W.W. has importance only as an illustration of a stable American economic process." It is largely a symptom of a certain vicious economic situation — a social sore on the body politic.[1]

Although the I.W.W. is a characteristic product of Western migratory labor, it develops sporadically wherever labor conditions are bad, wherever there are hordes of unskilled immigrant laborers, wherever causes of unrest and agitation are smouldering and are ready to be fanned into flames. Such was the situation in Lawrence, Massachusetts, in 1912. The failure of the American Federation of Labor to meet the needs of leadership in such communities has left the field to the exploitation of the I.W.W. Their leaders have developed a capacity for taking command in such situations and for using them to obtain sensational publicity.

[1] Parker: *The Casual Laborer and Other Essays*, pp. 113–24. Reprinted from the *Atlantic Monthly*, vol. cxx, pp. 658–62.

WESTERN FEDERATION OF MINERS

A new type of unionism was developed in the United States by the formation of the Western Federation of Miners at Butte, Montana, in May, 1893. It grew out of the conditions existing in the mining States of the Far West, especially in Colorado, Montana, Nevada, Idaho, and Arizona. Because of these conditions its activities were far more violent than those followed by the unions in the older parts of the country. The new organization grew slowly to 1896 and rapidly from that year to 1900. By 1900 it had a large following in the mining States. It affiliated with the American Federation of Labor in 1893, but withdrew in 1897, because of lack of harmony as to policies and methods. A number of years later, in 1911, it rejoined the Federation. By that time it had become more conservative and was engaged in bitter controversies with the I.W.W.

From 1893 to 1905 the Western Federation of Miners "figured in the most strenuous and dramatic series of strikes in the history of the American labor movement." One of the most violent contests began in 1902 over the eight-hour day for all miners in Colorado. The mine-owners crushed it with the aid of the Governor and the military. Later efforts were made to destroy the miners'organization and were answered by various acts of violence culminating in the assassination of ex-Governor Steunenberg of Idaho. Three leaders, charged with complicity, were brought to trial in 1907, and, after a struggle of eighty-four days, a verdict of "not guilty" was rendered. These leaders, Charles H. Moyer, William D. Haywood, and George A. Pettibone, were described by President Roosevelt as "undesirable citizens."

This new phase of the labor movement gradually became national in its influence by coöperation with forces that were hostile to the conservative policy of the American Federation of Labor. A minority of Socialists had continued for years to try to commit the older organization to socialism. They urged the uselessness of its purely industrial policy and the advantages of political action. The failure of a number of strikes, the use of the injunction by the courts, and the increasing hostility of big business, led to widespread criticism of the older trade-union policy. These conditions predisposed many unionists to listen to the arguments of the advocates of more aggressive methods. Gradually a considerable number of workers became converted to the *industrial* form of organization in preference to the *craft* form of the older Federation.

The idea that the labor union should be used as the organization for the operation of industry was taken up by Haywood, Debs and St. John in the years from 1902 to 1905. As "revolutionary industrial unionists," they proposed that the labor union should be regarded as the growing cell of society, thus becoming the nucleus out of which the coming social order should grow. With this constructive idea they joined the violent methods which their experience had led them to feel were the essential features of a vigorous and effective campaign upon the part of the workers. They substituted "direct action" for the conservative policy of the American Federation. The form of organization and the methods used were the distinctive marks of a new development in the history of the labor movement in the United States.

FORMATION OF THE I.W.W.

The I.W.W. had its beginning in an informal conference held in Chicago in the fall of 1904 by six men of prominence in the labor and socialist movement. These men believed that the labor movement in America was becoming powerless to obtain real benefits for working-men and women. Plans were made for a larger meeting, and for a letter of invitation to be sent out to about thirty persons of importance in radical labor and socialist circles. The letter invited them to a "secret conference to discuss ways and means of uniting the working-people of America on correct revolutionary principles, regardless of any general labor organization of past or present, and only restricted by such basic principles as will insure its integrity as a real protector of the interests of the workers." The "secret conference" was to meet in Chicago, January 2, 1905.

The "January Conference" was attended by twenty-three persons, representing nine different organizations. During the three days' session plans for a new labor organization were discussed and worked out. A "manifesto" was drawn up, which contained an indictment of "things as they are" in the trade-union world; plans for the new type of labor organization; and a call for a convention to form the new union.

The manifesto discussed certain modern tendencies in the labor movement. It pointed out that "trade divisions among laborers and competition among capitalists" were both disappearing. "The machine process" was "more and more tending to minimize skill and swell the ranks of the unskilled and unemployed." These results were fatal to labor groups divided according to the tool used. The employers were united on the industrial plan.

The craft form of organization was severely criticized. It made solidarity impossible, for it generated "a system of organized scabbery, where union men scab on each other." It resulted in "trade monopolies, prohibitive initiation fees, and political ignorance." It dwarfed "class consciousness," and tended to "foster the idea of harmony of interests between employing exploiter and employed slave."

The remedy proposed was "one great industrial union embracing all industries, providing for craft autonomy locally, industrial autonomy internationally, and working-class unity generally." The American Federation of Labor, as the representative of the craft form, was the subject of bitter attack. The idea was "to form a new central body, into which existing unions and unions to be formed could be admitted, but not to form rival unions." Organized laborers, however, were only a part of the concern of the conference. The ninety-five per cent of those gainfully occupied, who were unorganized, were also the objective of its efforts.

The convention called by the manifesto met in Chicago, June 27, 1905, with two hundred persons in attendance. It was "a gathering remarkable and epoch-making in more ways than one," and its activities were fundamental in the history of industrial unionism. Before its adjournment it had organized itself as the Industrial Workers of the World.

Probably the most striking characteristic of these two hundred radicals was the very great variety of occupations represented — at least forty distinct trades. There was also a very wide range in the structural types of the unions represented. Forty-three organizations were finally seated. Delegates were of two classes: those with voting power and those sent to take note of the proceedings and to report back. About one third were authorized to support the new organization, and these delegates exercised practically the whole voting power of the assembly. Most of these delegates came from five organizations, including the Western Federation of Miners, and from the latter came the great bulk of the funds for establishing the new union. Numerically and financially, it held the balance of power.

A few men really dominated the convention. Eugene V. Debs was the best known and he contributed his contagious enthusiasm, his eloquence, and his optimism. Ever since his organization of the American Railway Union, he had believed in the "One Big Union." William D. Haywood came from the West with his years of experience as a leader of the Western Federation of Miners. But the most striking figure was Daniel De Leon, a man with a university education and a graduate of the law school of Columbia University. He had obtained control of the Socialist Labor Party in the early nineties and had been chiefly responsible for the splits in that party which had finally resulted in the formation of the Socialist Party. Under his leadership the Socialist Labor Party had maintained a shadowy existence. His antagonism to trade-unionism had been extreme ever since his break with the Knights of Labor in 1895. Hillquit asserted that his "Socialist Trades and Labor Alliance had a record of having caused more disputes and schisms within the Socialist labor movement in America in recent years than any other factor, and its affiliation with the new movement was fateful for the latter."

"These, then, were the elements of the heterogeneous labor mass, which were to be worked up together into 'One Big Union.' The thing that made union possible in any degree was the binding influence of common antipathies. It has been suggested that all were at one in being opposed to a capitalistic society. They had no difficulty in making common cause of their mutual hatred of the capitalistic scheme of things. They were perhaps even more able to unite because of common opposition to certain things which they believed were helping to perpetuate the capitalist system. Most prominent and powerful of these was the craft form of labor organization.[1]

[1] Brissenden: *The I.W.W.: A Study of American Syndicalism*, in *Columbia University Studies in History, Economics and Public Law*, vol. LXXXIII, chaps. I, II; Brooks: *American Syndicalism*, chaps. VI, VII.

The adjournment of the convention, July 8, 1905, left the new organization in a very chaotic condition. The delegates had been so exclusively occupied with "the problem of building up 'one big union' out of many little unions, and the task of working out a harmony platform of law and policy on which all could come together, that the matter of business management was almost entirely neglected."

The industrial-union idea made marked headway among the trade unions during the first year of the I.W.W. Organizers were sent to places where serious friction existed between trade-unionists and the American Federation of Labor. The I.W.W. paid very little attention to the unorganized, but devoted its energy largely to the reformation of the craft union. Only in later years has it even approximately lived up to its avowed policy of organizing the unskilled and floating laborer.

But these controversies with craft unions were not the only serious problems with which the I.W.W. had to contend. It was threatened with wholesale defection, and very soon actually suffered in some quarters. The severest blow came from the withdrawal of the Western Federation of Miners in 1907. In fact, the Federation ceased to be active in the affairs of the I.W.W. after the second convention in September, 1906. In addition, most of the strikes undertaken during the first fifteen months were unsuccessful.

The second convention witnessed the first split in the ranks of the I.W.W. The friction at this time seemed to be chiefly personal, while the second schism in 1908 was due primarily to differences over principles and policies. From the beginning there had been a smouldering antagonism between the poorer and less skilled groups of workers and the more highly skilled and organized groups — the "revolutionists" or "wage-slave delegates" on the one side and "the reactionaries" or the "political fakirs" on the other.

Involved with these controversies was trouble stirred up by the members of the two Socialist parties.

These conflicts manifested themselves chiefly in charges and counter-charges of graft, corruption, and abuse of official power. The "revolutionists" gained the upper hand, deposed the president, and abolished the office, but the old officers retained possession of the headquarters and the funds. An appeal to the courts resulted favorably to "the revolutionists," but they were left in a rather forlorn position, since the Western Federation of Miners had supported their opponents, and that organization had been the main source of financial support. De Leon had been one of the leaders of "the revolutionists," and he had added one more to the number of splits for which he was responsible.

No actual division of the I.W.W. occurred in 1906. The "revolutionists" led by De Leon were nominally successful in that year, but they found themselves deprived of financial resources by the withdrawal of the Western Federation of Miners. Debs did not attend the 1906 gathering, and the Socialist Party was less actively interested, leaving only De Leon out of the "big three" of the first convention.

THE SPLIT OF 1908

In 1908 the I.W.W. split into two factions: the Detroit I.W.W. and the Chicago I.W.W. or "Bummery." These divisions continued till 1915, when the Detroit group assumed the name of the Workers' International Industrial Union. De Leon was the leader of the Detroit organization until his death in 1914. The Chicago group has been the active body since 1908 and has conducted most of the strikes and free-speech campaigns in which the I.W.W. has been engaged.

The question of "political action" was the overshadowing issue at the convention held in September, 1908. For four days the convention did practically nothing but debate the question whether the Socialist Labor Party, through Daniel De Leon, was trying to control the I.W.W. This struggle was merely a prelude to the contest over the retention of the political clause of the preamble to the constitution which was fought out on a personal issue — the admission of De Leon as a delegate. His supporters accused their opponents of trying to make the I.W.W. a "purely physical force body," while the De Leonites were charged with attempting to subordinate the interests of the I.W.W. to those of the Socialist Labor Party. Since De Leon was the leader of the political element in the I.W.W., the anti-parliamentarians probably felt that they must eliminate De Leon in order to make it possible for the delegates from the West to get rid of the objectionable political clause. Consequently De Leon was not seated.

With De Leon removed from the convention, the proposal to strike out the words "political field" was adopted and the "straight industrialists" had accomplished their purpose. The records and property of the organization remained with the successful faction which thus became entitled to be regarded as the *de facto* I.W.W.

The other faction held a convention in Paterson, New Jersey, and elected a new set of officers. They declared the proceedings of the Chicago Convention illegal, and read the "anarchist usurpers" out of the organization. They regarded themselves as the "*bona fide* industrial unionists." New York City was first selected as the location for the national headquarters, but within a few months the headquarters were established in Detroit, Michigan. This faction never attained a strength at all comparable to that of the direct-action group. To a very large extent it was merely a new name for the Socialist Labor Party.

The I.W.W. which has been most widely advertised in the United States is the "Chicago, or Direct-Actionist, or Anarcho-Syndicalist, or Anti-Political, or Bummery, or Red I.W.W." It is the I.W.W. which has been actively engaged in the strikes at Lawrence, Massachusetts, Wheatland, California, and many other places, and in "free-speech" fights at Spokane, Fresno, and San Diego.

In 1908 the direct-actionists were left in almost as weak a condition as their opponents, the doctrinaires. The weakness of the latter has been chronic. The former developed greater strength because they modified their theories sufficiently to apply them to the actual conditions of economic life. "They have been strikingly successful as gadflies — stinging and shocking the bourgeoisie into the initiation of reforms."

But for some time after 1908 they scarcely more than kept alive. Only in 1911 they began to increase their membership in a halting and fitful way. Levine, writing in the "Political Science Quarterly" in September, 1918, described the organization as having "shrunk to a mere handful of leaders, revolutionary in spirit and ideals, and persevering in action, with a small scattered and shifting following and an unsatisfactory administrative management." [1]

Free-Speech Fights

In 1909 the I.W.W. appeared as "the militant jail and soap-box belligerent in the free-speech fight." Since that year they have attracted as much attention by "their dramatic free-speech controversies with municipal authorities here and there as they have by the time-honored resort to the strike." The Pacific Coast is the best field for these conflicts. "Labor is more mobile there, and when the

[1] Levine: "The Development of Syndicalism in America," in the *Political Science Quarterly*, vol. xxviii, pp. 451–79.

organizers in any particular town are arrested for preaching revolution a more effective call to 'foot-loose Wobblies' for an 'invasion' is possible. On the Pacific slope 'the Wobblies' almost literally broke into the jails by hundreds. They came to speak, but with the nearly certain foreknowledge that they would be collared by the police before they said many words. They simply crowded the jails, and in this way, as they intended, clogged the machinery of municipal administration by making themselves the guests of the city in such numbers as to be no inconsiderable burden to their real hosts, the taxpayers."

The same tactics were used in nearly every instance. Whenever a local union became involved in a free-speech fight, it notified the general office, and the information was sent to all local unions with the request to send any members that were free to go to help. The national organization did not in any way manage or finance these contests. Their management was left to the unions interested.

A policy of sullen non-resistance on the part of the I.W.W. results in wholesale jailing by the authorities. The trouble begins when the authorities try to repress I.W.W. speakers because their remarks are "seditious, incendiary, unpatriotic, immoral... profane or vulgar." The result almost invariably is the same as if an attempt were made to smother an active volcano. The ideas get expressed more bitterly, and those who try to do the smothering are apt to use questionable methods of suppression. The violence of the aggressive representatives of the I.W.W. is met by the violence of the defenders of the law.

In the fall of 1909 there were three important free-speech campaigns conducted by the I.W.W. These were at Missoula, Montana; Spokane, Washington; and New Castle, Pennsylvania. In 1910 small contests were conducted during the spring and summer in Wenatchee and Walla

Walla, Washington, and in the fall a much more important one at Fresno, California, which lasted until March, 1911. From this time until the end of 1913 hardly a month elapsed without some sort of a free-speech fight between the I.W.W. and the municipal authorities in some part of the United States. From 1909 to 1913, there were at least twenty of these contests, continuing under I.W.W. direction for periods varying from a few days to more than six months.

The most remarkable of these contests was the one at San Diego, which lasted from February, 1912, until late the following summer. Governor Hiram Johnson appointed a special commissioner to investigate the disturbances. Mr. Harris Weinstock, the commissioner, carefully followed up "the stories of brutality and cruelty of the self-constituted citizens' committee of vigilantes," and in his report he says that he was "frank to confess that when he became satisfied of the truth of the stories ... it was hard for him to believe that he was not sojourning in Russia, conducting his investigation there instead of in this alleged 'land of the free and the home of the brave.'"

The Lawrence Strike — The "Crest of Power"

In 1912 the I.W.W. came into national prominence. From Lawrence, Massachusetts, to San Diego, California, they stirred the country with their strike and free-speech propaganda. There were more strikes and free-speech fights in 1912 and 1913 than during any other corresponding period in the history of the organization. This period, however, was marked by the prominence of "the then strange and novel syndicalist strike propaganda of the I.W.W." During this time more than thirty strikes ran their course in different parts of the country.

"Overshadowing all others in importance was the gigantic strike of the textile workers at Lawrence. This great struggle set new fashions in strike methods. It Americanized the words, 'sabotage,' 'direct action,' and 'syndicalism,' and revealed to the hitherto ignorant public the manner and effectiveness with which these alleged French importations could be applied to an existing industrial situation. Lawrence, together with San Diego, and one or two other 'free-speech' cities, really introduced the Industrial Workers of the World to the American public. The organization and its activities were known to students of the labor problem and to others who happened to be on the spot when a fight was on, but they were not known to the great body of citizens. Lawrence and the free-speech fights made the name of this little group of intransigeants a household word, hardly less talked about and no whit better understood than the words 'socialist' and 'anarchist.'"

The strike began January 11, 1912, when about fourteen thousand textile operatives left their work. During the strike, which lasted until March 14th, the number was increased to twenty-three thousand. The immediate cause was a reduction of earnings, due to a State law which became effective January 1, 1912, and which reduced the working hours for women and for persons under eighteen years of age from fifty-six to fifty-four per week. At the beginning only a small number of the operatives were organized. A few of the skilled crafts, composed chiefly of English-speaking workers, had their unions, but these contained only about twenty-five hundred members. The I.W.W. had some years before established an organization and claimed a membership of one thousand. It was estimated, however, that in January, 1912, there were not more than three hundred paid-up members.

Early in the strike, Joseph J. Ettor and William D. Haywood, I.W.W. officials, came to Lawrence and assumed leadership. They preached "solidarity," "passive resistance," "direct action," and "sabotage" as means to victory. There were acts of violence on the part of police and the militia as well as on the side of the strikers. There is strong evidence of at least one attempt on the part of the business and commercial interests to discredit the strikers by "planting" dynamite in three places. Later a business man of the city, who had no connection with the strikers, was "convicted of conspiracy to injure by the planting of dynamite," and was fined five hundred dollars.

The result of the strike was a decided victory for the strikers. Some thirty thousand textile workers secured an increase in wages of from five to twenty per cent. In addition, as an indirect result of the contest, increases in wages were granted to thousands of employees in other textile mills in New England. A significant fact also was that the highest percentages of increases were given to the unskilled workers.

Furthermore, this strike demonstrated that it was possible for the unskilled and unorganized workers, most of whom were immigrants of different nationalities, to carry on a successful strike. It also demonstrated the power of a new type of labor leader over ignorant and unskilled immigrant workers.

The Lawrence struggle stirred the country with the alarming slogans of a new kind of revolution. Socialism was respectable by comparison. The I.W.W. frankly ignored the rules under which "the capitalist game" is played. Lawrence was not an ordinary strike. It was a social revolution on a small scale. It was a class war waged with the ultimate purpose of overthrowing the wage system and establishing industrial democracy. The I.W.W. frankly rejected "current ethics and morality as bourgeois and therefore inimical to the exploited proletarian." They denounced the Church and the flag as made to serve commercialism and to exploit labor; Jingo patriotism made the enlargement and conquest of markets its end and aim.

The Lawrence strike marked "the crest of power" of the I.W.W. as an organization. It has never been strong numerically and the character of its membership makes it subject to very great fluctuation. After the close of the successful contest at Lawrence, its organizers claimed 14,-000 members in that city, while in October, 1913, there were only 700.

According to Levine, the total paid-up membership in 1913 was 70,000, distributed as follows: textile industry, 40,000; lumber industry, 15,000; railroad construction, 10,-000; metal and machinery, 1000; and miscellaneous, 4000. The members in the textile industry were located in the East; those in the lumber industry were in Washington, Oregon, Louisiana, and Texas; the railroad construction workers were in Washington, Oregon, and British Columbia.

Brissenden believes that Levine's estimate was furnished by the general office of the I.W.W. and that it was "unquestionably much too high." His own conclusions fix the membership at about 15,000 in 1913, 11,000 in 1914, and 15,000 in 1915.

At the meeting of the American Economic Association in December, 1913, Professor Hoxie compared the "numerical insignificance" of the I.W.W. with the American Federation of Labor. He said that in 1913 the I.W.W. had paid-up membership amounting to (1) less than one one-hundredth of the membership of the American Federation; (2) less than one sixtieth of the voters of the Socialist ticket in 1912; (3) less than one twentieth of the membership of a single industrial union in the A.F. of L.; (4) less than six one-thousandths of the general body of organized workmen; (5) less than one in two thousand of American wage-workers.[1]

Main Ideas of I.W.W.-ism

As already pointed out, the main ideas of I.W.W.-ism were of American origin. The conditions existing in France led to the establishment of the Confédération Générale du Travail there, while in this country the Western Federation of Miners and the I.W.W. grew out of the situation that had arisen in the mining States of the Far West. The actual experiences of the lower grades of workers resulted in a conception of political parties very similar to that of the revolutionary syndicalists of France. They reached the same conclusion — that conservative trade-unionism and political socialism could not greatly improve the condition of the unskilled wage-earners.

The I.W.W. had no direct contact with French syndicalism before 1908. In that year William D. Haywood went to Europe and met some of the leaders of the C.G.T., and in 1910 he attended the International Labor and Socialist Congress at Copenhagen. Before the period of personal contacts the leaders had read the writings of Pouget, Sorel, Lagardelle, and others of the French syndicalist school. As one of them told Mr. Brooks: "One or two of us knew that trade unions were called *syndicates* in France, and that *sabotage* meant some sort of a row with the boss, in which labor got back at him with new tricks. It enabled the men to hold on to their jobs while the strike was still carried on." [2] But actual influence did not come until the characteristics of the I.W.W. had been hammered out in the fires of the American labor movement.

[1] *Brissenden: The I.W.W.: A Study of American Syndicalism*, chaps. XI, XII, XIV; *The New Republic*, vol. VIII, p. 95.
[2] Brooks: *American Syndicalism*, p. 75; Parker: *The Casual Laborer and Other Essays*, pp. 105–07.

As Kirkup declared, in his "History of Socialism," "the United States provides a soil which exactly suits syndicalism," [1] and, consequently, the I.W.W. is the American counterpart of syndicalism. Similar ideas developed simultaneously in America and in France. In England the same opinions have been put forth by the Guild Socialists.

These three movements agree in their denunciation of the workings of modern representative democracy. Furthermore, they only state in stronger terms what many citizens express mildly in their comments upon modern political life. Criticism of the modern democratic state is really a commonplace in our contemporary life. French syndicalists and the American I.W.W. separate themselves from the Guild Socialists and the independent voters in the United States because they endorse and use violent methods to accomplish their demands.

The French syndicalists and their American collaborators insist that "no genuine democracy is possible in industry until those who do the work in a business (from hired president to hired common laborer) control its management." They have developed a crude and inadequate mechanism for this purpose. The industrial union in their opinion is to be "the administrative unit in the future industrial democracy." Actually this demand merely means that some of our democracy — some of our representative government — ought to be extended from political into economic life. Those who support these views "ask that industry be democratized by giving the workers — all grades of workers — at least a share in its management. They ask to have the management of industrial units transferred from the hands of those who think chiefly in terms of income to those who think primarily in terms of the productive process." They would have one-man control of in-

[1] Kirkup: *History of Socialism*, p. 296.

dustry "supplanted by economic democracy in nearly all civilized states."

"Let the workers run the industries" is the radical or revolutionary way of stating what more conservative people mean when they talk about representative government in industry. Whether the "currently accepted model of the Prussian state" is the best and only way to run an industrial enterprise is a "moot point," and the syndicalists and industrial unionists have challenged the Prussian method. Whatever merit there may be in their position, they are "grotesquely unprepared for responsibility" and evidently do not see how "unimportant is their much-talked of sabotage method. They have challenged the autocratic method, but have done it very crudely and with a weird misplacement of emphasis. They whisper it in a footnote, as it were, to their strident blackface statements about method." They declare that if workers are not allowed a voice in the management of industry, the remedy is sabotage.

THE I.W.W. AND THE WAR

During recent years the methods and tactics of the I.W.W. have exposed them to charges of disloyalty in addition to the criticism aroused by their violent and revolutionary activities. It is bad enough to practice sabotage, conduct free-speech campaigns, and lead unskilled and ignorant foreigners in such a strike as that at Lawrence in time of peace, but such methods, in time of war, certainly constitute disloyalty, if they do not actually spell treason. With patriotism fully aroused by the German threats to the world, it was inevitable that the I.W.W. should be regarded with greater suspicion and even with hatred by most people. Any statement made in explanation of their conduct must not be interpreted in terms of excuse or extenuation. They are intended simply to call attention to facts and conditions that ought not to be neglected.

Carleton Parker, in his illuminating article in the "Atlantic Monthly" in November, 1917, undertook to describe the I.W.W. attitude toward the war. He pointed out that for them there was only one war, and that was the class war which had no national boundaries. They quoted the increase in the prices of meats, textiles, and shoes, and the increase of earnings of the steel and munition companies; they added also the increase of farm tenancy; and they declared that they did not see why they should go out and get shot to save the kind of life they enjoyed.

Contrast this attitude with that of the fifty thousand volunteers for the Officers' Training Camps, and you have the patriotism reflected from "a rich background of social satisfactions, which in the mind of the young officer had sprung from his country, America. Not only the self-sacrificing quality of this patriotism, but the very patriotism itself, depends on the existence of these social satisfactions. Cynical disloyalty and contempt of the flag must in the light of modern psychology come from a mind devoid of national gratitude and for whom the United States stirs no memory of satisfaction or happiness."

Professor Irving Fisher, of Yale University, expressed a similar opinion when he stated that "the war revealed great industrial discontent in our country, and our consequent weakness in time of stress and emergency. Lack of loyalty and lukewarmness of patriotism appeared more common among industrial workers than elsewhere. The I.W.W. we regarded as distinctly disloyal. . . . The fault of the I.W.W. is not primarily with its members, but with our existing social and industrial system. There is something radically wrong, of which the I.W.W. is a symptom. . . .

"The German Government did everything for the working-man *before* the war. Therefore, when the war came the laborer felt that he owed his country something. He was willing, in return, to make sacrifices for his country. That was his attitude subconsciously, at least, even if not reasoned out. It is upon this subconscious sense of gratitude that patriotism and morale are, always in the last analysis, dependent. . . .

"The members of the I.W.W. . . . rebelled, like the small boys of a large city without playgrounds who break windows for excitement. When boys become so destructive, we give them not a jail sentence, but a place to play; or at any rate the Juvenile Court recognizes that the delinquency is simply a miscarriage of the boys' legitimate instincts.

"The I.W.W. workman is the naughty boy of industry. We have not given him the outlet which he must have. The very energy which breaks through and makes him destructive would, if enlisted for constructive work, have made him a more useful workman than his more docile and less energetic brother." [1]

Professor Hoxie, writing before the war, declared that a "large proportion of our organized workers are probably temperamentally conservative and would never become revolutionary unionists no matter what the industrial development. A growing portion of the workers — largely as the result of our recent immigration — are temperamentally radical. In so far as they become unionists at all, they are bound to be revolutionaries. Between these extremes are the floaters, the negative mass, perhaps the largest proportion of the workers. They will be swayed by their asso-

[1] Fisher: "Humanizing Industry," in *The Annals*, vol. LXXXII, pp. 83–85.

ciates and by industrial and political conditions. . . . In times of prosperity they will become satisfied and temperate; in times of stress, radical. Political disability and casual work, such as the migratory worker suffers, will draw them into the revolutionary camp. Reforms — workmen's compensation, health and safety legislation, old age pensions — will tend to make them supporters of the existing system. Militant action by employers' associations and trusts, and unfavorable legislative action and court decisions, will make militants of them." [1]

Recent experience has shown the fundamental soundness of these opinions. In the words of John Graham Brooks, than whom there is no wiser and better-informed observer of industrial and social conditions in the United States, the I.W.W. has performed "the service of the awakener." It brings no promise of constructive purpose. The heated energies of direct action should be held in real restraint by some great aim like that which coöperation offers. [2]

SELECTED REFERENCES

1. Brissenden: *The I.W.W.: A Study of American Syndicalism.*
2. Brooks: *American Syndicalism: The I.W.W.*
3. Parker: *The Casual Laborer and Other Essays*, pp. 91–124.
4. Parker: "The I.W.W.," in the *Atlantic Monthly*, vol. cxx, pp. 651–62.
5. Levine: "The Development of Syndicalism in America," in the *Political Science Quarterly*, vol. xxviii, pp. 451–79.
6. *Report on Strike of Textile Workers in Lawrence, Mass.*, 62d Congress, 2d Session, Senate Document no. 870.
7. Hunter: *Violence and the Labor Movement*, Preface and chap. x.
8. Baker: "The Revolutionary Strike," in the *American Magazine*, vol. lxxiv, pp. 19–30.
9. Tridon: *The New Unionism*, chap. vi.
10. Hoxie: *Trade-Unionism in the United States*, chap. vi.

[1] Hoxie: *Trade Unionism in the United States*, pp. 173, 174.
[2] Brooks: *American Syndicalism*, pp. 225, 234.

11. Macy: *Socialism in America*, chap. IX.
12. Marot: *American Labor Unions*, chap. IV.
13. Orth: *The Armies of Labor*, chap. IX.
14. Edwards: "Manufacturing 'Reds,'" in the *Atlantic Monthly*, vol. CXXVI, pp. 119–21.
15. Fry: "The Under Dog," in *The Outlook*, vol. CXXVI, pp. 18, 19.
16. Savage: *Industrial Unionism in America*.

CHAPTER XI

THE NEW UNIONISM

A NEW type of trade-unionism is presented by the unions in the clothing industry. The workers in this industry, largely of foreign birth, were for many years notoriously exploited. Their unfortunate condition, due to overcrowding in the tenements, to occupational diseases and to underpayment, overwork, and seasonal unemployment, was a favorite topic for the agitator, reformer, and social worker. Spontaneous and unorganized strikes occurred from time to time, but without permanent results. Then came a sudden victory, and almost within ten years the clothing workers have come out of the sweatshops and have advanced to a leading position in American organized labor.

Of the unions now existing, the most important are the International Ladies' Garment Workers' Union, with jurisdiction over all branches of ready-made women's and children's garments; the Amalgamated Clothing Workers of America, which embraces the majority of workers in the manufacture of men's and boys' clothing; the United Garment Workers of America, which officially has the same jurisdiction as the Amalgamated, but exercises actual control only in the overall industry; the United Cloth Hat and Cap Makers of North America, which, in addition to those indicated by its title, includes a large number of millinery workers; the International Fur Workers' Union of the United States and Canada, and a few other organizations of a miscellaneous character.

These unions are strongest in the branches of the clothing industry in which immigrant labor is chiefly employed and large-scale production has shown the least development. They have thoroughly organized the makers of cloaks, suits, dresses of all kinds, waists, and overcoats. They are waging a vigorous struggle for the makers of shirts and collars. They are just beginning to be successful with the corset-makers. There are practically no unorganized makers of cloth hats and caps, but many non-union workers are still to be found in the millinery trade.

None of the unions existed before 1890, and only one — the United Garment Workers — has had a continuous existence since before 1900. The history before 1900 is therefore filled with scattered and mostly unsuccessful, though persistent, efforts at organization. Many of the leaders who to-day are at the head of the strong and successful unions were then attempting the seemingly impossible and they never gave up hope. With infinite patience the Yiddish press and the socialist intellectuals tried to educate the masses, and little by little laid the foundations for later success.

The industrial form of union was adopted partly because of the theories of the leaders and partly because of the character of the industry. The craft division represents an earlier era in labor organization suited to the then existing situation, while the unions in the clothing trades, coming much later and with a free field, took on the form that fitted the ideas of the leaders and the conditions of the industry. The industrial form was the natural result.

UNITED GARMENT WORKERS

In 1891 the first national union — the United Garment Workers — was formed in New York. Thirty-six delegates were present from New York, Boston, Chicago, and Philadelphia, and they elected American-born non-socialist officials, because it was thought on account of their knowledge of the language and customs that they could better conduct the affairs of the union. Socialist resolutions were also passed and accepted by the officers to gain the support of the radical delegates. The new union immediately affiliated with the American Federation of Labor. Not long after the officers began a warfare on all socialist activities and ever since the United Garment Workers has been anti-socialist.

The membership never grew large, and it survived because of its Federation charter and its control of the union label. Some of the cheaper ready-made suits, and a large proportion of the overalls, are bought by union labor. No label is authentic except the one endorsed by the American Federation of Labor, the label is protected by the United States registry, and as long as the Federation supports the garment workers' union, the officials can, by granting or withholding the label to manufacturers, maintain almost a personal monopoly of the labor supply. So complete has become the reliance of the United Garment Workers upon the union label that the principal association of employers with which it now makes collective agreements is the Union-Made Garment Manufacturers' Association. This association consists chiefly of overall manufacturers in the smaller cities who employ largely native-born operatives.

United Cloth Hat and Cap Makers

After the United Garment Workers, the oldest national union is the United Cloth Hat and Cap Makers, which was organized in 1901 by delegates from nine locals, three in New York and one each in Chicago, Philadelphia, Boston, Detroit, Baltimore, and San Francisco. The first convention adopted a radical policy and did not affiliate with the American Federation of Labor. The union was drawn into a jurisdictional controversy with the Federation and in 1902 decided to amalgamate with that body. It has always maintained its socialist principles and has frequently been in opposition to the larger policies of the Federation. The union has consistently represented the radical attitude in the annual meetings of the Federation.

Immediately after its formation, the new organization began a fight against long hours, home work, and sweatshop conditions. In December, 1903, the largest manufacturer in New York precipitated a ten-weeks' struggle by a lockout. The result was a victory for the union. A general organization of manufacturers followed, which was preliminary to a national attack on the union during the winter of 1904–05. The New York strike lasted thirteen weeks and there were general strikes or lockouts in Chicago, San Francisco, New Haven, Cleveland, Detroit, and Cincinnati. The contest was decisive, resulting in the establishment of the union shop and a greatly enlarged membership. It was the first lasting success won in the needle trades.

The United Cloth Hat and Cap Makers now consists of forty-six locals in twenty-five towns with a membership of about fifteen thousand. It is the only union in the clothing industry which has succeeded in establishing a universal closed shop. In the millinery trade the organization is strong except in the custom retail shops. The strike of the cap makers in 1919 won every demand, including the forty-four-hour week and the substitution of week work for piece work. A millinery strike, however, was not so successful, partly on account of the jurisdictional dispute with the United Hatters, which had been in existence since 1915.

INTERNATIONAL LADIES' GARMENT WORKERS' UNION

Local unions of women's cloakmakers were among the transitory organizations which appeared and disappeared in the early years of the labor movement in the needle trades. In June, 1900, the International Ladies' Garment Workers' Union was organized by delegates from New York, Philadelphia, Baltimore, Newark, and Brownsville. Soon afterwards the Chicago and San Francisco workers joined. The International adopted a socialist constitution, affiliated with the American Federation of Labor, and has retained its affiliation, although, like the cap makers, it has often disapproved of the policies of the Federation.

Originally the plan was to duplicate the success of the United Garment Workers with the union label, and between 1900 and 1907 the struggle continued with very little success. In 1907, the reefer makers, led by refugees from the Russian Revolution of 1905, carried on a strike which lasted for nine weeks and won most of their demands. This victory made it seem possible to win results through strong organization and fighting tactics.

In 1909 another mass movement resulted in substantial gains for the women workers. A small local of waist and dressmakers in New York called a strike, expecting about three thousand to respond. Instead thirty thousand left their work. No such strike of women had before been known or thought possible. The public was aroused to the sufferings of the needle-workers. The more liberal churches and newspapers gave the strike much attention. Substantial gains were made and the membership of the local was greatly increased.

This struggle stimulated the cloakmakers to renewed activity; they joined the union in large numbers and were eager to repeat the success of the waistmakers. In July, 1910, the great strike was called which lasted ten weeks and resulted in the first collective agreement in the ready-made clothing trade — the so-called "Protocol."

For five years the protocol remained in force while the workers achieved under it progressive improvement in material conditions. Friction, however, was continuous and increasing, and in May, 1915, the manufacturers abrogated the Protocol, charging that the union had not lived up to the agreement.

Efforts to avert the impending struggle failed, and in April, 1916, the employers' association ordered a lockout. The contest lasted fifteen weeks and ended by a victory for the union. A new agreement, modified in favor of the workers, was made for a period of three years and its conclusion witnessed another successful strike.

These repeated victories gave a great impetus to the organization in New York and throughout the country. The union is one of the few in the country which has been able to organize women in large numbers. The membership includes not only cloakmakers and waistmakers, but workers on house dresses and kimonos, white goods, raincoats, embroidery, and corsets. In 1920 the International officially reported 102,000 paid-up members. It is the sixth largest union in the American Federation of Labor, being surpassed only by the Mine Workers, Carpenters, Machinists, Electrical Workers, and Railway Carmen.

Amalgamated Clothing Workers of America

Naturally the success of the makers of women's garments made the workers in the men's clothing trades more and more restless from 1907 to 1913. A general strike in Chicago in the fall of 1910 resulted in an agreement with the large and progressive house of Hart, Schaffner & Marx, which employed about seven thousand persons.

In New York in 1912 a strike vote was submitted to union members and overwhelmingly carried. The actual membership of the United Garment Workers was about five thousand. Yet approximately fifty thousand went out shortly after the strike call. Repeated efforts to settle the strike were made, but were rejected by the votes of the strikers. Finally a proposal to submit the controversy to arbitration was accepted by the president of the garment workers upon his own responsibility without a referendum. The action effectually broke the strike, but intensified the ill-feeling against his administration which already existed. The arbitration award gave substantial concessions, but made no provision for peaceful settlement of future difficulties.

Dissatisfaction culminated at the national convention at Nashville, Tennessee, in October, 1914. An insurgent convention was held which elected its own officers. A series of legal skirmishes followed, which established the right of the original organization to retain its name and the union label, while the insurgent locals were permitted to keep the funds in their treasuries. In December, 1914, the insurgents held a second meeting in New York, adopted a democratic constitution and the title of Amalgamated Clothing Workers of America.

Probably the claim of the insurgents to represent a majority of the membership of the United Garment Workers was sound, since they included almost all the delegates from the large locals in New York and Brooklyn, Chicago, Boston, Rochester, Baltimore, and Philadelphia, besides a few from Syracuse and Cincinnati, while the loyal delegates came from small locals in scattered towns and largely represented workers in overall factories controlled by the union label.

The insurgents charged the officers of the organization with the misuse of the union label, with employment of their powers to make money for themselves, with private understandings with the manufacturers, and with efforts to disfranchise the opposition locals. The officers declared that the insurgent movement was promoted by outsiders and intellectuals, that it was founded upon race prejudice and aimed to secure exclusive control for the Jews.

When the insurgents at Nashville elected delegates to the convention of the American Federation of Labor, the credentials committee of the Federation decided not to recognize them and their decision was sustained. Repeated attempts to bring about recognition have been rebuffed by Mr. Gompers and the other officials of the Federation, on the ground that secession cannot be tolerated in the labor movement. There is good ground, however, for assuming that the existing conservative administration of the Federation is not in sympathy either with the form or the aims of the Amalgamated.

The jurisdictional controversy has not seriously interfered with the success of the Amalgamated. A collective agreement in New York was signed in July, 1915, providing machinery for the adjustment of disputes. The formal agreement was later destroyed, but informal understandings took its place. A general strike in December, 1916, gained the forty-eight-hour week for all members of the union in New York. This struggle, involving nearly sixty thousand workers, was the first in the clothing industry to be financed entirely with funds raised from the locals concerned. Successful strikes in Baltimore, Toronto, Montreal, Chicago, Boston, and other centers increased the membership. Early in 1919 the Amalgamated gained the forty-four-hour week — one of the first unions to win this concession.

In 1921 the Amalgamated Clothing Workers numbered nearly two hundred thousand members. The United Garment Workers pay to the American Federation of Labor a per-capita tax on forty-six thousand members. Hence the insurgent movement of 1914 has grown into an organization four times stronger in membership than the one from which it seceded. In structure the Amalgamated is industrial and very democratic in government. The rules for voting permit the rank and file to control the action of the officials very closely. The philosophy of the organization is a form of reformist socialism.

THE PROTOCOL OF PEACE

The first of the collective agreements in the clothing industry was the Protocol of Peace entered into on September 2, 1910, between the Cloak, Suit, and Skirt Manufacturers' Protective Association and a number of locals of the International Ladies' Garment Workers' Union.

In the first place, the Protocol recorded the concessions made to the union as a result of the strike. These concessions included regulations regarding mechanical power, the abolition of home work and subcontracting, and the preferential union shop, the authorship of which is usually attributed to Mr. Louis Brandeis. The preferential union shop was defined as one in which union conditions were adhered to, and in which, when engaging an employee, the employer shall give preference to a union member.

The Protocol also established a judicial system consisting of a board of arbitration, whose decision was to be accepted as final in all future controversies, and a committee on grievances to deal with minor disputes. Finally it founded the joint board of sanitary control, containing representatives of employers, employees, and the public, to establish sanitary standards and see that they were carried out.

In this system there was no sharp division of functions. The board of arbitration, made up of a representative of each side and of the public to act as chairman, was not only a final court of appeal to give interpretations of the fundamental law, embodied in the Protocol, but it had power to revise wages and hours, or settle any other dispute that might arise.

The joint committee on grievances, consisting of representatives of each side with no impartial chairman, not only decided minor disputes, but had power to devise legislation to direct its own procedure and to make effective the basic law. In the same way the joint board of sanitary control combined legislative, judicial, and executive functions.

At first the committee on grievances consisted of two representatives from each side, but it was soon increased to five and its name changed to the board of grievances. Two chief clerks were appointed, one for the union and one for the manufacturers, to oversee the investigation of disputes. The representative of the union was the manager of the protocol department of the union, and the representative of the association was the manager of its labor department.

Whenever a dispute arose, the first attempt to settle was between the shop chairman and the employer. If this failed, a complaint was filed. When a complaint was filed by a union member, it went to the union's chief clerk; when it was filed by an employer, it went to the association's chief clerk. The chief clerk forwarded the complaint to the other clerk, and, if either side was clearly in the wrong, the matter was settled by a few words from the labor manager to the employer or from the protocol manager of the union to the shop workers.

If the case was not clear, an investigation was made by deputy clerks one for each side, acting together. If they disagreed, the dispute went before the whole board of grievances, and, if that was deadlocked, the matter came before the board of arbitration, where the representative

of the public had the deciding vote. This arrangement resulted in the disposal of clear cases of violation of the
Protocol by subordinate representatives of the two parties
acting in concert, while more complex disputes went before
the higher boards.

Between April 15, 1911, and October 31, 1913, 7656 complaints were filed. About ninety per cent were adjusted
and dropped by deputy clerks, nearly eight per cent were
adjusted by chief clerks, two per cent were adjusted by the
board of grievances, and one per cent were decided by the
board of arbitration.

Apparently the system was working well, and it would
seem as if the rank and file should have been satisfied. Nevertheless friction existed and was increasing. Complaints
of the union led to an intensive investigation of the working of the machinery of adjustment. The result showed
that in only nine cases out of 7656 complaints did the board
of grievances deadlock. Three of the cases were complaints
of manufacturers against shop strikes, two were complaints of employees against discrimination, two were
against irregular price settlement, one was against a shop
lockout, and one — involving twelve separate cases —
was against non-payment for a holiday.

The two most frequent complaints by the union were
discrimination against individuals and alleged wrongful
discharge. The most frequent complaint of the association
was against the shop strike or stoppage of work. It is
highly significant that in the complaints most frequently
presented, decisions satisfactory to the complainant were
least frequent.

In an attempt to meet the request of the union for a
change in the machinery and for greater promptness in decisions, the board of arbitration, on January 24, 1914, established a committee on immediate action, to consist of

the two chief clerks and a third impartial person. This committee was given power to decide all questions submitted to it by the chief clerks except those involving Protocol law. An appeal from its decisions could be taken direct to the board of arbitration.

The new committee did not solve the problem. The questions regarding the right of discharge and the shop strike constantly grew more difficult. They involved the interpretation of the preferential union shop plan and its application in dull seasons.

Finally the manufacturers' association abrogated the Protocol on May 20, 1915, giving as a reason the recurring shop strikes. Public opinion was strongly against the manufacturers, and as a last effort to prevent industrial warfare Mayor Mitchel appointed a council of conciliation composed of prominent citizens. After over three weeks of public hearings the council drafted a settlement raising the scale of wages, renewing the Protocol, and granting the right of review in all cases of discharge. The decision was at once accepted by the union, and was afterwards reluctantly ratified by the association. During the ensuing year the conflict grew more intense and, in April, 1916, the manufacturers again abrogated the Protocol and declared a lockout. The "right of discharge" was declared to be the fundamental issue at stake.

A bitter general strike which lasted fourteen weeks proved that the union was too strong to be destroyed. The issue was debated at length in newspaper advertisements. Finally the president of the union made a statement which became the basis of negotiations. He conceded to the employer "the right to increase or decrease the number of his employees to meet the conditions in his factory and to retain such of his employees as he may desire on the basis of efficiency." The right to strike against any employer who exercised the power to discharge arbitrarily or oppressively, or used it as a weapon to punish employees for union activity, was explicitly retained. The negotiations resulted in a new agreement embodying certain specific concessions to the union.

The judicial system of arbitration under the Protocol was not renewed and the agreement was limited to three years. The right of hiring and discharge was retained by employers and the right to strike in individual shops was retained by the union. The preferential union shop was also retained and further defined. Hours and conditions of work were somewhat modified.

As a result the relations of the manufacturers and the workers were not better than before. Friction was not abolished, but it was frankly recognized, and the strain of attempting to settle it was removed from the agreement itself. Unjust discharges, shop strikes, the recurrence of dull seasons, and the general lack of order in the industry made constant trouble. The anti-union manufacturers in the association seemed bent upon breaking down the agreement.

Early in 1919 the new struggle came. The union not only preserved its former gains, but improved its position. The forty-four-hour week and increased wages were gained, but the chief victories concerned the points of contention left open by the agreement of 1916. The permitting of shop strikes and local stoppages had prevented the standardization of wages; the strong locals had obtained all they could from the employers, while the weak ones had been left behind. To remedy this inequality week work with minimum rates was in many cases substituted for piece work, and where piece work was retained, minimum rates were worked out by methods which had been adopted earlier, but had not been systematically and universally applied.

A method of reviewing discharges was also adopted. Any worker discharged after his first two weeks had a right of appeal. His case was first reviewed by the chief clerks or their deputies, and if they were unable to agree, by an "impartial chairman" — a new office created as a substitute for the former "representative of the public." The impartial chairmen were paid by both sides, and were chosen for their familiarity with industrial problems and their neutrality of outlook.

With a method of review provided, shop strikes were forbidden and a part of the machinery of arbitration was renewed. A grievance board was established, with the impartial chairman holding the deciding vote, to pass on disputes under the agreement. The duration of the agreement was limited as in 1916.

The joint board of sanitary control created by the original Protocol consisted of two representatives of the union, two representatives of the manufacturers, and three representatives of the public. Both parties contributed an equal amount to its support. The abolition of home work in the making of women's clothing removed the greatest menace to the workers and the public, but much remained to be done.

In addition to inspection and encouragement of better conditions, the board conducted educational work of a preventive nature in safety and sanitation, established coöperative medical and dental clinics for the workers, and assisted the union in founding a tuberculosis sanatorium. Both dental clinic and sanatorium are supported entirely by the unions.

The best proof of the usefulness of the board of sanitary control is shown by the fact that when the Protocol was abrogated, it continued to function with the consent and financial support of both union and employers.

The Hart, Schaffner & Marx Labor Agreement

The first important agreement in the manufacture of men's clothing was adopted in Chicago in 1911 by Hart, Schaffner & Marx and their seven thousand employees. It came as the result of a four months' strike which began early in October, 1910.

Like many of the strikes in the clothing industry, it was a spontaneous outbreak, beginning with twenty workers in one shop and spreading until forty thousand were out. The grievances were long hours and low pay, deductions from wages through fines, and charges for material and power, overbearing foremen, and the absence of any machinery of adjustment. Demands were formulated only after the strike had become general. They included provisions intended to remove the grievances to which the workers believed themselves subjected.

A settlement was negotiated between the manufacturers and the officers of the United Garment Workers, but it was overwhelmingly defeated by a referendum vote of the strikers. A large citizens' committee was then formed to investigate the dispute. The committee reported that conditions in the factories were bad, that the workers were underpaid and overworked, and that they were subject to many petty tyrannies. It recommended some form of shop organization which would give the employees representation and a voice in determining the conditions under which they worked. To all demands of the strikers and appeals of the public, the manufacturers replied by a denial of bad conditions. They declared that the strike was the result of agitation and that they had nothing to arbitrate.

Meanwhile the strikers were assisted by the Chicago Federation of Labor and by the Women's Trade Union League. The Teachers' Federation, liberal churches, and public leaders gave their support. On November 28, 1910, the Board of Aldermen decided to mediate and appointed a committee which suggested a conference. Hart, Schaffner & Marx and a few others accepted the plan, but most of the employers maintained their original position.

A strike organization was perfected to relieve destitution among the workers. Supplies were bought in bulk and then rationed out. In this way twenty-two carloads of food and two hundred thousand loaves of bread were distributed; twelve thousand families were supplied weekly. In all, nearly one hundred thousand dollars was spent for relief, and of this sum all but twenty-five thousand dollars was contributed by working-people.

The conference between representatives of Hart, Schaffner & Marx and the strikers arrived at a basis for settlement which omitted the objectionable features of the first offer. On December 24th, the proposition was submitted to the Hart, Schaffner & Marx employees, but they refused to benefit by a peace which did not extend to the people in other shops. Finally, on February 3d, the strike collapsed and the workers returned to their places without conditions. Meanwhile Hart, Schaffner & Marx and their employees had come to an agreement similar to the one previously rejected. The rest of the clothing workers had learned their strength and, consequently, the struggle was merely postponed. It broke out again several times during succeeding years until in the summer of 1919 a majority of the employers signed a collective agreement.

By the settlement made between Hart, Schaffner & Marx and their employees, better wages, hours, and conditions were granted, the way was cleared for the presentation of complaints, and a permanent board of arbitration was established. Provision was not made for the recognition of the union or for the union shop. Successive improvements were made without actual break in relations so that to-day the preferential shop exists, and the agreement is in other respects among the most satisfactory in the country.

It was found that the labor complaint department, representing the undertaking of the firm to adjust disputes from above, did not prove satisfactory to the workers, and that an increasing number of cases was referred to the board of arbitration. In April, 1912, a trade board was established to investigate and to attempt to settle disputes before they were referred to the arbitrators. The trade board corresponded to the board of grievances in the Protocol, and like it was composed of an equal number of members from each side, but the union members had to be employees of the firm. Unlike the New York board, however, the trade board had an impartial chairman. It was given power to appoint chief deputies and deputies like the chief clerks and deputy clerks in the Protocol.

As in New York, the deputies succeeded in adjusting most of the grievances, while the trade board settled most of the others. Very few came before the arbitrators. By far the greater number of the employees' grievances concerned discharge and the employer was most bothered by shop strikes.

The success of the Hart, Schaffner & Marx agreement in avoiding general strikes is due to a number of factors. The union was dealing with one firm engaged in quantity production, making a good quality of clothing, and having a high standing in the trade. The product was assured a reasonably steady sale through advertising. The employer was therefore able to maintain standards a little in advance of those ruling in the industry and to eliminate inequalities. Seasonal fluctuations were considerably modified. The firm was wise enough to yield points gradually as the union gained strength and increased its demands. The equilibrium of power between the organized workers and the employer has been maintained since 1911.

Another reason for the success of the Hart, Schaffner & Marx agreement was the presence of two men, both in the same shop, one an employer and one a worker. The employer was Joseph Schaffner, who had built up a large business in Chicago, and who had retained a more than ordinary interest in his employees. When the great strike came in 1910, he felt very badly, but, instead of assuming that he was right and the workers wrong, he began to inquire into the whole subject of relations between employers and employees. He discovered that, as his business had grown larger, the old personal relationship between him and his workers had become impossible. He did not know his own men.

So he employed a man who was entirely outside of the industry to study the problem. The man was Professor Earl Dean Howard, the pioneer labor manager in American industry. There are now over fifty such managers in the clothing trade alone, many of them formerly college professors.

The new department gradually assumed certain functions in which the workers had a direct interest. Its chief duties came to be the maintenance of a system for the prompt discovery and investigation of any abuses or complaints among employees; the recommendation of measures designed to eliminate the source of complaint; protecting the employer's interests in the board of arbitration and the trade board; negotiating with the business agents of the unions; administering all discipline in the factories; general oversight of all hiring; the administration of all welfare work; and responsibility for the observance of State and municipal regulations as to child labor, health, and safety, as well as for the observance of all agreements with the unions or decisions of the two boards.

In the same shop there was a young Jewish clothing cutter named Sidney Hillman. He was about twenty-four years old at the time. He was born in Russia and educated in a rabbinical school. He became an active revolutionist against the old imperial government and was arrested and imprisoned. While in prison he read every book upon economics and political science he could obtain. When he was released, he left Russia, spent a year in Manchester, England, and then came to Chicago, where he worked first for Sears, Roebuck & Co., and later in the shops of Hart, Schaffner & Marx. His ambition was to become a lawyer, but when the strikes began, he found himself in a position of leadership, and was the principal agent on the part of the unions in working out the labor agreement of 1911.

In 1914, when the split came in the United Garment Workers which resulted in the formation of the Amalgamated Clothing Workers of America, Sidney Hillman was elected general president. Although excommunicated by the American Federation of Labor, the new organization spread with extraordinary rapidity and practically dominates the workers in the men's garment trades of the United States.

One important influence in this growth has undoubtedly been the able management of its chief executive. Hillman is outspoken in his disapproval of violence, he courts the approval of the disinterested public, and trusts entirely to the reasonableness of the positions taken to win. He is quietly persistent and absolutely trustworthy in his statements and in his promises. While in Chicago, though it was known that he and the head of the firm were in frequent consultation, he retained the entire confidence of a union made up of more than a dozen different nationalities

— to such an extent that, with no effort on his part and without his previous knowledge, he was chosen the national leader of the new organization of clothing workers.

The Protocol and the Hart, Schaffner & Marx Agreement are typical of the arrangements set up in other branches of the clothing industry and in other cities. Outside of the Hart, Schaffner & Marx plant, there was comparatively little union organization in Chicago until 1919. In the early months of that year a series of strikes involving fourteen firms occurred and union membership was rapidly extended. On May 12th, members of the Wholesale Clothiers' Association, including several firms of large size, signed agreements. Similar agreements were concluded by members of the Wholesale Tailors' Association on May 21st. These agreements were condensed versions of that of Hart, Schaffner & Marx. At present nearly all the employers are organized in the Chicago Industrial Federation of Clothing Manufacturers. Practically the whole industry is now under the board of arbitration. There are two trade boards, one for Hart, Schaffner & Marx, the other for the rest of the market.

In New York the factories are, on the average, much smaller than in Chicago, and there are a multitude of "contractors'" shops making up clothing for the larger manufacturers. Competition is, consequently, more bitter and conditions are more unstable.

A considerable section of the New York market is not under the terms of any regular agreement. Most of the smaller manufacturers and contractors have no definite agreements, and yet work under arrangements which give the unions a high degree of control over their establishments. The number of New York shops working under informal understandings with the union is not definitely ascertainable, but it is probably large.

Experience with agreements in Rochester, as in Chicago, has been favorable. Until 1918 unionism had made little progress, though several strikes had occurred. In July of that year a strike for a wage increase took place in one factory and threatened to spread. Arbitration was agreed upon and the award was accepted as applying to the entire industry. Thenceforward the Amalgamated Clothing Workers rapidly gained in membership. In February, 1919, an agreement was reached between the employers' organization and the Amalgamated. This agreement has been continued with modifications and renewals to the present time — the last renewal made in April, 1922, continues for three years. One large Rochester firm, Michaels-Stern & Co., has signed no agreements. A strike in 1919 against this firm led to injunctions and a suit for damages.

The Amalgamated Clothing Workers have agreements in Baltimore with the principal manufacturers of men's clothing, individually, and not through an association. The largest plant in the city concluded its first agreement in 1916. This was renewed in 1919 on a closed union shop basis. It was again renewed, with a preferential union shop provision and with other modifications in January, 1921, to run to May, 1922. Another large establishment after labor difficulties in 1918 concluded an agreement which was renewed in July, 1919, and was in force until the firm went out of business in the winter of 1920–21. About the same time four Baltimore firms severed relations with the Amalgamated and strikes resulted. The majority of the clothing firms, employing about ninety per cent of the wage-earners, continued under agreements.

New York, Chicago, Rochester, and Baltimore are the four leading American clothing centers. Besides these places the Amalgamated Clothing Workers have agreements with associations of employers in Boston, Cleveland,

Montreal, and Toronto. Agreements with associations of individual firms have also been concluded in Philadelphia, Cincinnati, Indianapolis, Milwaukee, St. Paul, Minneapolis, Louisville, and a number of other cities.

In July, 1919, the National Industrial Federation of Clothing Manufacturers was formed to secure greater uniformity of action in labor matters in the various clothing centers. At the beginning, the new body was composed of representatives of clothing manufacturers of New York, Chicago, Baltimore, and Rochester. Later Boston, Montreal, and Toronto came under the same system. The Federation is confined to markets and establishments working under agreements with the Amalgamated, which agreements provide impartial machinery for the settlement of disputes.[1]

STRUCTURE AND POLICY

The differences between the old and the new unionism are not so much in the form of organization as in their attitude toward the methods and purposes of the labor movement. The old unionism aims only at immediate betterment of the conditions of the working-people, while the new regards such improvements as merely a means toward a larger end based upon a disbelief in the final necessity of profit-making capitalism. Socialist intellectuals as leaders found an environment that made it possible for them to carry on their propaganda for the abolition of capitalism.

The large number of small and changing firms, the keen competition among both employers and workers, and the seasonal character of the needle trades made it seem impossible to hope for material improvement without the

[1] *Experience with Trade Union Agreements — Clothing Industries.* Research Report no. 38. National Industrial Conference Board, June, 1921.

abolition of the existing industrial system. Organization had to be built upon a class consciousness looking toward complete economic emancipation. The creation of this consciousness took years of agitation and education. The failure of the United Garment Workers was one of method; the success of the Amalgamated Clothing Workers was due to the recognition of the facts and needs of the situation. The preamble of the Amalgamated is the fullest and most recent statement of the underlying philosophy of the new unionism.

Its philosophy causes the new unionism to take a wider interest and a more active part in the life of the labor movement as a whole than does the old. Every battle of labor anywhere it regards as its own. Financial assistance has been given by the clothing workers generously in every struggle where it has been needed. To the steel strikers the needle trades pledged half a million dollars and before its close had actually contributed as much as any other group of unions, including those who officially called the strike. The clothing unions have remained, as far as they could, within the American Federation of Labor, in spite of their objections to the policies of its leader. Affiliation is regarded purely as a sign of loyalty to the working-class.

WORKERS' EDUCATION

Every labor union is, in a sense, an educational institution. The broader the principles upon which a labor organization is built, the greater is its educational value. The union which limits its activity to the betterment of its own craft necessarily offers fewer opportunities for education than one which considers its work for the immediate improvement of the industry as merely a step toward full industrial and political democracy for all people. Their fundamental philosophy made it seem essential to the unions in the clothing industry from the beginning to devote attention to subjects with which the older unions never concerned themselves. In this sense educational work began in the needle trades with their first attempts at organization.

The first decade of the twentieth century was the time when all the great organizations in the clothing trades were built up. During this period the unions made repeated efforts to organize educational work. They appointed educational committees, had lectures at regular meetings, and arranged musicales. The Rand School of Social Science was established in 1905, and it met to a great extent the demand for systematic education which existed among the active members of the union. The Rand School has always drawn a very considerable proportion of its students from the clothing workers. The Workmen's Circle, a Jewish fraternal order, also increased its educational activities which reached an increasing number of Yiddish-speaking people.

Pioneer work in systematic education in the labor movement in America, as well as in the needle trades, was begun by the International Ladies' Garment Workers' Union. In 1914 the general executive committee appointed a special educational committee, which at first tried to take advantage of existing educational institutions. Arrangements were made with the Rand School for a number of courses to be carried on under the joint direction of the International educational committee and the school. Some other similar enterprises were undertaken by the same committee and by local unions. In 1916 the convention of the International adopted a plan for an extensive educational campaign and voted five thousand dollars for it. In 1918 the plan was extended and ten thousand dollars appropriated.

The International has in its national office in New York a special educational department working under the supervision of the educational committee appointed by the president of the organization. This department conducts classes in New York City, and also advises and helps local unions in New York and in other cities in planning and carrying on their own educational work. In New York the International has secured the coöperation of the Board of Education for the use of public school buildings and the assignment of teachers for their English classes. Eight public schools in the various residential sections serve as "Unity Centers" where numerous classes in English, economics, literature, and physical training are conducted for the ladies' garment workers. These centers have about twelve hundred pupils and are a means of getting large groups of workers to receive instruction.

More advanced educational work is provided under the name of the Workers' University of the International which meets on Saturday afternoons and Sunday mornings in the Washington Irving High School. The business agents, other officers, and members of the rank and file of the local unions attend the classes. The registration is three hundred.

The Unity Centers and the Workers' University are intended to reach the more active and serious-minded groups. The Extension Division undertakes to create an interest in education in the great mass of the membership. Its work consists not only in organizing special lectures to which all the members are invited, but also in arranging concerts and entertainments. These are very popular and are provided for the membership which is unprepared or unwilling to avail itself of the opportunities offered by the Unity Centers and the Workers' University.

Another educational enterprise is the United Labor

Education Committee which was established in 1918. When it was started it was intended to be the central body for workers' education, but this expectation has not been realized. The committee consists of about thirty local unions and several central bodies in New York City. Finances are provided for by dues paid by the locals according to membership.

The committee believed that some new methods should be devised if the educational work was to reach the large masses of the labor movement. It was thought that the classroom method could reach only a limited number, because weariness and exhaustion after the day's work and lack of preliminary education make it difficult for working-people to attend classes.

Mass education was developed most successfully in unemployment and strike service. These activities were carried on during periods of unemployment when people were free during the day. It proved impossible to do intensive work because unemployment psychology is not conducive to intensive educational work; it is, however, favorable to extensive educational work which creates a certain atmosphere. This work was done by having unemployment meetings in the union halls. The programme usually was made up of two parts; an entertainment of music, singing or recitation, and a lecture. After the lecture there was a discussion. Sometimes a series of lectures on a single subject was arranged. These unemployment meetings had a large attendance, ranging from sixty to four hundred, with the larger figure more usual. Similar opportunities during strike periods were made use of in the same way.

Besides the unemployment and strike service, lectures before local union meetings were also undertaken. To bring education before the regular union proved to be very difficult. The members insisted that it interfered with their activities and with the routine business of the union. The active members were the ones who controlled the unions and they were rarely to be found at general lectures or at social activities. At the same time they comprise the most important element in organized labor. To a limited degree the committee was successful in its effort.

In addition use was made of the forum. Dramatic recitals were also arranged. The organization of a Workman's Theater was started, but failed. Some classes were conducted, but with only moderate success.

At first the Amalgamated Clothing Workers of America were affiliated with the United Labor Education Committee, but in 1920 the Amalgamated decided to concentrate upon its own educational work. Accordingly a department of education was fully organized with a national director and regional directors. No definite appropriation was made, but there was no lack of funds. A lockout in New York, with disturbances in Philadelphia, Newark, Baltimore, and Boston, impaired considerably the ambitious plans of the new department. Chicago and Rochester were the cities least affected and they therefore led in educational progress. The plans followed were similar to those of the United Labor Education Committee for mass education, local union lectures and classes. A number of scholarships at the Rand School were provided and a temporary day Labor College established.

Already the American experiments in workers' education have been of many kinds. There has been education for labor given by wealthy benevolent trustees, as in the Cooper Union; there has been the Rand School on a party basis; and there have been schools organized on the basis of the consumers, as in the schools of the coöperatives.

There have been schools for the groups of producers; a single union, like the International Ladies' Garment Workers' Union and the Amalgamated Clothing Workers; groups of unions, as in the United Labor Education Committee; the Central Labor organization of a city, as in the Boston Trade Union College; and the State Federation of Labor, as in Pennsylvania. This last group of undertakings represents the really vital part of a new educational effort in the United States.

Previous to 1918 there were only four experiments in existence. Two new schools were added in that year. In 1919 four new schools were organized, while 1920 witnessed the establishment of thirteen additional ones, nine of which were in Pennsylvania. During the first three months of 1921 three more were added and plans were under way for opening a number in the fall.

A questionnaire sent out early in 1921 brought returns from twenty-six enterprises in twenty-two cities. Included in the list were: the Educational Department of the Amalgamated Clothing Workers of America, New York; the Amherst Classes for Workers; the Baltimore Labor Class; the Boston Trade Union College; the Cleveland Workers' University; the Workers' Educational Association of Detroit; the Work Peoples' College of Duluth; the Educational Department of the International Ladies' Garment Workers' Union, New York; the Minneapolis Workers' College; the Trade Union College of Greater New York; the Pennsylvania Labor Education Committee; the Philadelphia Trade Union College; the Pittsburgh Trade Union College; the Rand School of Social Science, New York; the Rochester Labor College; the St. Paul Labor College; the Seattle Workers' College; the United Labor Education Committee, New York; the Trade Union College of Washington, and the National Women's

Trade Union League. Three of these schools provide for resident students.[1]

The new unionism represents the most constructive wing of the labor movement in the United States at the present time. Its leaders, many of them socialist intellectuals, regard social reorganization as inevitable. At the same time they recognize that a long period of education is necessary before any of their more extensive plans can be carried into operation. The preambles to the constitutions, such as that of the Ladies' Garment Workers, which provides for the support of a party whose aim is the abolition of the capitalist system, must not be taken too literally, since they are intended in part to conciliate the more radical elements. Education of the workers occupies a much larger place in the unions in the clothing trades than in the older craft organizations.

In 1920 the Amalgamated set a new precedent when it voted to establish standards of production. If the workers are ever to control industry, they must do away with inefficiency and slacking on the job. Somehow production must be increased and maintained so that high wages and good conditions of work may seem practicable to the employer and the consumer. Inefficiency is an instinctive expression of dissatisfaction and lack of interest; it can be removed only as the worker feels a pride in his job. By laying emphasis upon increased control of the process, the root source of loafing and even of sabotage is reached. It is the only complete cure for the conflict between labor and capital over productivity in industry.

Leaders like Sidney Hillman are conservative enough to appreciate the facts of the situation in industry. They

---

[1] *Workers' Education in the United States. Report of Proceedings of the First National Conference on Workers' Education,* held in New York City, April 2, 3, 1921, pp. 133, 134.

realize that the development of machinery for the exercise of the laborer's share in the control of the conditions of work must precede the assumption of control, if such a distant goal is ever to be reached. The chief interest of the leaders is in the organization of such machinery rather than in the immediate reorganization of the industrial system. Any view which overlooks the difference between some of the published statements and the actual working policy of the leaders will fail to evaluate the new unionism in the clothing industry correctly.

SELECTED REFERENCES

1. Budish and Soule: *The New Unionism.*
2. Cohen: *Law and Order in Industry.*
3. Baker: *The New Industrial Unrest: Reasons and Remedies,* chaps. XV, XVI.
4. Tridon: *The New Unionism.*
5. Tannenbaum: *The Labor Movement.*
6. *The Annals,* July, 1920.
7. *The Hart, Schaffner & Marx Labor Agreement.*
8. Gleason: *Workers' Education.*
9. *Workers' Education,* in *Proceedings of the First National Conference on Workers' Education,* New York City, April, 1921.
10. *Constructive Experiments in Industrial Coöperation between Employers and Employees,* in *Proceedings of the Academy of Political Science,* January, 1922.
11. Commons: *Trade Unionism and Labor Problems* (Second Series. 1921), pp. 534–61.
12. Commons: *Industrial Government.*
13. Leiserson: *Constitutional Government in Industry,* in *Proceedings of American Economic Association,* vol. XII, pp. 56–79. (1921.)
14. *Experience with Trade Union Agreements — Clothing Industries.* Research Report no. 38, National Industrial Conference Board, June, 1921.
15. *The Clothing Workers of Chicago, 1910–1922,* published by the Chicago Joint Board, Amalgamated Clothing Workers of America.

CHAPTER XII

SOCIALISTS AND THE WAR

SOCIALISTS have fought vigorously against militarism from the beginning of their organized activities and they have exerted considerable influence against war in several European crises. They opposed colonization, forbade their members to vote for appropriations for the army and navy, advocated compulsory arbitration of international disputes, and discussed the general strike as a means of preventing war. Although opposing offensive warfare, they did not go on record against defensive warfare.

The fiftieth anniversary of the first International was planned to be held in Vienna, August 23, 1914, but was prevented by the outbreak of war. During the last days of July, when war was imminent, Socialists met at Brussels, held a great anti-war demonstration, and called their congress to meet in Paris, August 9th, with the question of war as the chief topic for discussion. Anti-war mass meetings were held throughout Europe.

Before the date set for the Congress, Germany had invaded Belgium in the attack on France, and Socialists in both these countries rushed to the defense of their home lands. German Socialists voted for the war budget as a defense against the threatened invasion from Russia. In England the Independent Labor Party opposed the war, but the Labor Party as a whole supported it after its outbreak. Thus, under the pressure of the sudden rush of events in the summer of 1914, the Socialist opposition to war was overwhelmed and failed to have any effective retarding influence.

American Socialists were the only ones far enough away

from the great conflict to be able to act logically and freely according to their opinions. In a general way their position was characterized by a militant anti-war attitude and by peace activities. Irresponsibility and an inability to discriminate as to the relative importance of interests was clearly manifest in their expressions of opinion.

EARLY DECLARATIONS

August 12, 1914, the Committee on Immediate Action of the Socialist Party issued a manifesto in which it expressed its sympathy with the workers of all nations, pledged its support to the Socialist parties of Europe in their fight for peace, and urged the national administration to open "negotiations for mediation," and extend "every effort to bring about the speedy termination" of the "disastrous conflict." The manifesto also reiterated the party's "opposition to this and all other wars, waged upon any pretext whatsoever; war being a crude, savage, and unsatisfactory method of settling real or imaginary differences between nations, and destructive of the ideals of brotherhood and humanity to which the international socialist movement is dedicated."

Two days later the same committee urged the Government to seize "the packing-houses, cold-storage warehouses, granaries, flour mills, and such other plants and industries as may be necessary to safeguard the food of the people. . . . When the Government controls the industries, the exportation of foods to Europe can be prevented. The rulers of Europe, unable to secure food for their armies, will be forced to call off their soldiers." The slogan, "Starve the war and feed America," was put forth both to meet the rising cost of living at home, and to aid in bringing about the end of the war by cutting off the supply of food to the belligerents.

The committee also advocated "that the exportation of money and of munitions of war be prohibited. The United States must not aid the powers of Europe to continue their fratricidal strife." Since the enforcement of these proposals would have injured the Allies much more than the Central Powers, such suggestions practically resulted in the assumption of a pro-German position by American Socialists. Their abstract anti-war theory prevented them from seeing any difference between the warring countries. Their recommendations were severely criticized at the time.

In September, the party cabled to the Socialists in ten European countries urging them to use their influence to induce their Governments to accept mediation by the United States. It was suggested that the conference should be held at The Hague or Washington. A few days later the National Executive Committee proposed that an international Socialist congress be called in Europe or America and offered "to pay all the necessary expenses of five delegates from every nation entitled to twenty votes, and in proportion for the delegates from every nation, the minimum to be two delegates, according to the representation established by the International Socialist Bureau." The subjects for discussion were to be "ways and means to most speedily and effectively stop this war, and such other matters as may pertain to the subject of World's Peace." This conference did not materialize, although a conference of Socialists from neutral nations was called to meet in Copenhagen, January 15, 1915.

When the sinking of the Lusitania occurred in May, 1915, the National Committee addressed a manifesto to the American people, warning them against the influence of the interests, which they claimed were trying to stampede the United States into war. It contended that "no disaster, however appalling, no crime, however revolting, justifies the slaughter of nations and the devastation of countries.

"The destruction of the Lusitania and the killing of hundreds of non-combatants, men, women, and children, on board the steamer, brings more closely home to us the fiendish savagery of warfare and should inspire us with stronger determination than ever to maintain peace and civilization at any cost."

At the same session of the committee a peace programme was adopted which had been widely discussed in the party press beforehand. The proposed terms of peace advocated an international federation of the world, universal disarmament, the extension of democracy, and the removal of the economic causes making for war. It also urged the application of the principle of "no indemnities, no forcible annexations, and the free development of nations." As a means for bringing about disarmament, it recommended "the abolition of the manufacture of arms and munitions of war for private profit, and the prohibition of exportation of arms, war equipment, and supplies from one country to another." Again abstract theory led to a conclusion favorable to Germany and hostile to the Allies.

The only Socialist Congressman, Meyer London, in December, 1915, introduced a resolution calling upon the President to convene a congress of neutral nations which should offer mediation to the belligerent nations. The resolutions also contained suggestions for peace terms which were considered prerequisite to the securing of a just and durable settlement. The following principles were laid down: evacuation of invaded territories; liberation of oppressed nationalities; plebiscite for Alsace-Lorraine, Finland, and Poland; removal of political and civic disabilities of Jewish people wherever such exist; freedom of the seas;

gradual concerted disarmament; and the establishment of an international court of arbitration with the commercial boycott as a means of punishment.

THE CAMPAIGN OF 1916

At every crisis of affairs the Socialists reiterated their opposition to war. No disregard of national rights seemed to them to warrant the entrance of the United States into a war which they believed to be the inevitable outcome of the capitalistic system of industry. The presidential campaign of 1916 gave them an opportunity to wage nationally the contest which they had carried on intermittently since the outbreak of the war. The adoption of a platform presented a chance to frame a comprehensive statement of the position they held after the struggle had been going on for nearly two years.

The platform reaffirmed the "steadfast adherence" of the Socialist Party "to the principles of international brotherhood, world peace, and industrial democracy." It declared the Great War "one of the natural results of the capitalist system of production," and urged the working-class to take advantage of the opportunity to force disarmament and to advance the cause of industrial freedom. It pointed out that "the workers in Europe were helpless to avert the war because they were already saddled with the burden of militarism. The workers in the United States are yet free from this burden and have the opportunity of establishing a working-class policy and programme against war. It advocated opposition to "military preparedness, to any appropriations of men or money for war or militarism, while control of such forces . . . rests in the hands of the capitalist class. The Socialist Party stands committed to the class war, and urges upon the workers in the mines and forests, on the railways and ships, in factories and fields, the use of their economic and industrial power, by refusing to mine the coal, to transport soldiers, to furnish food or other supplies for military purposes, and thus keep out of the hands of the ruling class the control of armed forces and economic power, necessary for aggression abroad and industrial despotism at home."

As measures to insure peace under the capitalist system, the platform recommended a referendum vote before the declaration of war, the abandonment of the Monroe Doctrine, "perhaps our greatest single danger of war," because it was likely to be used to retain Central and South America "as a private trade preserve," the immediate independence of the Philippines, and a congress of all neutral nations to mediate between the belligerent nations, to be called by the United States.

The candidates, Allan L. Benson and George R. Kirkpatrick, secured their nominations mainly for the reason of their conspicuous opposition to war and militarism.

Again, in February, 1917, when diplomatic relations between the United States and Germany were plainly approaching the breaking-point, the Emergency Committee of the Socialist Party urged an embargo "upon all shipments of whatsoever kind from the United States to any and all of the belligerent countries." It referred to a similar demand made by the party in August, 1914, under the slogan, "Starve the war and feed America." The committee believed such action would terminate the war in Europe and remove danger of war from the United States. In addition, it would release large amounts of food for home consumption and reduce the rising prices. Finally, such action was the only way in which the country could take a genuinely neutral position. It had not been neutral, but had violated the spirit of international law "by shipping munitions and other supplies to one side when it was prevented by that side from shipping them to the other."

Protest against war was made on the occasion of the severance of diplomatic relations with Germany, and immediately before the actual declaration of war the Socialists demanded that the people be given an opportunity to express their opinion through a referendum vote upon the matter.

The St. Louis Convention

Upon the formal declaration of war by Congress, the National Committee called an Emergency Convention "to consider the war policy of the party and to take such measures as would be deemed advisable to inaugurate a movement for a speedy termination of the war." The call met with the general approval of the party, and nearly two hundred delegates from all parts of the country assembled in St. Louis during the second week of April, and proceeded to determine the position of the organization upon the questions of war and militarism.

The convention elected a committee on war and militarism of fifteen members, which met for two days and presented three separate reports: a majority report, signed by eleven members; a minority report, drawn up by three of the committee, which approved the position of the majority, but expressed it in different terms; and a second minority report, signed by only one member, John Spargo.

Of these reports the first received one hundred forty votes, and became therefore the official action of the convention. The first minority report received thirty-one votes, while the remaining one only received five votes. As neither of the latter had obtained the required number of votes, they could not be submitted to the referendum vote of the members. At the request of a number of delegates, including some who voted for the majority report, John Spargo prepared a declaration of war policy, which under the party rules could be submitted if signed by fifty delegates. It was signed by fifty-two members and accordingly was submitted. By an overwhelming vote, 21,639 to 2752, the members of the Socialist Party supported the official recommendations of the St. Louis Convention.

These recommendations reaffirmed the party's allegiance to internationalism, proclaimed its unalterable opposition to the war, declared that modern wars as a rule had been caused "by the commercial and financial rivalry and intrigues of the capitalist interests in the different countries," condemned the failure of the country before the war to observe real neutrality, expressed the opinion that the war would not advance the cause of democracy, and asserted that the people of the United States had "no quarrel with the people of Germany or any other country."

"In all modern history there has been no war more unjustifiable than the war in which we are about to engage . . . the Socialist Party emphatically rejects the proposal that in time of war the workers should suspend their struggle for better conditions. On the contrary, the acute situation created by war calls for an even more vigorous prosecution of the class struggle, and we recommend to the workers and pledge ourselves to the following course of action; continuous, active and public opposition to the war; unyielding opposition to all proposed legislation for military or industrial conscription; vigorous resistance to all reactionary measures; consistent propaganda against military training"; extension of organization among the workers "to enable them by concerted and harmonious mass action to shorten this war and to establish lasting peace; widespread educational propaganda to enlighten the masses as to the true relation between capitalism and war"; and "to protect the masses of the American people from the pressing danger of starvation which the war in Europe has brought upon them, and which the entry of the United States has already accentuated."

The Declaration of War Policy, drawn up by Spargo, simply recognized the war as a fact and urged the party "to try to force upon the Government, through pressure of public opinion, a constructive programme." Furthermore, it must seize the opportunity presented by war conditions to advance its programme of democratic collectivism. In furtherance of these aims, it proposed the conscription of wealth, the socialization of industry, no conscription of men without a referendum as in Australia, the establishment of communications with Socialists within the enemy nations to bring about a democratic peace at the earliest possible time.

In June, the Emergency Committee issued a proclamation appointing July 4th as the day upon which the people were to assemble in mass meetings and demand that the Government submit conscription to a referendum of the people, and that it issue a clear and definite statement of the objects for which the war was to be waged.[1]

THE SOCIAL DEMOCRATIC LEAGUE

Following the acceptance of the majority report of the Emergency Convention by the party referendum, a number of well-known Socialists, chiefly "intellectuals," resigned their memberships and formed the Social Democratic League which in January, 1919, claimed a member-

[1] Trachtenberg: *The American Socialists and the War:* a documentary history of the attitude of the Socialist Party toward war and militarism; Spargo: *Americanism and Social Democracy*, pp. 257–326; Laidler: *Socialism in Thought and Action*, pp. 454–58; Walling: *The Socialists and the War*, pp. 378–92, 463–78; *The American Labor Year Book*, 1917–18, pp. 50–53, 373–79.

ship of 1100. Several of those who resigned published letters giving reasons for their action.[1] One of them, Rose Pastor Stokes, published a so-called "Confession" in the "Century Magazine" in January, 1918. Among the group of "intellectuals" who left the Socialist Party were John Spargo, Upton Sinclair, W. E. Walling, Charles Edward Russell, Allan Benson, J. G. Phelps Stokes, Jack London, A. M. Simons, and W. J. Ghent. In addition, other members became inactive or were expelled. The party was thus left more completely in the control of the anti-war faction than it had been before.

In September, 1918, the Social Democratic League, of which John Spargo was president and W. E. Walling was secretary, issued a programme of social reconstruction after the war. This programme was in the form of an eighteen-page pamphlet and declared the object of the League to be the "practical advancement of democratic socialism." It endorsed the fourteen principles set forth by President Wilson in his address of January 8, 1918, and the peace terms of the Inter-Allied Socialist Conference held in London, February 22, 1918.

"Democratic socialism," in the words of the programme, "in opposition to the so-called socialism of the Prussians, demands more organization and a better organization of society only in such forms as promote the freer and fuller development of the individual. The socialism at which we aim has nothing in common with the regimentation that Socialists of Prussia are forced to accept in fact and cannot get rid of in their thinking — submerged as they are in the vast sea of Prussian Kultur. The democratic state, and still more the democratic Socialist state, exists to extend the opportunities and the freedom of all its citizens, to

[1] Spargo: *Americanism and Social Democracy*, pp. 315–26; Stokes: "A Confession," in the *Century Magazine*, vol. xcv, pp. 457–59.

stimulate individual initiative, and through producing the maximum of individual development to produce the most efficient of all social systems."

After-the-war socialism, according to the programme, will be "freer, more democratic, more radical, and more practical than pre-war socialism." Any attempt "to revive the purely destructive communism of 1870" will be a failure. "No movement that aims to govern in behalf of a minority, ignoring both the skilled workers, manual and mental, and the great mass of agriculturists, can speak for social democracy, whether that movement be called Bolshevism or Syndicalism."

Furthermore, the programme urged that the tendency of the war to introduce democratic control over industry should be developed and greatly accelerated at its close.

As a national policy for the United States, it proposed "the retention of much of the machinery for mobilizing labor created during the war, especially the federal employment service and the national War Labor Board; the extension of Government insurance at the close of the war to the entire civilian population, to cover— without burden upon the insured — sickness, accidents, old age, and unemployment; the fixing of maximum prices and rents; the establishment of a national department of health, with a secretary of health in the President's Cabinet, as a means for retaining under Government control the medical and hygienic services organized for war purposes; the establishment of a national department of education, with a secretary of education in the President's Cabinet, and various other educational improvements, such as raising the minimum school age to eighteen years; the continuance and extension of all such Government ownership and control as has been established; the Government control of capital through loans, both national and international; and coöperatives, both of consumers and producers, for the purpose of eliminating the parasite middleman and bringing the price of a commodity paid by the consumer somewhat nearer to the price received by the producer."

Permanent peace could be secured only "by making permanent and developing that economic coöperation of the democratic nations already initiated on a vast scale and in many directions since the war — at the same time extending the circle of nations included in this coöperation by admitting, first, the neutrals and then the present enemy nations — as rapidly as they give sufficient evidence of their final acceptance of the principles and practice of international democracy."

Moreover, such economic coöperation was "an indispensable preparation for their political federation." If it could be successfully practiced for a period of years, the federation of all nations of the world that accepted the principle that "governments derive their just powers from the consent of the governed" would become practicable. Politically and economically backward regions could then be organized into "probationary states under international protection, bearing to the United Democracies of the World a relation resembling that which the American Territories have borne to the United States."

This programme was described as having met the "unanimous approval of all members of the administrative and executive committees" of the Social Democratic League of America.[1] It provided a constructive and comprehensive platform of principles upon which to meet the demands of new problems and situations. It discarded the abstract anti-war position of the majority of the Socialist Party. Undoubtedly it was too optimistic and suggested too large a scheme to be immediately practicable, but it pointed in

[1] *The Survey*, vol. XL, pp. 673, 674.

the direction of progress. The real leaders of Socialist thought and action were in this group and their loss to the Socialist Party has been fatal to any usefulness it might have had for these days.

About the same time the Executive Committee of the Socialist Party adopted a programme for the use of Congressional candidates in the fall elections of 1918. The platform was also approved by the conference of party officials. It made no reference to the military conduct of the war nor to the kind of military victory that was desirable. It ignored the platform adopted at St. Louis in April, 1917, and confined itself to "suggestions for the securing of a democratic peace and to questions of an economic, political, industrial, and diplomatic nature." In the opinion of many members of the party, this programme was the nearest approach in the United States to the platform of the British Labor Party issued in June, 1918.[1] Compared with that platform and the programme of the Social Democratic League, just discussed, it was inferior in breadth of vision and in the character of its specific proposals.

The Elections of 1917

In spite of the defection of a group of leaders, the rank and file of the Socialist Party increased during 1917. The growth was particularly manifest in the larger cities where the anti-militarist attitude of the party attracted support. The gain was remarkable in the urban districts of the East and Middle West, and was the more significant since the Socialist vote for President had declined from approximately 900,000 in 1912 to 590,000 in 1916, a loss of about forty-five per cent. As it was an odd year, the municipal elections, with the exception of a few State elections, were the only ones held. These city elections were unique, for

[1] *The Survey*, vol. xl, pp. 640-42.

they were waged not only on local but on international issues. The old parties attacked the Socialistic on the issue of patriotism, labeling them as traitors and charging them with seeking to bring about a separate peace with Germany.

The most noteworthy campaign was that of Morris Hillquit for Mayor of New York City. There were three other candidates, Mayor John P. Mitchel, Fusion candidate, John W. Hylan, the Tammany candidate, and William M. Bennett, the Republican nominee. Hillquit pledged himself to continue the efficiency methods of Mitchel and to extend the educational facilities of the city. He also urged municipal ownership of public utilities and "America's immediate withdrawal from the war even at the expense of a German peace." He refused to subscribe for Liberty bonds. The convention which nominated him also demanded the repeal of the Conscription Act. Plainly the issue was between patriotism and obstruction of the progress of the war.

And yet, in spite of his position upon the war, Hillquit polled 145,895 votes, 90,000 more than the Republican candidate and within 10,000 of Mayor Mitchel's vote. Compared with the election of 1913 the Socialist vote showed an increase of approximately 425 per cent, nor was the Socialist gain confined to the vote for Mayor. It extended to other candidates and the Socialists elected ten assemblymen — a gain of eight — six aldermen when they had never before elected one, and a municipal court judge for the first time. Hylan, the Tammany candidate, was elected, receiving 313,871 votes.[1]

Mr. J. G. Phelps Stokes believed that only about forty thousand Socialists of good standing voted for Hillquit and

[1] Douglas: "The Socialist Vote in the Municipal Elections of 1917," in the *National Municipal Review*, vol. VII, pp. 131–34.

his anti-war policy. The additional hundred thousand ballots came, in his opinion, from pro-German and pacifist voters.[1]

The other returns from cities east of the Mississippi and north of the Ohio in the autumn elections of 1917 also showed great gains for the Socialists. Election figures from fifteen cities indicated that out of a total vote of 1,450,000 the Socialists polled 314,000, or 21.6 per cent. This was over four times the proportion of the vote usually cast for Socialist candidates in these cities. Had they polled an equal proportion in 1916, their total vote for president would have been nearly 4,000,000.

Such a sudden growth in the Socialist vote was due to several causes: (1) opposition to the war was undoubtedly the chief reason; (2) resentment at the action of the Post-Office Department in suppressing many radical papers; (3) discontent due to economic pressure caused by rising prices.[2]

During the early part of 1917 a conference was held in St. Louis, which was attended by representatives of the Progressive Party, Prohibitionists, and other liberal and radical groups, and at which arrangements were made for a more formal gathering at Chicago in the autumn. As a result the National Party was organized at Chicago, October 4, 1917, by delegates from five groups — the Progressives, Prohibitionists, Single-Taxers, Social Democrats, and Independents, the latter embracing spokesmen for the women's party. A tentative platform, intended to be submitted to another conference to be held in 1918, was adopted after many hours of discussion. It was substantially the one drafted by John Spargo, formerly a promi-

---

[1] *The Survey*, vol. xxxix, pp. 299, 300.

[2] Douglas: "The Socialist Vote in the Municipal Elections of 1917," in the *National Municipal Review*, vol. vii, pp. 138, 139.

nent member of the Socialist Party and later identified with the Social Democratic League.

The platform was strongly socialistic, but declared allegiance and loyalty to the Government during the war. The new party leaders proposed to elect "half a dozen United States Senators and between twenty and forty members of the House of Representatives," in 1918, and in 1920 to "march upon Washington and take possession of the Government."

Instead of the realization of the ambitious scheme, just outlined, the new party figured in a few districts and a few States west of the Mississippi, such as Washington, Montana, and Minnesota. Of course the actual results in votes were unimportant, and the National Party ceased to exist, or perhaps it would be more correct to say that the various elements fell apart to attempt another amalgamation later. Some of the supporters of the party were active later in connection with the "Committee of 48."

THE ELECTIONS OF 1918

During 1918 the average membership of the Socialist Party was 74,519, as compared with 83,284 for 1916 and with 80,694 for 1917. Its continued opposition to the war, the wholesale suppression of Socialist papers and meetings, the fusion of the old parties against it upon a patriotic basis and the effect of increase of wages upon the workers, led to a decreased vote for Socialist candidates in 1918 as compared with 1917.

The most noted victory occurred in Milwaukee where Victor L. Berger was again elected to Congress after being defeated in 1912, 1914, and 1916. Eleven Assemblymen and three State Senators, together with the entire county ticket, were also elected by the Socialists. In April, Berger had been a candidate for United States Senator, as an open advocate for immediate peace with Germany. He received "a rather startling number of votes, about 97,000," out of a total of less than 375,000.

In New York the Socialist vote for Governor increased about one hundred twenty-five per cent. The total State vote increased nearly forty-two per cent. On the other hand, Meyer London, the only Socialist Congressman, was defeated for reëlection by a fusion of the Republicans and Democrats against him, and eight out of the ten Socialist Assemblymen were not returned. In Minneapolis also the Socialists failed to reëlect the Mayor chosen by them in 1916. On the whole their showing in the State and Congressional elections of 1918 was considerably less satisfactory than in the municipal contests of 1917. In the cities, where the pro-German voters were more numerous and could act in masses, the anti-war policy of the Socialists undoubtedly strengthened them. The conditions were less favorable in 1918 than in 1917 because of the larger areas and the smaller population.

DIVISIONS AMONG THE SOCIALISTS

The inevitable result of the controversy in the Socialist Party which began at the convention held in St. Louis in April, 1917, was a serious division in its ranks. The constructive and thoughtful leaders, who tried to reconcile the abstract principles of the party with the facts of the European situation produced by the World War, were driven out, leaving the shaping of its policy in the hands of the more revolutionary and less discriminating members. The overwhelming endorsement of this group by the party referendum confirmed the virtual expulsion of most of those in the party who believed in the effectiveness of political action and in the use of peaceful means to attain their aims.

Before August, 1914, the dominant element in the Socialist parties in nearly every country was the group which placed the greater emphasis upon the importance of participation in the so-called bourgeois parliaments. This group aimed at gaining a majority in these representative bodies with the object of obtaining legislation which would in the end overthrow capitalism and put in its place industrial and social democracy. Reform measures were, therefore, regarded as conducive to the ultimate realization of the aims of socialism. Members of this group have long been familiar under the name of "moderate" or "opportunist" Socialists. Probably, the English Fabians, led by Sidney Webb, have been the best examples of this section.

Opposed to the moderates have been the revolutionary Socialists, who have contended that political action produced only negligible results, and that mass action alone can achieve the emancipation of the workers. They depended chiefly upon the general strike and other industrial weapons. The syndicalists in France are the best representatives of this last group; the I.W.W. are their American counterpart.

In 1912 the two factions engaged in "a battle royal" in the national convention of the American Socialist Party. The moderates won and an article providing for the expulsion of advocates of sabotage, violence, or other forms of crime, was inserted in the party constitution. As a result of this action William Haywood, a leader of the I.W.W., was recalled from the National Executive Committee.

The outbreak of the European War, and especially the startling features of the Russian Revolution, gave a new impetus to the revolutionary group. Just as German Socialism moulded the thought and action of the parliamentary Socialists, so Russian Bolshevism has been the influence back of the recent activity of the revolutionary wing.

After the Emergency Convention in April, 1917, the removal of the more moderate leaders gave fuller opportunity to the advocates of violent methods within the Socialist Party. These elements were also an easy prey for the pro-German propagandists, who were watching for every opportunity to stir up trouble. They helped to lead up to the anti-red hysteria that developed after the cessation of hostilities.

After the signing of the armistice, there was an influx of new members into the Socialist Party. They came from the Russian and other language federations of the party and from certain radical groups who found it difficult to function in more revolutionary organizations. This influx added to the increasing opposition to those who were in control of the party machinery.

Early in 1919 the protestants began to form a left wing section, which maintained its own press, organizers, collected dues, and issued membership cards. It endorsed a manifesto similar to that of the Russian International and required adherence to the platform. It captured numerous branches and made efforts to obtain control of the national machinery by electing its candidates to the National Executive Committee. On the face of the returns it elected twelve out of the fifteen members of that committee in the spring of 1919.

Rumors of election irregularities on the part of the left wing were widespread, and the National Executive Committee, late in May, decided to have the election results determined by the Emergency Convention called for August 30, 1919, although its term of office legally expired on June 30th. It also suspended seven out of the twelve language federations and expelled three State organizations — Michigan, Massachusetts, and Ohio. These organizations were charged with various violations of the party regulations, but actually the causes given were probably largely technical, and the real reasons were more fundamental. The contest was for party control between somewhat conservative revolutionists and much more radical ones.

The left wing section held a convention in New York City in June, 1919, which consisted of "ninety-four delegates representing twenty States, and chosen especially from large industrial centers, 'the heart of the militant proletarian movement.'" A difference of opinion developed at the outset on the alternatives of organizing immediately a new party, or of continuing the fight for the control of the old Socialist Party, at least until the August convention. The proposal to organize a new party at once was defeated by a vote of 55 to 38, whereupon thirty-one delegates, chiefly from the Russian federations, withdrew. Later this minority issued a call for a convention to meet in Chicago, September 1st, for the purpose of organizing a Communist Party. The majority held to the plan of gaining control of the old party and elected a national left wing council to carry on the contest. By August 1st, this council became convinced that the organization of a Communist Party was generally supported by their adherents and consequently joined in the call for a convention for such a purpose.

Another meeting during the summer was that of the alleged new executive committee, elected by the revolutionary faction. The left wing candidates declared that the action of the old committee in holding the election decision until the convention in August was illegal. They tabulated the returns, announced their election, and called together the "new executive committee." They met in Cleveland, reinstated the suspended groups, planned for "the real Socialist Party Convention" in Chicago, and elected an executive secretary. They also decided to continue their fight for control of the Socialist Party. Thus, a few months after the organization of the left wing movement, there were three national divisions in process of formation, represented by the left wing convention, the proposed Communist party, and by the "new executive committee."

THE CHICAGO CONVENTIONS

Late in August, 1919, several hundred delegates came to Chicago to attend the conventions called to meet there by the different social and revolutionary groups. The Socialist Party met on the second floor of Mechanics Hall. The "left-wingers" had rented the floor below for caucus purposes. Saturday morning, August 30th, the date when the Socialist Party Convention was scheduled to meet, the left-wingers began to occupy the hall reserved for the Socialist Party delegates. A struggle for possession followed and the police were called in to clear the hall. This contest and particularly the fact that the police were summoned by the Socialist Party officials, was regarded as proof that the old party had become a "counter-revolutionary" organization.

About one hundred and fifty delegates from twenty-five States were seated in the Socialist Party Convention without contest. The chairman for the first day, Seymour Stedman, was elected over the leader of the left-wingers by a vote of 88 to 37. The following three days were largely taken up with debate over the admission of contested delegates; about twelve were admitted and seventeen excluded. Before the contests were settled, the leader of the left-wingers announced the withdrawal of all left-wing delegates, and their departure took place without disturbance. Twenty-six of the uncontested delegates left the convention hall.

From that time the business of the Socialist Party Convention moved steadily and with comparative smoothness. Numerous delegates remained who in general took the left-wing position.

COMMUNIST LABOR PARTY

Sunday evening, August 31, 1919, the seceding delegates were called to order on the lower floor of Mechanics Hall by the national secretary, elected by the executive committee organized at Cleveland in the summer by the twelve new members, whose election had been questioned by the existing party committee and referred by them to the August Convention.

The first contest occurred over a motion to unite with the Communist Party which had grown out of the June meeting of left-wingers in New York City. Tuesday morning, September 2d, when coöperation with the Communist Party was found to be impossible, they organized a separate group known as the Communist Labor Party of America.

The chief debate in this convention centered around the use of political or industrial methods in the advancement of the objects of the party. The industrial unionists won by a two to one vote — 46 to 22. Following this vote, Louis Boudin, of New York, bolted the convention, declaring that he had not "left a party of crooks to join a party of lunatics." A number of delegates followed his lead.

During its deliberations the convention approved the principles of the Third or Russian International and urged "the establishment of the dictatorship of the proletariat." It asserted that "not one of the great teachers of scientific socialism has ever said that it is possible to achieve the social revolution by the ballot." It favored mass action in the shop as the most important means of capturing the State power. It also recommended organized propaganda of industrial unionism and suggested the development of labor organizations along the lines of the shop steward and shop committee movements.

The Communist Party

September 1, 1919, the Communist Party opened its first regular convention at "Smolny Institute," Chicago. The meeting was in marked contrast to the other two because of its youth; the majority of the delegates seemed to be in their twenties. The machinery worked smoothly. "Machine politics" in the Socialist Party were replaced by "revolutionary discipline" in the Communist Party; the former were "cumbersome" when compared with "the beautifully oiled steam roller" of the latter. There was also a new terminology. In place of "class struggle," "surplus value," and "coöperative commonwealth," there appeared "revolutionary communism," "dictatorship of the proletariat," and "revolutionary mass action." Marxian terms were replaced by Bolshevik phrases.

One of the bitterest fights was waged over the relation of the Communist Party with the Communist Labor Party. The proposal to appoint a committee to confer with the latter organization developed a contest between the English-speaking minority and the Russian majority. The proposal was first voted down, then reconsidered and a conference committee appointed. The two committees met, but could find no common ground. Apparently there was no fundamental difference in principles or beliefs between the two groups; the distinction was largely in personality and in point of view. The dominant elements in the Communist Labor Party were English-speaking, while in the Communist Party the foreign groups were in control.

The constitution was very different from any document of a political party ever formulated in the United States. One provision excluded from membership any person "who has an entire livelihood from rent, interest, or profit." For some time it seemed that this provision would exclude Rose Pastor Stokes. She finally convinced the delegates that she was occasionally exploited by her publishers and was allowed to remain. Later she became a sergeant-at-arms.

Rejecting parliamentary action, the constitution laid chief emphasis upon industrial movements. It favored big industrial struggles for its major campaigns, participation in mass strikes as a step toward a general strike, and agitation for the organization of a general industrial trade union.

Meanwhile, the Socialist Party, purged of the elements that formed the two Communist parties, worked out "a more consistently radical programme than it had ever before attempted." The Wisconsin delegation formed the extreme right, while a group of left-wingers also remained in the old party.

The party distinguished itself from the Communist and Communist Labor parties by insistence upon parliamentary action as one of the means of establishing socialism, but it by no means ignored industrial action. While maintaining that "its chief function as a party" was to wrest "the political machinery from the hands of the ruling class," it deemed its "paramount duty" was to point out that "industrial organization must take the place of the craft union." It took a distinct step toward the soviet idea when it favored industrial representation based on occupational groups.

American socialism now comprises "a moderate right wing, a vacillating center left, and an extremely radical left wing." It is impossible to determine accurately the numerical strength of the three divisions. Before the recent split in its ranks, the Socialist Party had a membership of approximately 100,000. It still claims 55,000 and concedes 35,000 and 10,000 to the Communist and Communist Labor parties respectively. The Communist Party claims 60,-000 and estimates that the Socialist and Communist Labor parties have 25,000 and 10,000, leaving 5000 unaccounted for. The Communist Labor Party claims 30,000 for itself, concedes 25,000 to the Communist Party, which leaves 45,-000 still in the Socialist Party. Probably a safe estimate would give about 46,000 to the Socialist Party, 40,000 to the Communist Party, and 14,000 to the Communist Labor Party. In May, 1920, the United Communist Party was formed by a merger of the Communist Labor Party and a part of the Communist Party. This party in turn merged with a Workers' Party formed in December, 1921.[1]

Generally speaking, the disintegration in the structure of American socialism is due to the conflict between a "programme of opportunism and an ultra-revolutionary platform leading to the establishment of a proletarian dictatorship." The breach is a logical result of a similar crisis in European socialism, in which the moderates still adhere to the older Second International, while the revolutionists accept the leadership of Lenin and Trotzky in the so-called Third or Russian International.

As in Europe, these lines of division were appearing in the United States even before 1914, and discontent gained greater momentum after the outbreak of the World War, and particularly following the Russian Revolution and the triumph of the Bolshevists. Differences that might have been compromised or postponed during peace times became violent and irreconcilable under the impact of war

[1] Watkins: "Revolutionary Communism in the United States," in the *American Political Science Review*, vol. xiv, pp. 14–33; Laidler: "The Present Status of Socialism in America," in the *Socialist Review*, vol. viii, pp. 33–37, 106–14; Watkins: "The Present Status of Socialism in the United States," in the *Atlantic Monthly*, vol. cxxiv, pp. 821–30.

conditions. Hence the situation in this country in which we have three distinct organizations, in addition to the group of "intellectuals" forced out of the Socialist Party at the time of the St. Louis Convention of April, 1917.

What the outcome may be is still in the rather remote future. Apparently the revolutionary element is in the ascendancy and the older political and parliamentary socialism is waning. Significantly, the new groups are describing themselves as "communist" parties and the term "socialism" is falling into disuse.

In his letter of resignation from the Socialist Party, dated May 30, 1917, John Spargo declared that his withdrawal did not mean his renunciation of socialism. His retirement was due to a profound conviction that the Socialist Party had ceased to be "an efficient instrument for the advancement of socialism." For a long time he had felt that the Socialist Party was "probably the greatest single obstacle to the progress of socialism in America." [1]

Graham Wallas, reviewing "The History of the Fabian Society" in 1916, suggested that the future of socialism as a world movement is doubtful. "Some great leader may turn international socialism into a world-purpose. . . . Or, as I [Wallas] myself think it to be more probable, the word 'socialism' may go the way of 'natural rights,' and the 'greatest happiness principle,' and in our new need we may find a new name for our hopes." [2]

SELECTED REFERENCES

1. Trachtenberg: *The American Socialists and the War:* a documentary history of the attitude of the Socialist Party toward war and militarism.
2. Spargo: *Americanism and Social Democracy*, pp. 159–85, 257–326.
3. Walling: *The Socialists and the War*, pp. 378–92, 463–78.

---

[1] Spargo: *Americanism and Social Democracy*, p. 317.
[2] *The New Republic*, vol. VII, p. 204.

4. Laidler: *Socialism in Thought and Action*, pp. 454–74.
5. *The American Labor Year Book*, 1917–18, pp. 50–53, 373–79.
6. Stokes: "A Confession," in the *Century Magazine*, vol. xcv, pp. 457–59 (January, 1918).
7. Douglas: "The Socialist Vote in the Municipal Elections of 1917," in the *National Municipal Review*, vol. vii, pp. 131–39 (March, 1918).
8. Watkins: "The Present Status of Socialism in the United States," in the *Atlantic Monthly*, vol. cxxiv, pp. 821–30 (December, 1919).
9. Watkins: "Revolutionary Communism in the United States," in the *American Political Science Review*, vol. xiv, pp. 14–33 (February, 1920).
10. Laidler: "The Present Status of Socialism in the United States," in the *Socialist Rêview*, vol. viii, pp. 33–37, 106–14 (December, 1919, January, 1920).
11. *The American Labor Year Book*, 1919–20, pp. 400–33.
12. Benedict: *The Larger Socialism*, chap. v.
13. Ghent: *The Reds Bring Reaction.*

CHAPTER XIII

THE NONPARTISAN LEAGUE

Since the disappearance of the Populist Party through its absorption in the Democratic Party under the candidacy of Bryan in 1896, and the development of the Progressive movement in the Republican Party largely through the national leadership of Roosevelt, there have been no successors to the numerous third parties which from the seventies to the nineties of the last century were characteristic features of Western life. The farmers' movements, the Grangers, the Greenbackers, and the Populists, seem to have culminated in the Progressive Party of 1912.

Undoubtedly the influence of the European War largely accounts for recent tendencies in American politics, but it is noteworthy that twenty-five years have now elapsed without any signs of the development of one of these minor parties. And the years since 1912 seem to indicate that the Progressive movement has ceased to be an active factor in our political life. Apparently both Progressives and Standpatters were united in supporting the candidacy of Senator Harding. Again, in the contest over the League of Nations and the ratification of the peace treaty, Progressives and conservatives agreed. The Progressive movement may revive after a time, but for the immediate future there is little prospect of its influence, except as an historic force growing out of the earlier conditions of Western life.

From 1915 to 1920 a farmers' organization, known as the Nonpartisan League, and originating in North Dakota, grew to a point where it claimed a membership of about 230,000 persons in thirteen Western States — all except Wisconsin being west of the Mississippi River. The States in the order of the number of members of the League are North Dakota, Minnesota, South Dakota, Montana, Nebraska, Colorado, Wisconsin, Idaho, Washington, Kansas, Texas, Oklahoma, and Iowa. "North Dakota has become the home center and the source of moneys and supplies for a new political party which shall be founded upon discontent, and whose ultimate object, besides bettering the political and financial fortunes of its leaders, shall be the destruction of the middleman, the industrial entrepreneur, and the so-called capitalistic classes, and even the destruction of the private ownership in land itself." [1]

Earlier agrarian political movements had never made great headway in North Dakota. This fact can be most easily explained by the composite character of the population. The first settlers were Scotch, English, and Irish, who located in the lower Red River Valley in the northeastern corner of the State. Next farmers of American birth followed the Northern Pacific Railroad across the prairies to the Missouri. The biggest single element of the population was composed of Norwegians, whereas in Minnesota there has been a heavy colonization of Swedes. Germans and "German-Russians" later formed a fourth element. They settled largely in the south-central and southwestern parts of the State near the Missouri River.

Naturally, the situation threw into the hands of the native American stock a larger share in the control of political affairs than their numbers warranted, since racial differences prevented common action among the other elements. Such a condition lent itself to the "boss" system. North Dakota thus became a commonwealth controlled by men whose business was politics. The "boss" came in with the railroads and owed most of his power to them.

Another consequence of the mixed racial conditions was

[1] Bruce: *The Non-Partisan League*, p. 2.

that two thirds of the population of the State were not deeply stirred by granger political movements in the pioneer days, and the consciousness of their political power did not dawn upon the farmers until a generation had passed after statehood.

The State was mildly infected by successive epidemics of reform legislation and there was some rivalry between progressives and standpatters. Direct primary laws, the creation of a State railroad commission, and some direct legislation amendments to the Constitution at length led to the fight on economic issues in which the League was born. The *marketing of grain* played a similar part to that of the railroad and the currency in the Granger, Greenback, and Populist agitations.

BEGINNINGS OF AGITATION

The awakening of the farmers of North Dakota was the outcome of their efforts at economic coöperation. Experience with farmers' elevators and with the terminal grain markets convinced them of the need for public regulation of these agencies. They felt themselves the victims of many economic grievances; they began to grow impatient at the control of the State Government by bankers, lawyers, merchants, and professional politicians; and they focused their opposition in a demand for "State-owned terminal elevators."

Signs of unrest became evident ten years before the birth of the League, and, consequently, it should not be given the full credit nor all the blame for stirring the farmers to revolt and it did not create the issues. No attempt has been made, even by the opposition to the League, to deny that the farmers had been exploited. The League was simply the first political organization to come forward with a positive and definite programme of relief.

The first to agitate for an improvement of the existing situation were the president and some of the professors of the State Agricultural College at Fargo. In the course of their work they found a condition that was plainly unfavorable to more regular and more profitable agricultural production. Small grains alone were the "money" crops, and the great bulk of these grains were shipped out of the State almost immediately after the harvest. They went to Minneapolis, St. Paul, Duluth, and Buffalo for milling or export.

The stock-raising industry was small because screenings and mill feeds to be obtained in large quantities had to be shipped from Minneapolis or a more distant point. At any rate, the price of feed in North Dakota was fixed by the price at the terminal markets plus the freight. The location of the big packing-houses in St. Paul and Chicago added further difficulties to the problem of feeding cattle.

Besides, there was a great economic waste, due to the impoverishment of the soil by the shipping out of the State of millions of dollars' worth of soil values, in the shape of natural fertility.

Finally, the same college professors pointed out other evils in the market situation. They explained how the "docking" of grain resulted in double profit to the big terminal elevators; how grain-mixing resulted in an output of the higher grades in excess of the purchases by the elevators of those grades; and how the grain speculation and manipulation of the market resulted in low prices, when the farmers' obligations compelled them to sell, and in high prices only when the grain had passed into the hands of the speculators.

The group of college reformers found among the "coöperators" willing workers to help them in their campaign for better conditions of production. Considerable headway had been made by an organization known as the Equity Society, which in North Dakota operated as the North Dakota Union of the American Society of Equity. Its object was to promote coöperative effort among farmers, both in buying and selling. It did not engage in business itself, but encouraged the formation of buying and selling societies upon the basis of the "Equity plan," by which each member or stockholder was to have only one vote, regardless of the amount of his stock.

After the establishment of a large number of local elevators in the State and with the support of farmers generally throughout the State, the leaders in the Equity movement organized a society, known as the Equity Coöperative Exchange, to handle business in the central market. Townspeople generally frowned on the invasion of the central market by the Equity Exchange, which started a general share-selling campaign, opened an office in St. Paul, and began to solicit shipments of grain. This struggle was at its height when the League was formed. In a number of places the use of town halls and even streets was denied to representatives of the Exchange, and such actions aroused the latent resentment always existing between the farmers and the townspeople. The later political adventures of the farmers were considerably influenced by their experiences with the Equity Society.

It is claimed that the credit for the first suggestion of a terminal elevator to be owned by the farmers was made in some resolutions passed by the North Dakota State Bankers' Association in 1906. These resolutions asked the legislatures of Wisconsin and Minnesota to amend their grain-grading laws so as to remedy injustices to North Dakota farmers, and concluded with the statement that, if they failed to obtain redress through legislation, they recommended the grain-growers of their State to coöperate for the building of home and terminal elevators. The report of a committee of the Association, made the same year, confirmed the prevailing opinions among farmers and their friends as to the unfair treatment of North Dakota grain-growers by Minnesota storage elevators.

The first attempt to meet the situation took the form of State-owned elevators at the so-called terminal markets — Minneapolis, St. Paul, and Duluth. An amendment to the State Constitution, permitting the State to build or buy a terminal elevator, and to acquire property *outside the State* for that purpose, was adopted by the legislature in 1909. It was again approved in 1911 and was ratified by popular vote in 1912.

Meanwhile an agitation for the creation of a grain market *within the State* arose, and a second constitutional amendment, making it possible to build a terminal elevator within the State, went through the processes of adoption and became a part of the constitution in 1914. These proposals had the backing of some bankers and many merchants and were adopted by large majorities.

In 1915 the legislature authorized members of the board of control — the board officially in charge of such business matters — to investigate and report plans for the construction of State-owned elevators. After several months the board reported against the whole project, and, consequently, a tax to create a State elevator fund imposed by a former legislature was repealed. A bill to appropriate funds for the construction of an elevator was also defeated. Apparently a majority of the legislature accepted the report as conclusive in the matter. Popular opinion did not follow the course of the legislature, and was not so readily convinced that the project should be dropped, because a few State officials had been persuaded by interested parties that the State could not succeed in the grain business.

Origin of the League

While the legislature was in session, the North Dakota Union of the American Society of Equity was holding its annual session in Bismarck. The convention was stirred by the report of the board and determined to force the legislators to act in spite of the adverse report. Delegations visited the legislature and demanded hearings before committees. These hearings developed bitter controversies, and during one of the arguments an angry legislator was reported to have demanded by what right a "bunch of farmers come down here to browbeat the legislature," and ended by advising them to "Go home and slop the hogs." This remark became a slogan in the fight of the farmers against the dominant political group. Whether these exact words were ever used, the farmers had found that lobbying was a failure, even when backed by an expression of the will of the majority of the people of the State.

When the farmers received their rebuffs from the legislature, the man who was to be the leader of the League was with them at Bismarck. He was not a leader nor even a member of their organization, but a mere hanger-on and observer watching events.

Arthur C. Townley was thirty-five years old in 1915. He was a western farm boy, born in northwestern Minnesota of native American parents. He graduated from the high school and for two seasons afterwards he taught school in the neighborhood of his home. At that time he was a voracious reader. Finally he grew tired of books and decided to try farming, locating in the extreme western part of North Dakota near the Montana border.

In his first experience as a farmer, he manifested the same disposition to lead that has since become his chief characteristic. He was impatient with small operations.

Working with horses was too slow for him, and he persuaded a number of farmers to combine with him and purchase a tractor and ploughs. Later he bought a second tractor, and, by running both from early daylight to late at night, he established a ploughing record that would be hard to equal. The season proved dry and, when the prospects were at the worst, Townley withdrew and allowed his partners to parcel out the remainder of the seed, divide the equipment, and take their own individual chances. Rain came soon after his departure and those who had been with him in a sort of farming syndicate prospered. Townley spent the following winter as a plasterer's helper traveling over all the Northwest from North Dakota to the coast.

Anxious to try again, he returned to the place of his failure where money was being made in flax. He had two fairly successful seasons and expanded his holdings until he began to be spoken of as a "flax king," and as a highly successful farmer. His third season was the disastrous one of 1912, when he had incurred heavy obligations for the purchase and rent of land and for equipment to be paid for out of the crop. The season was dry and the crop short, and in addition the price broke sharply under a market attack by speculators. Townley's brief prosperity was ended.

With time for reflection, he began to relate his troubles and those of his brother farmers to his economic studies. He found sympathy for his plans for reform among the Socialists and became active in the Socialist Party movement. Accepting most of their criticisms of the existing economic and political order, he reached the conclusion that the course to follow was "to organize on the basis of a simple and practicable programme of changes which could be put into execution and tested by experience before proceeding to other, more revolutionary things." He was impatient with the Socialist tendency to extreme theory rather than to action.

The various issues and reforms before the people of the State at that time seemed to him to furnish the basis for a new political alignment that might result in improved economic conditions. "Among these was the State-owned elevator coupled with the project for state-owned flour mills. The single-tax theory, in so far as it applied merely to the exemption of farm improvements, was being discussed and was widely favored. Rural credits on a new basis to reduce exorbitant interest charges were being nationally discussed, and were a particularly live topic in North Dakota, where the farmers had been for years the prey of conscienceless usurers and mortgage sharks. Over across the line in Canada they had achieved crop insurance on a general taxation basis, and big coöperative organizations had compelled the Government to assist them by financing elevators and storage warehouses at railroad terminal and central points."

After over a year's absence from the State, Townley returned and became an organizer for the Socialist Party. He began to "organize" the farmers into the Socialist Party. While he was tramping around from place to place seeing as many farmers as he could in a day, he decided that, if he had a Ford car, he could sign many more members and pay for the Ford. He went to a farmer Socialist of some means who helped him to get the necessary money. So he worked with the Ford and got many more members. If one man could do this with one car, why could not a hundred do it? Townley went to the Socialist State Committee with the problem. The committee discussed it, and it was brought before a State convention with the result that Townley resigned as an organizer. He believed that he had support enough in the convention to have had his plan adopted, but he did not think there was use of going on. Too many of the Socialists seemed to him "as conservative as the old parties. Offer them a plan by which they could really accomplish something instead of merely talking, and they were afraid of it." Having parted company with the Socialists, and with another plan beginning to develop, Townley went to the State Capital to observe the farmers and the legislature.

Before Townley left Bismarck, his idea had taken definite form. He had become convinced that the farmers were ready for a new organization, and that they would desert the old parties and the old leaders if anything were offered them which held hope of bettering conditions.

Organization of the League

Among the farmers at the Equity meeting of 1915 was Fred B. Wood, of Deering, McHenry County, in the north-central part of the State. He was a man of about fifty years of age with two grown sons, prominent in the Equity movement, and a successful farmer, whom Townley had met in the course of his organizing work for the Socialist Party. He renewed the acquaintance and confided his plan to him. Wood agreed to lend his name and influence to make it a success. He invited Townley to come to his farm in the spring and he would help him start the new enterprise.

Townley appeared at the Wood farm even before the snow had gone. A long conference followed in which Wood's two sons also joined. Early the next day, Howard Wood and Townley started out to call upon the neighbors. The results were to be a test of the plan. Wood furnished the introductions and Townley did the talking. This arrangement later became the method used in the League organization work. An early convert would act as a "booster" in a township, going along with an organizer and introducing him to his neighbors. Sometimes an organizer hired a capable farm hand, and took him along to take the place of the farmer on the plough or hay wagon while the farmer listened to his arguments.

The first day's work was a success, and there were a dozen members of the League at its close. Within a short time a few of the first converts signed notes to enable Townley to buy a car. Next a force of organizers was created; some were farmers and some were former Socialist speakers and writers. A temporary office was established at Minot in the northwestern part of the State. An "executive committee" was selected — Townley named himself as president, and the elder Wood was vice-president. The programme was as follows:

"State ownership of terminal elevators, flour mills, packing-houses, and cold-storage plants.

"State inspection of grain and grain dockage.

"Exemption of farm improvements from taxation.

"State hail insurance on the acreage tax basis.

"Rural credit banks operated at cost."

The programme was not original with Townley. It was "the accrued product of several years of discussion." It contained the ideas of the leaders in the farmers' coöperative organizations and these were approved by learned and scientific authority.

And yet these items were not the central thing in the League's propaganda. Townley realized that an organization was necessary to hold the allegiance of men for any considerable length of time. So the organizers talked "organization" to the farmers, first, last, and all the time. They told them that they could never get what they wanted from the State Government unless they organized as others did to get it.

Progress was made; names and checks and cash began to roll into the headquarters at Minot. At first the dues were $2.50 a year. Later they were increased to $6, and then to $9. After the first successful campaign, dues were fixed at $16 for two years, corresponding with the terms of State officials.

Before midsummer the first year, there were ten thousand members enrolled, and when winter came there were twenty-six thousand. The Nonpartisan League was an established fact in North Dakota. In September, 1915, the "Nonpartisan Leader" began to be issued as the official publication of the League, and its establishment marked the end of the first period in its history — a period of the swift and secret growth of a potent idea into organized working form with a self-appointed leader.

THE ELECTIONS OF 1916

The first great task of the League was the capture of the State in the general elections of 1916. Plans began to be developed early in the year. Township or election precinct caucuses were held throughout the State on February 22d. Great emphasis was placed upon these meetings by the leaders. By March 1st, reports were all in from the local caucuses and the results were exceedingly satisfactory. Politicians were rejected as delegates, and in a large percentage of cases those chosen were men who protested against their selection because of their lack of experience, and who urged the choice of others in their places. These were the men who would choose candidates for the legislature and delegates to the State Convention which would name the candidates for State offices.

During the first three weeks of March, the legislative district conventions were held, at which candidates were selected for the lower house of the legislature — one to

four in number according to the population of the district
— and one candidate for the State Senate in half of the districts, since Senators were elected for four years, and consequently only half were elected at each general election.
These district conventions selected the delegates to the
State Convention. The rule generally followed was the appointment of the legislative candidate who received the
highest vote at the district convention.

Late in March the League delegates met in State Convention at Fargo to nominate candidates for Governor and
other State officials. The nominee for Governor was Lynn
J. Frazier, the son of a pioneer homesteader of native
American stock. He was forty-one years old, a graduate of
the State University, but little known outside of his own
community. He was a successful farmer, a good neighbor,
and an earnest prohibitionist. He had voted the Republican ticket all his life, and his father, who had been regarded
as a "temperance crank," had also been a Republican.

For State offices the League endorsed four men who
were recognized candidates for positions, but for the remaining eight places, aside from the Supreme Court,
farmer candidates and League members, unknown to
office, were nominated. For the three Supreme Court
vacancies they named a member of the faculty of the
State University School of Law, a practicing lawyer, who
also owned a farm, and an eccentric old man who had been
one of the first lawyers to locate in the State.

Such was the make-up of the ticket in North Dakota
which "agitated the office-holders, perplexed the politicians, and set the whole State to wondering whether they
were witnessing a huge joke or a revolutionary political
movement."

Immediately following the nomination of candidates
for State offices, "Grand State Convention mass meetings"

were held, which were addressed by Frazier and the other men upon the State ticket.

During April and May, because the farmers were busy sowing grain, no attempts were made to hold public meetings, but between June 1st and 28th, when the primaries were held, a whirlwind canvass was carried on, chiefly by a series of "picnics" — all-day meetings to which the farmers came for many miles in their wagons or automobiles, and which were, to strangers, the most interesting feature of a campaign unique in several respects. The League candidates and Townley spoke at these "picnics."

In the week before the primaries a special train was chartered and, as the "Frazier Special," it made a round trip of the State, north to Grand Forks, west to Williston, south to Beach, and back to Fargo. Frazier spoke frequently from the car platform, and at every stop many farmers came to hear him.

Primary day, June 28th, there occurred one of the most violent and long-continued thunderstorms in the history of the State. It seemed impossible that there could be much of a farmer vote. In spite of adverse weather conditions, Frazier defeated his opponent, receiving 40,000 votes out of a total of approximately 75,000. The other farmer candidates ran close to him. The League candidate for Governor was thus assured of sufficient votes to win in the fall elections. His opponent was a "progressive" Democrat, who did not make an active campaign.

The League had been helped in its primary campaign by other farm organizations, the Equity, Farmers' Union, and the Grange. The state master of the Grange, a farmer preacher, had campaigned for the League candidates and had been a delegate to the State Convention.

An incident of the summer was the capture of the Republican State Committee by League representatives. No special effort had been made to obtain control of the committee, but it came as a result of the general success of League candidates. A majority of the committee members were also League members, and, after some skirmishing by opponents, a platform similar to that of the League was accepted. Before this was done, Frazier had announced that his campaign would be for the League programme no matter what the State Committee might do. Under these circumstances the Republican party machinery was in control of the League and its leaders. Only the election of Supreme Court members required much attention after the victory at the primaries.

At the November election, the League candidates for the Supreme Court won by large majorities and all the men endorsed for State office were elected. Control of the lower house of the legislature was obtained by the election of 81 Leaguers out of a total of 113 members. Twenty-two candidates had been endorsed for the twenty-five Senate vacancies. Eighteen were elected, leaving the control of the upper house an open question, dependent upon the conversion to League ideas of some of the "holdover" Senators.

In the presidential and senatorial campaigns, the League officers tried to maintain neutrality, but the Republican candidates were benefited by the fact that the League representatives were on the Republican ticket. The Republican candidate for United States Senator won by a large vote, although President Wilson carried the State by a narrow margin.

LEGISLATIVE RESULTS IN 1917

When the new legislature assembled in January, 1917, no difficulty was experienced in organizing the lower house by the Leaguers, as they controlled over two thirds of the membership. The expectation of winning the support of enough of the holdover Senators to obtain a majority in the upper house soon proved hopeless. One of the eighteen League Senators was found to be only lukewarm, leaving seventeen instead of the twenty-five required for a majority in that body. The League also suffered the defection of the Lieutenant Governor, who appointed committees having in all important cases a minority of League members. Evidently the opposition forestalled the League and lined up the Senate against the farmers. This situation explains the course followed by the League during the legislative session. Without the control of the upper house very little could be accomplished.

Only by the amendment of the State Constitution could all the items of the League programme be enacted into law. Authority was needed to permit the State to engage in other industries than the operation of a terminal elevator, to allow the issue of bonds to finance such industries, to permit the exemption of farm improvements from taxation, and to make possible taxation to provide for hail insurance.

The methods provided for changing the constitution were slow, making impossible the completion of the League programme much before 1919 or 1920. To obtain speedier action the League leaders determined to ignore the usual methods of amendment and to have the legislature frame a new constitution. It was to be submitted to the people and was to replace the existing constitution as soon as it had been adopted by popular vote.

Accordingly the new constitution appeared as House Bill 44, in the form of a concurrent resolution, which after setting forth the constitution as a whole, then provided for a special election at which the constitution should be presented to the people. The new constitution was in fact the existing constitution with a number of changes giving the authority necessary to accomplish the purposes desired by the League.

The counter effort of the opposition was the introduction in the Senate of a bill for a special election for delegates to a constitutional convention.

Both sides tried to influence public sentiment to exert pressure upon the legislature. When Bill 44 came to a vote in the House, eighty-one favored it and twenty-eight voted against it. Three days later it came up in the Senate, and was indefinitely postponed by a vote of 29 to 20.

The League claimed that the defeat of the measure was "a betrayal of the farmers' interests and a defiance of the mandate of the people of the State, who had twice specifically voted in favor of State-owned terminal elevators and had given the League candidates huge majorities in the 1916 elections." The reply of the opposition was that the procedure was "revolutionary" and had not been an issue in the election. They declared themselves ready to grant constitutional revision by "constitutional" means. Apparently the position of the opposition was sound and the burden of proof rested with the League, which was proposing unusual methods to accomplish more speedily results that could in due time be obtained by regular constitutional processes. The League leaders felt the need of haste to satisfy and hold in line their newly organized forces.

Every item in the League programme, except a terminal elevator and State grain grading, met with insurmountable obstacles under the existing constitution. A serious obstacle also existed to the terminal elevator project because of a lack of means to finance it except by taxation. To inaugurate State ownership of elevators meant the use of not less than a million dollars, and for the joint mill and elevator projects, five million were considered desirable. Expert advisers believed that the two should be started together and as a unit. The debt limit imposed by the State Constitution did not permit the issue of bonds even for the terminal elevator.

There was some difference of opinion among the League supporters as to the course to be followed. To divide them still more, the opposition drafted a bill, making an appropriation of $300,000 for a terminal elevator "to carry out the instructions of the people." It passed the Senate and came up in the House on the final day of the session. After some changes in conference, it also passed the House, League members dividing upon it. Governor Frazier promptly vetoed the measure, and his action does not seem to have been seriously questioned by his supporters.

The League legislators did not give all their attention to constitutional changes intended to inaugurate their economic programme. They passed an amendment to the constitution giving votes to women, extended suffrage to women on all offices and all questions where there was no constitutional bar, passed a State Grain-Grading Act, a Torrens Title Registration Law, a law guaranteeing deposits in State banks, reduced the rate of assessment on farm improvements to five per cent, passed freight rate laws to reduce freights, and created a state highway commission with increased appropriations for good roads.

Probably the Grain-Grading Act of the 1917 legislature was the most important single enactment. There had never been an effective system of grain-grading in North Dakota under the theory that, since virtually all the grain raised there was sold on the Minnesota market and Minnesota had a very elaborate system, there was no need for North Dakota to provide for grading its grain.

The League's advisers believed that this conclusion was fallacious. What was wanted was honest enforcement of whatever grades were used at the primary markets, together with honest weights and honest accounting. The League Bill created two departments, one of warehouse accounting and supervision, and another of grain inspection and grading. It gave up the old plan of many salaried inspectors and compelled buyers of grain to procure licenses as grain inspectors. Such licenses could be revoked for violation of State regulations or for misgrading or short weighing. The elevator or warehouse employing the buyer could not buy grain until he had regained his standing or another buyer had been licensed in his place. A few months of operation of this law showed more uniform and higher grading of grain, and indirectly it improved the prices paid for the various grades.

In 1919 a much more drastic act was passed which conferred upon the inspector the additional power to fix prices as well as grades. Though attacked by a farmer-elevator company, the constitutionality of the act of 1917 was sustained by the Supreme Court of the State. The new act was attacked in the United States courts in a case which involved the Interstate Commerce Act. It was there held unconstitutional as an interference with interstate commerce and because the Federal Government had itself undertaken the grading of grain.[1]

Thus the end of the 1917 legislative session saw but one of the planks in the League platform actually enacted into law. The League had been balked by constitutional provisions and by the holdover Senators. It faced the task of providing some means for the amendment of the State Constitution in order to make its programme possible of accomplishment and of winning enough more Senate votes

[1] Bruce: *The Nonpartisan League*, p. 98.

to give control of that body, while holding its majority in the lower house.

The League again won in North Dakota in 1918, re-electing Governor Frazier and gaining control over both houses of the legislature. All the amendments to the constitution proposed by the League to make its programme effective were also approved by popular vote. A complete Congressional delegation of League representatives was chosen.

LEGISLATION OF 1919

Since the results of the elections of 1918 gave the League full control of the legislative machinery and constituted a popular referendum upon its programme, nothing stood in its way in carrying out its proposals. The principal measures which became law during the 1919 session of the legislature were as follows:

1. An "Industrial Commission" was created, consisting of the Governor, the Secretary of Agriculture, and the Attorney-General, to have control of State-owned financial and commercial industries.

2. Provision was made for the operation by the Industrial Commission, through a "mill and elevator association," of State-owned grain warehouses and elevators and State-owned flour mills, and for a bond issue of $5,000,000 to give working capital.

3. Creation of the Bank of North Dakota, with an initial capital of $2,000,000 to be supplied by a bond issue; this bank was to be the sole depository of public funds and was to act as a rediscount and reserve bank.

4. The Home Building Association of North Dakota, another activity of the Industrial Commission, was established for the purpose of receiving deposits for home buying and building purposes and lending funds for the

same on low interest rates and an amortization scheme of payments.

5. Provision was made for levying a graduated tax upon incomes to be based upon data in the possession of the Federal Government, which by law is made available to the States. This tax made a distinction between "earned" and "unearned" incomes.

6. Creation of a hail insurance fund to be obtained from an acreage tax on all tillable land and from assessments on all land, the owners of which desire the benefit of hail insurance.

7. Exemption of all farm improvements from taxation and in towns of homes to the value of one thousand dollars, furniture to the amount of three hundred dollars, and additional personal property to the value of three hundred dollars.

8. Classification for taxation purposes of all land, exclusive of improvements, at one hundred per cent of true value, tangible property of public utilities, bank stock and other income-producing properties at one hundred per cent, and live stock, merchandise, and other personal property, including farm equipment, at fifty per cent of true value.

9. Creation of a workmen's compensation commission and provision of assessments against all employers to furnish sickness and accident compensation for all workers.

10. Regulation of the hours and conditions of labor for women, including an eight-hour law.

11. Provision for mine inspection and the regulation of working conditions in mines.

12. Levying a tax to provide a fund for the buying of homes for returned soldiers or assisting in their education, each soldier to draw twenty-five dollars a month for every month spent in the national service.

13. Establishment of a single "official newspaper" in each county for all legal and public printing, the newspapers to be selected in each county biennially by popular vote.

14. The Minnesota plan of distance tariffs on railroads was put in force in North Dakota to prevent discrimination against the State in railway freight rates.[1]

The more noteworthy features of this new legislation were the plan for a State bank similar to the federal reserve banks and the home building law. The former provided means for the handling of the financial parts of the League's industrial and economic programme, while the latter enabled persons to obtain homes. Critics of one as socialistic were embarrassed by the individualistic aspect of the other. In both cases the power of the State was intended to be used for the benefit of its citizens as a whole.

Of this great body of new legislation, the more important bills were passed with an "emergency clause," by which they became law immediately, but their defeat in a referendum election would act as a repeal. Thirty thousand signatures were required to call a special election, but seven thousand were sufficient for their reference to the next regular election.

Governor Frazier announced that he would use the power granted to him and call a special election if half the required number of signatures was obtained. It was claimed that more than thirty thousand signatures were turned in, but there were charges of irregularity in the methods used in getting the names. The special election was held June 26, 1919, and resulted in the approval of

[1] Gaston: *The Nonpartisan League*, pp. 285–87; *The New Day in North Dakota*, a pamphlet issued by the Industrial Commission of North Dakota in 1919.

every one of the measures by "majorities ranging from 6914 to 13,256 in the case of the Bank of North Dakota Bill." The latter bill therefore received the greatest popular support.

As soon as the organization of the Industrial Commission had been completed, steps were taken for the opening of the Bank of North Dakota. A director general, a pioneer banker in the State, was appointed; a building was rented in Bismarck and a staff of clerks assembled. Although springing up incidentally to the development of rural credits, the bank was the first to get into active operation, and commended itself to a wider number of people than any other of the new enterprises.

In November, 1919, the selection of Grand Forks as the site of the first large State-owned mill and elevator was announced, together with the plans for the construction of a mill of the most modern type, having a daily grinding capacity of three thousand barrels of flour.

ACTIVITY IN OTHER STATES

North Dakota has been the scene of the chief activities and successes of the Nonpartisan League. In that State only has it been in actual control of the machinery of government. The beginning of its national activity came in January, 1917, when national headquarters were opened in St. Paul. Organizers had started work in western Minnesota in July, 1916, immediately after the success in the North Dakota primaries of that year. Soon after others were at work in the northern tier of counties of South Dakota and in eastern Montana. The plan followed in these States was practically the same as in North Dakota. In the place of a "president," the title by which Townley was known in his own State, a "State chairman" was chosen for each of the other States. In reality Townley actually became the accepted head of a national organization, the National Nonpartisan League.

Minnesota has been the only other State in which the League has been strong enough to challenge the power of the old party politicians. Conditions, however, were less favorable and success, consequently, was less definite and complete. Combination with other dissatisfied elements was necessary. The League candidate for Governor in the primary elections of 1918 was defeated by the regular Republican candidate by approximately 50,000 votes, although the League candidate polled 150,000 votes, three times its membership in the State at the time. In addition, it carried thirty out of the eighty-nine counties for its legislative candidates. The results also indicated that a large proportion of the Union labor vote was cast for the League. Had not the issues of the campaign been complicated by the introduction of the anti-war views of their candidate for Governor, a somewhat better showing might have been made.

After the defeat of its candidate in the primaries, the League joined with organized labor in the nomination of an independent candidate for Governor. In the fall elections this candidate polled 111,948 votes, while the Republican nominee received 166,515 votes. The League elected 11 Senators and 26 members of the lower house. Added to the labor representatives from the cities, there appeared to be a working group of 30 League-Labor representatives out of 67 in the Senate, and 60 out of 131 in the House. Defections on various measures during the session materially reduced this possible strength. The League alarmed and threatened Republican supremacy in Minnesota, but it was still far from occupying anything like its position in North Dakota. The opposition is much stronger in Minnesota and control of the State Government can only come from a coalition of the farmer-labor vote.

In 1918 also complete State tickets were nominated in South Dakota and Idaho, and in Colorado, Montana, and Nebraska State Conventions were held and candidates named in as many districts as there seemed any prospect of victory. In Nebraska seven members of the lower house and one Senator endorsed by the League were elected. In addition, several others who ran without League endorsement were elected and were supporters of the League programme. In Colorado two State Senators and two Representatives in the legislature were elected.

Montana had a larger proportion of League members considering its population than Colorado or Nebraska, but organization was too incomplete to make any serious bid for control. A League State Convention endorsed Jeanette Rankin, Congresswoman from the State, as a candidate for the United States Senate. In South Dakota five Senators and eight Representatives were elected. The net results of the 1918 elections in the States outside of North Dakota were not such as to give great encouragement for the future.

When the "Nonpartisan Leader," the official publication of the League, was moved to St. Paul from North Dakota, January 1, 1918, the total membership was about 150,000. The close of the work of organization at the end of that year found around 200,000 names upon the membership lists. North Dakota and Minnesota contained nearly half of that number, while South Dakota and Montana furnished almost half of the remainder, with Nebraska, Idaho, and Colorado next in order. Washington, Texas, Iowa, Kansas, Oklahoma, and Wisconsin completed the total. Evidently the four States of North Dakota, Minnesota, Montana, and South Dakota comprised the heart of the movement. Outside of these States the Nonpartisan League had only scattering strength. Labor and socialistic groups may coöperate with it at times, but there is little indication of permanent fusion.

THE DECLINE OF THE LEAGUE

The election successes of 1918 and the legislation of 1919 marked the climax of the accomplishments of the Nonpartisan League. The autocratic control exercised by Townley was bound sooner or later to bring about revolt. The first rebels came from among the leaders in the Society of Equity who believed in coöperation rather than State ownership, but really serious opposition did not appear until 1919, when the Attorney-General, William Langer, the State Auditor, and the Secretary of State raised the standard of revolt. All these men had been members of the League and had been elected as its candidates. They did not claim to be opposed to the organization as an organization and they did not renounce their allegiance to its original industrial programme. Their opposition was clearly stated by Langer in a number of public addresses made during the primary election of 1920 in which he said:

"Three years ago when a candidate for Attorney-General, I publicly pledged my best efforts to serve all of the people of the State. That pledge I have kept. I have been Attorney-General for all of the people and have not permitted myself to become the chattel, rubber stamp, plaything, or tool of A. C. Townley, or any other political boss.

"I have honestly used my utmost endeavor to carry out the platform upon which I was elected. On the other hand, Townley has made no honest effort to carry out that programme, but has acted at all times from selfish motives and has built up a personal political machine, which is controlled absolutely by him, and which not only extends to the newspapers and banks which he has organized, but extends into the very legislative halls of the State, and even controls many State officials." [1]

At the primaries of 1920, a general opposition ticket was placed in the field by the conservatives. Although they failed to nominate Langer, their candidate for Governor, by a few thousand votes, they carried nearly all the eastern and more prosperous counties and succeeded in nominating their candidates for State Auditor and Secretary of State as well as two out of three members of Congress. They also nominated enough members of the lower house to assure them the control.

"The most noticeable feature of this revolt was that autocracy, excessive taxation, and mismanagement were the only grounds on which a united opposition could be based, and that, though the leadership of the League was opposed, its industrial programme was endorsed." [2]

In the fall of 1920 the conservatives were generally successful. In Minnesota their victory was decisive and resulted in the election of the regular Republican candidate for Governor by a plurality of about 145,000 and of the remainder of the ticket, including the conservatives' candidate for Supreme Judge, by even larger majorities. The conservatives also reclaimed the control of thirty counties which had been carried at the primaries by the Nonpartisans, and thus obtained the complete control of both houses of the legislature. The losses in Minnesota were bitter blows to the Nonpartisans. Much had been expected of Minnesota, and much reliance had been placed on the fact

[1] Bruce: *The Nonpartisan League*, pp. 200–05.
[2] *Ibid.*, 212, 213.

that it contained not merely discontented farmers, but a large number of radical laborers. The coalition between city workers and the farmers failed to materialize.

A coalition of the Republicans and Democrats in Montana resulted in a sweeping victory in the fall election, though the Nonpartisan League had captured the primaries of the dominant Democratic Party and had succeeded in nominating their candidate for Governor.

In Colorado, where the Nonpartisans had captured the Republican primaries, a similar coalition was formed with similar results. In South Dakota there were three parties in the field, the Democratic, the Republican, and the Nonpartisan. The result was a sweeping victory for the Republicans, the Nonpartisans apparently taking second place. In Wisconsin, the Nonpartisan candidate for Governor was elected. He was, however, a La Follette rather than a Nonpartisan candidate and, with the exception of his election, the Nonpartisan successes were negligible.

In the fall elections the Nonpartisans supported Governor Frazier and the rest of their successful nominees on the Republican ticket and created an independent ticket for the offices for which their opponents had named their candidates. The regular Republicans or conservatives formed a coalition with the Democrats and agreed to support the Democratic State ticket with the exception of the offices for which their candidates had been named. Both Republicans and Democrats united in supporting the various initiated measures which opened the books of the Bank of North Dakota to inspection and safeguarded its investments, and which no longer made it obligatory on the county treasurers to deposit their funds therein; which repealed the State Sheriff Law, restored to the State Superintendent of Public Instruction the powers formerly possessed by that official, repealed the State Press Law, and the law making it a criminal offense to criticize the industrial programme of the League. These measures were the most objectionable of the laws passed during the legislative session of 1919.

The Democratic Governor was defeated by only 4630 votes. The conservatives elected their candidates for State Superintendent of Public Instruction, Secretary of State, State Treasurer, and Justice of the Supreme Court, two members of Congress, and enough members of the legislature to obtain the control of the lower house by from three to six votes. They lost control of the upper house by only one member, but they secured the passage of all the initiated measures.

In spite of the reëlection of Governor Frazier and the League candidates for Attorney-General and State Auditor, the result was an emphatic vote of lack of confidence. The votes for the initiated laws ranged from 19,231 to 8173, and the votes for the successful conservative candidates were about the same as those cast for the initiated measures. Senator Harding received 159,211 votes, while Governor Frazier only received 117,118. Dr. E. F. Ladd, the Nonpartisan candidate for United States Senator, received 130,614 votes, the highest vote of all the candidates.

For a time it seemed as though the results of the election of 1920, together with the strained financial situation which the sudden decrease in the price of wheat and other farm products in the fall of that year occasioned, might result in a compromise between the two factions.

Not only were a number of the weaker banks compelled to close their doors, but the packing-house of the Society of Equity, located at Fargo, found itself confronted with a deficit of over $700,000 and was forced to suspend operations. In addition, the Bank of North Dakota became seriously embarrassed and the further construction of the grain elevator and mill at Grand Forks had to be discontinued as well as the operations of the home building and rural credit board.

Evidently something had to be done by the bankers and business men of North Dakota, for a condition of general State insolvency would ruin the banker and business man as well as the farmer. The result was a meeting of the Bankers' Association, followed by a conference with a number of the Nonpartisan leaders, and the formulation of a plan by which the Bankers' Association agreed to underwrite the State bonds to an amount necessary to complete and operate the mill and elevator at Grand Forks, to operate the mill at Drake, to underwrite and aid in selling some $3,000,000 of farm mortgages, held by the Bank of North Dakota, and as far as possible to aid the League in carrying out its industrial experiments. A plan was also worked out for the assistance of the smaller banks.

One condition, however, was imposed, and that was that the legislature of 1921 should not establish any new enterprises and that for the present no additional State industries should be launched.

At first it seemed probable that an agreement would be made, but with the meeting of the legislature the conservative forces were surprised by a recommendation in the Governor's message which advocated the purchase and operation of a State-owned lignite coal mine, and later by a refusal to concede to the demand that the State industrial activities be confined to those which had already been provided for. The Industrial Commission, composed of Nonpartisans, declared that the proposition of the bankers was "a plain attempt on the part of the financial interests, presumably Wall Street financiers, to dictate the political, financial, and industrial policies of the State of

North Dakota and requiring a surrender of the sovereign powers of the State to manage its own affairs, and to permit the dictation and interference with the independence and liberty of the free people of a sovereign State."

Though the Nonpartisans controlled the Senate, the conservative majority in the lower house made it possible to block the administration measure for a State-owned coal mine, to order a legislative investigation of the State industries, and to publish the report of the examination of the affairs of the Bank of North Dakota made in 1920. This report disclosed the actual insolvency of the Bank of North Dakota and of the Scandinavian American Bank of Fargo, which had been largely used in financing the Nonpartisan movement and its industrial programme.

The Recall Election of 1921

Finally the failure of all efforts at compromise resulted in the formulation of a plan for the recall of the Nonpartisan officials and the initiation of measures which would change the personnel of the Industrial Commission and would transform the Bank of North Dakota into a rural credit agency of the State Government.

A controlling element in the whole affair was the conviction of the conservatives that the Nonpartisan finances were in a hopeless state of confusion and collapse. One element in the opposition urged a recall election at once, relying on the discontent among the farmers due to the fall of prices of farm products; the other element preferred to wait until the primaries in June, 1922, for further action. The element for immediate action prevailed and the recall election was set for October 28, 1921.

The Independent Voters' Association, the name under which the conservatives figured in the recall campaign, entered the contest with a platform which promised to give a fair trial to part of the Nonpartisan League programme. They proposed amendments and initiated laws that would limit the issue of State bonds to $7,500,000 instead of $17,000,000; which would authorize $2,500,000 to complete the Grand Forks terminal elevator and mill; the issuance of $250,000 to wind up the affairs of the Home Builders' Association, the liquidation of the bank of North Dakota, and the creation of a rural credits bureau to take over the farm loan business of the bank.

R. A. Nestos, of Minot, who had, as State's Attorney of Ward County, made a great reputation as a vigorous officer for law enforcement, was nominated to run against Frazier. At the recall election Nestos and the other two candidates on the Independent ticket won by a few thousand votes over Frazier and his two fellow officials. The measures directed against the State industrial programme failed. Nestos, a man of high character, has always been very progressive and promised in his campaign that, if elected, he would give the State enterprises a fair trial under the operation of competent men who understood such business.

Apparently the League programme has suffered a permanent breakdown. "The plan of making the State of North Dakota a self-contained unit financially was fundamentally erroneous. The State is mainly devoted to one industry, agriculture, and largely to one crop. Money is easy or tight in all localities at one and the same time. For this reason the State does not make a well-balanced economic or financial unit in itself. Moreover, North Dakota is a comparatively new State; it has always used outside capital to its advantage and can continue to do so. The idea of corralling all the loose funds at the capital of the State and of getting along without aid from outside was a mistake." [1]

---

[1] *The National City Bank Monthly Letter*, April, 1921.

Accordingly, the election results of 1920 and 1921 and the economic situation seem to have spelled defeat for the Nonpartisan League. An interesting movement which has aroused heated controversies, and has also raised the hopes of many people, is disappearing as have so many similar undertakings in the past. Townley's idea, a Ford car, and $16 produced a remarkable organization. Just what its final influence may prove to be remains for the future to show us. Certainly, it emphasizes the value of leadership — leadership plus a sound constructive programme.

SELECTED REFERENCES

1. Bruce: *The Nonpartisan League.*
2. Gaston: *The Nonpartisan League.*
3. Russell: *The Story of the Nonpartisan League.*
4. Boyle: "The Agrarian Movement in the Northwest," in the *American Economic Review*, vol. VIII, pp. 505–21 (September, 1918).
5. Gillette: "The North Dakota Harvest of the Nonpartisan League," in *The Survey*, vol. XLI, pp. 753–60.
6. Ruhl: "The North Dakota Idea," in the *Atlantic Monthly*, vol. CXXIII, pp. 686–96 (May, 1919).
7. Devine: "North Dakota — The Laboratory of the Nonpartisan League," in *The Survey*, vol. XLIII, pp. 684–89.
8. *The New Day in North Dakota*, a pamphlet issued by the Industrial Commission in 1919.
9. Langer: *The Nonpartisan League, Its Birth, Activities and Leaders.*
10. Carroll: "The Recall in North Dakota," in *National Municipal Review*, vol. XI, pp. 3–5 (January, 1922).
11. *The North Dakota Industrial Programme*, a report on the organization and progress of North Dakota State industries issued by the Industrial Commission, June, 1921.
12. Laws and constitutional amendments authorizing the North Dakota Industrial Programme, issued by the Industrial Commission, June, 1921.

CHAPTER XIV

THE NEW FARMERS' MOVEMENT

DURING the latter part of the World War there was much discussion of reconstruction and a great deal of vague reference to a new social order which was to come as a result of the peace settlement. The world was to be made safe for democracy. The actual application of this principle was taken seriously by the workers and industrial democracy became the central feature of the discussion of reconstruction. Democracy in industry came to be accepted as the immediate goal to be attained.

The shortage of labor, due to military demands and to the after-war boom in the United States, emphasized this phase of reconstruction. Labor was in a position of strategic strength and the skilled and organized workers proceeded to take advantage of this situation. Wages were sharply increased and productive efficiency declined. Labor unrest, illustrated vividly by the coal and steel strikes of 1919, spread rapidly. Conservative labor leaders were threatened in their control by radical leaders supported by the rank and file of the organizations. "Outlaw" strikes added to the seriousness of the situation.

Until the spring of 1920 prices and wages continued to rise. The first signs of a downward movement in prices appeared in May and had become quite evident by October. The spread of industrial depression deprived wage-earners of their bargaining advantage and put them back in their pre-war position of dependence. The talk about industrial democracy came to an abrupt end. Its place was taken by the familiar story of unemployment.

In recent years the center of the stage has been taken by the farmers. The fall in the prices of farm products during the autumn of 1920 gave a still more serious aspect to business conditions. The drop in farm products let down practically one half of the industrial organization and rendered it unable to continue purchases from the other half on the same scale without a general adjustment of the basis on which exchanges are made. The farmer has suffered not only a great direct loss of purchasing power, but a shock which will affect his mental attitude toward expenditures for some time.[1]

The immediate result has been the development of a new agitation among the farmers who have been on the whole quiescent since the decline of Populism. The recent demands of the representatives of farm organizations upon the Treasury and the Federal Reserve Board for financial aid in marketing crops and in holding them are reminiscent of the agrarianism of earlier periods. As then, so now there is a widespread conviction that agricultural products have an inherent value quite independent of the market price, and that the fluctuations and the fall in market prices are the result of speculative manipulations.

Furthermore, the loss had not been anticipated and discounted. The papers had been filled with accounts of world shortages in every kind of food and raw materials. Who would have predicted a spectacular fall in the price of wool and cotton, in corn and wheat, while all Europe was still hungry and in need of clothing? Lack of purchasing power explains why such a change has been possible, but farmers are not students of economics, and they cannot see why in a world where goods are moved on credits, based in the last analysis on future productive power, the workers of Europe should go unemployed and

[1] National City Bank, *Monthly Letter*, December, 1920.

hungry, while American materials and food heap up until prices fall below cost.

Such a situation invites a careful consideration of recent developments in typical Western States. Naturally we think first of North Dakota and the Nonpartisan League. Is the West to see such a movement sweep over it in the way Populism did in the nineties of the last century? A feature of the present as of the earlier period is the existence of a number of rapidly growing farm organizations of which the Farm Bureau Federation and the Farmers' Educational and Coöperative Union are typical. For fifty years the farmers have been protesting "at being mere growers of products, leaving the returns to Providence and the middleman." The new farmers' movement is the same protest grown efficient. The farmers have learned their lesson from capital and labor. They can play the combination game and they are also developing the art of economic coöperation. Where they are as numerous, well-to-do, and intelligent as they are in the grain-growing States, they are bound to establish, by economic action or political or both, a force of their own to balance the economic power of private business and industry.

The Farm Bureau

The best evidence that at last the farmers are organized to cope with the problems of distribution in an effective manner is to be found in the farm bureau movement which has had a very remarkable development in the last few years.

The farm bureau has grown out of the development of county agents, an instrumentality resulting from various attempts by both State and Federal departments of agriculture to induce farmers to put into practice the scientific methods provided by agricultural colleges and experiment stations. Beginning in the South in 1906 and extended to the North in 1911, the county agent plan was established in every agricultural county during 1917–18.

County agent work seeks to improve agriculture and to better conditions on the farm. The agent must act as an educator, as a practical farmer and as an organizer. He is a source of information for the farmers of his county. He speaks at farmers' meetings, assists at institutes and holds field schools, but his most effective work is that of actual demonstration on farms. Where there are organizations, he coöperates with them; where there are none, he tries to form one. In the South these organizations formed by the agents are usually called "County Farm Councils," while in the North they are known as "County Farm Bureaus."

A farm bureau is an association of people interested in rural affairs, which has for its objects the development within a county of the best system of agriculture, the establishment of community ideals, and the improvement of the well-being, prosperity, and happiness of country people. It seeks to accomplish its purposes through coöperation with the local, State, and national agencies which are doing extension work in agriculture and home economics.

The earlier conception of the farm bureau regarded it as an aid to the county agent in his work; more recently it has become a democratic, agricultural organization which studies the local needs and attempts to solve the local problems. The farm bureau is based upon the desire of the American farmers to unite for mutual self-help and coöperation and to get into closer touch with the governmental institutions and agencies of agriculture. It has been characterized as a clearing-house and as a chamber of agriculture corresponding to a city commercial club. It is non-political, non-sectarian, non-secret, and represents the whole farming population, men, women, and children.

Twenty-one of the thirty-three Northern and Western States had farm bureaus before the United States entered the war. On December 1, 1916, these twenty-one States had 287 farm bureaus with 98,654 members. To carry out its increased food production campaigns, the United States Department of Agriculture began a systematic organization of farm bureaus in the counties. On June 30, 1918, in twenty-nine States of the North and West there were 791 farm bureaus with 290,000 members. Three other States, Indiana, Oregon, and Washington, had county federations of farmers' organizations which functioned much the same as farm bureaus. Wisconsin alone had no county organization to assist in agricultural extension work.

The Iowa Farm Bureau Federation was formed, December 27, 1918, at a meeting at Marshalltown by delegates from seventy-two of the county farm bureaus. Each bureau has one official representative on the board of directors who has a vote. In no case may the county agent be selected as a representative. The board of directors annually elect a president, three vice-presidents, a treasurer, and an executive committee. The secretary is chosen by the executive committee, which consists of one member of the board of directors from each of the eleven Congressional districts of the State, with the State County Agent Leader and the Director of Agricultural Extension as *ex-officiis*, advisory members without a vote. All of the officers and directors must be actually engaged in farming and serve without pay, but are reimbursed for expenses incurred in performance of official duties.

One dollar of each membership fee received by the county farm bureaus may be used by the federation. There are no public funds to which it is entitled, and donations and gifts are its only other means of support. In the farm bureau membership drive late in 1919 about $300,000 was donated by members to the special working fund of the federation.

In November, 1919, the American Farm Bureau Federation was formed at Chicago by delegates from thirty-three States. A preliminary meeting had been held at Ithaca, New York, in February, 1919, at which a committee had been appointed to frame a tentative constitution and arrange for a later session. The Chicago meeting was the result of the work of this committee. Mr. J. R. Howard, of the Iowa Farm Bureau Federation, was elected president, S. L. Strivings of New York, vice president, and J. W. Coverdale, temporary secretary, until the next meeting, which was set for March, 1920.

The constitution stated the objects as follows: "To correlate and strengthen the State farm bureaus and similar State organizations of the several States in the national federation, to promote, protect, and represent the business, economic, social, and educational interests of the Nation, and to develop agriculture."

Membership in the Federation consists of State farm bureau federations or State agricultural associations formed on the farm bureau plan or a similar plan. The dues for a State are fifty cents for each individual farm bureau member of the State.

The governing body is a board of directors which meets annually. Each State is entitled to one director and an additional director for every twenty thousand paid-up members of county organizations. The directors must be actual farmers, and as soon as a director or officer becomes "a candidate for an elective or appointive State or national office," he must immediately resign. Each member is also entitled to one delegate and an additional delegate for every ten thousand farmers of the State. These delegates form a House of Delegates which sits with the directors and shares all their privileges except the right to vote.

The directors annually elect from their own number an executive committee of twelve members which has charge of the administrative affairs of the organization. The president and vice-president are *ex-officiis* members, and the Secretary of Agriculture of the United States and the Director of the States' Relation Service have the privilege of attending all meetings and may take part in all discussions, but have no vote.

The second session of the American Farm Bureau Federation was held in Chicago, March 3, 1920. Twenty-eight States were admitted to membership. Bureaus were created to study the transportation problem, the distribution of farm products, and the simplification of the income tax. A legislative bureau and a bureau of world statistics on supply and demand were also formed. J. W. Coverdale, of Iowa, was chosen permanent secretary. National headquarters were established at Chicago and legislative at Washington.

Early in December, 1920, the second annual convention of the Federation was held in Indianapolis. There were sixty-four voting delegates present representing thirty-two States. Organization work was reported to be in progress in all but three States. It was estimated that the Federation was supported by approximately a million and a half actual farmers, although the membership in the States affiliated was only slightly over eight hundred thousand. President Howard and Secretary Coverdale were reëlected.

The three strongest States as to membership in the Federation are Iowa, Illinois, and Ohio. Iowa leads with 123,000, while Illinois and Ohio have about 100,000. The predominance of the Middle West was shown at Indianapolis where the States from that section had thirty-six voting delegates compared with ten from the East, ten from the South, and nine from the Far West.

By comparison with the organization of other bodies of farmers, it is apparent that farm bureau strength is largely in previously unorganized territory. Perhaps the explanation is found in the fact that the Middle West has been quite prosperous until recently and has not felt the need of organization. In addition this territory is the grain-belt and general farming section where conflicts of interest are greater. The rapid growth of the farm bureau is partly due to the decline in the farm products, but also to the forced nurture due to the war and Government support and encouragement.

THE FARMERS' UNION

Another leading general farm organization is the Farmers' Educational and Coöperative Union of America which was organized in the South in 1903. Its greatest strength is now in Kansas, Nebraska, Iowa, and Oklahoma. It did not enter the grain-belt States to any considerable extent until 1913. There are twenty-seven State unions, most of them south of Kentucky and Virginia and west of the Mississippi. Current newspaper accounts credit it with a membership varying from 250,000 to 900,000.

The Farmers' Union has emphasized the need of the farmer to systematize his business by coöperation and to apply to it the principles of scientific commerce. Hence its chief activity has been devoted to the promotion of coöperative enterprise. It claims to do an annual business of one million dollars, twenty per cent of which represents savings to members. About two fifths of this business was done in Kansas and Nebraska. All coöperative associations are organized upon the Rockdale plan, and pay from six to eight per cent dividends on capital stock and distribute additional profits in the form of patronage dividends.

Until recently these two national farm organizations seem to have worked together without serious friction. In some instances there has been duplication of membership, and officials have coöperated in the support of legislative measures in the interest of farmers. Lately in Iowa there have been signs of conflict, and, at the State meeting of the Farmers' Union in September, 1921, a contest for the presidency resulted in the election of the candidate who stood for the maintenance of the complete independence of the organization from the Farm Bureau and for keeping it "strictly a farmers' organization." The opposing candidate was understood to favor coöperation with the Farm Bureau. The vote was 489 to 186. A resolution was unanimously adopted calling for the abolition of county agricultural agents as "unnecessary and useless." Another resolution instructed the officers to confer with representatives of the American Society of Equity on proposals for amalgamation.

It is too early to predict what will result from the recent activity of the farmers and their organizations. The Nonpartisan League is apparently on the wane. The inference is, therefore, that the farmers generally will not respond to any movement which offers a great or a revolutionary change in existing conditions and methods. The Farm Bureau has placed the emphasis upon education and better farming. It has been conservative and has kept out of partisan politics, but it must now meet the urgent economic needs of its constituents or give way to a more effective organization. The Farmers' Union has devoted itself especially to coöperative methods of marketing and of distribution.

State control of methods of distribution has failed to meet widespread approval and has not been worked out successfully in North Dakota. Nebraska's experience suggests a better way and one suited to the individualistic character of the Western farmer — that of voluntary coöperation in buying and selling.

Coöperation will accomplish the organization in purchasing and marketing that seems more and more necessary both for the producer and the consumer. It avoids the rigidity of State management and control and provides a considerable degree of coördinate action; it is more adaptable to varying conditions and gives more opportunity for individual initiative. It may be the next step in economic evolution.

Agricultural Credit

There are two outstanding problems which face the new farmers' movement: the provision of adequate agricultural credit and the orderly marketing of farm products. These two requirements are really only different phases of a common problem. Agricultural credit is essential if there is to be orderly marketing. The credit needs of farmers should be so arranged that it will not be necessary for them to throw their products upon the market as soon as the harvest is completed in order to meet urgent financial obligations. Some methods of obtaining advances upon their products, similar to those at the command of business men in towns and cities, must be devised. Credit for from six months to three years is essential to meet the farmers' needs as thoroughly as thirty to ninety-day loans provide for business men in urban communities.

During the Populist agitation of the nineties, this same problem gave rise to a demand for so-called "subtreasuries," which were to be established in every county that could show that it produced $500,000 worth of wheat, corn, oats, and cotton annually. Treasury notes were to be issued to the amount of eighty per cent of the value of the products. Fifty million dollars was to be appropriated to carry out the plan. This proposal grew out of the demand for more and cheaper money that characterized the period and it undertook to meet the same need that is now under consideration — agricultural credit to enable the farmer to market his products in an orderly manner throughout the year rather than to compel him to dispose of them in large part within from three to five months, when the market is sure to be glutted with prices showing the usual autumn dip. The Populist remedy was crude and impracticable, but it sensed a vital need.

As the grain trade has developed, the farmer has come to be more and more dependent upon the banker and middleman. The local elevator, the railroad, and the terminal market stand between the producer and the consumer. The margin between the prices received by the farmer and those paid by the consumer seems to the former unnecessarily wide. To reduce this margin coöperative elevators have been established. In many cases the result has been to raise the price of grain in the locality from one to three cents a bushel. Such an outcome undoubtedly was due to the widespread existence of pooling and of price agreements among the elevators. In the late nineties and the early years of the present century these arrangements were quite generally characteristic of country marketing conditions.

In the Northwest these practices were apparently very prevalent among the commercial line companies, which were largely developed in that section. Most of these companies had their headquarters in the terminal markets, and it was therefore a comparatively simple and easy thing to perfect arrangements as to competition between the houses of these companies at local stations. Farther south and east, in Nebraska, Iowa, and Illinois, where independents were relatively more important, both types were involved and the restriction of competition was accomplished through the various State associations of grain dealers, to which both the line and independent elevators quite generally belonged. The farmers were therefore justified in believing that prices were artificially manipulated to their disadvantage. Hence the impetus to the establishment of coöperative elevators after the middle or late nineties.

About 1900, or a little earlier, the farmers' elevator movement began to meet with determined opposition from the older types of houses. This warfare assumed the most serious proportions in the Chicago territory. In Iowa, Nebraska, and Illinois, the State associations of grain dealers refused recognition to coöperative or farmers' elevators.[1]

Besides the obstacle arising from the existence of agreements restricting competition in the marketing of grain, there was the problem of financing the country elevators. The line elevators usually procured their funds for buying grain from the head offices which were located in the larger centers where banking facilities were ample. The three main sources of loans for all elevators, as reported to the Federal Trade Commission, were as follows: from local banks, 41.58 per cent; from head offices, 34.99 per cent; and from commission houses, 10.44 per cent. Of the sources of loans for coöperative elevators, local banks constituted 56 per cent and commission houses less than 27 per cent. It is evident that local banking facilities are

[1] *Report of the Federal Trade Commission on the Grain Trade*, vol. I, pp. 82–93.

very important factors in the marketing of grain and largely control the farmers in their efforts to handle their own products in a coöperative way.

Local banking facilities in the grain States vary considerably. In the southern and eastern part of the territory the local banks are better equipped to finance the grain business than in the Northwest on account of larger deposits and capital. Many banks in the Northwestern grain States have comparatively small capital and their deposits are not large; also they are frequently under such limitations in regard to the amounts which they may loan to a single organization as to render their resources inadequate to the financing of the country grain business. Owing to this situation, moreover, interest rates are frequently higher than the grain producers are willing to pay for the financing of the crop.[1]

The number of banks and their total resources in the eight largest grain-producing States are given in the following table. For comparison the same figures are also given for New York, Pennsylvania, and Massachusetts:

	NUMBER OF BANKS	TOTAL RESOURCES (in thousands of dollars)
Iowa	1,763	1,287,916
Illinois	1,610	3,604,784
Minnesota	1,515	1,204,746
Kansas	1,349	602,067
Nebraska	1,196	638,497
Indiana	1,057	960,617
North Dakota	898	256,309
South Dakota	694	325,836
New York	1,056	13,455,441
Pennsylvania	1,546	4,719,209
Massachusetts	465	3,310,257 [2]

[1] *Report of the Federal Trade Commission on the Grain Trade*, vol. I, pp. 233–42.

[2] *Report of the Comptroller of the Currency* (1920), vol. I, pp. 255–46.

For at least eleven years Iowa has led all the States in the total number of banks, having approximately one to every 1250 persons. One explanation may be the high per capita wealth of the inhabitants; in 1912 it was $3539, while for the whole United States it was $1965.

Probably the chief explanation is to be found in the large volume of rural business tributary to the small town. The vast majority of the banks are in small places. One town of 200 has two banks, and another of 688 has three. The aggregate resources of one of these towns in 1920 was $2,453,617. Business is found in financing agricultural operations in territory tributary to the towns. These banks are largely owned by the farmers, active and retired. There is keen competition among the banks, and this fact, added to the accessibility of the banks to all the people, would seem to assure widespread service.[1]

In aggregate resources Iowa ranks after Illinois and is followed by Minnesota, Indiana, Nebraska, Kansas, South Dakota, and North Dakota. It is interesting to note that North Dakota, which stands at the bottom of this list, has been the State where the most radical agitation has developed in recent years against the situation in the grain trade.

Is there sufficient agricultural credit in Iowa? Was there too generous credit for land and stock speculation during the boom period of 1919? As has been shown, except for Illinois, Iowa has the greatest aggregate banking resources and has the largest number of banks widely distributed. If these questions are answered in the affirmative, then the problem arises as to the needs of the other States nearer the bottom of the list. Furthermore, we ought to compare the banking resources of a State like New York, with a thousand banks and $13,455,411,000,

[1] Preston: *History of Banking in Iowa*, pp. 353–56.

and Iowa or any of the other seven great grain-producing States, with their great number of banks and limited banking resources — $8,880,772,000 for the eight States, compared with $21,484,877,000, for the three States of New York, Pennsylvania, and Massachusetts.

Coöperative Marketing

Orderly marketing of farm products depends not only upon sufficient agricultural credit, but also upon the possession of machinery and information upon the part of the producers as to methods of handling their products during their transfer from the farm to the consumer. One way to attain this desirable result is by means of coöperative marketing. By experience gained in this way the farmers are enabled to compete with the established agencies, and in addition they learn by doing what is essential in the process of distribution. They will not make impossible demands and they will not be at the mercy of the middleman. Some progress has been made in this direction in several Western States in recent years. Among these States Nebraska, Minnesota, and Iowa have accomplished some notable results.

Nebraska

About twenty years ago, when the Populist movement was disappearing, Nebraska farmers began taking the local marketing of grain into their own hands. In 1911, when a law was passed providing for the organization of coöperative companies, there were less than two hundred grain elevators which could be claimed to be farmer-owned. None of these were truly coöperative, as the corporation law under which they were organized made no provision for the payment of patronage dividends, and there was no legal means to prevent the concentration of the stock in the hands of a few men. In 1921 there were 465 farmer-owned elevator companies.

The majority of these associations buy and sell not only grain, but other commodities, among which coal, lumber, mill feeds, tankage, and flour are the most common. More than a third ship hogs and a fourth ship cattle. A few handle hay, posts, paint, salt, and automobile supplies, and order potatoes and apples in carload lots in the autumn. There seems to be a growing tendency for the members of a coöperative elevator company to utilize their organization for the purchase of staple farm supplies. One farmer-owned elevator did a million-dollar business in 1919; three other companies passed the $900,000 mark, and many others handled grain and other goods valued at more than half a million dollars. The average business in 1919 for 185 companies was $281,000.[1]

In the earlier years of the coöperative movement the State Coöperative Elevator Association was the dominant factor and had more to do with pushing coöperation than all other organizations. Since the Farmers' Union has entered the field, it has done more organization work than the State association. It is responsible for at least one hundred and twenty-five of the more recently established elevators. Another result of the work of the Union has been the formation of more than one hundred coöperative stores. These stores are, as a rule, the result of local community action without any definite encouragement on the part of the State officials, except their general preaching of coöperation. There are also about half a dozen coöperative creameries controlled by Union members.

In addition to the grain elevators, stores, and creameries, there are a considerable number of live stock shipping

[1] Filley: *Coöperative Elevators*, pp. 11–13.

associations, the majority of which have been fathered by the Farmers' Union. A large per cent of the elevators also ship some stock as a side line. The Farmers' Union Live Stock Commission firm at South Omaha takes care of the business at that market and has branches at St. Joseph, Sioux City, Kansas City, and Denver.

Early in the development of the work of the Farmers' Union, a buying organization was formed in Omaha and known as the "State Exchange." It started out with a very small capital, borrowed from the general funds of the Union, and sold goods by mail, either to members direct, or billed them to a local secretary for distribution. Their overhead expense was very low, and, in one of the earlier years, they did a business of more than a million dollars at an expense of about two per cent and charged a gross margin of only about four per cent. Because of their low cost of doing business, they accumulated quite a surplus, but were always hampered by lack of capital. Later the Exchange was separated from the State Farmers' Union and a separate board of directors elected to manage its affairs. After this change was made, it was not possible to do business quite as cheaply as before, and in addition the Exchange carried a much larger stock of goods.

When the drop in prices came, the Exchange lost on goods on hand as did other wholesale houses. Fortunately, it had a rather lighter stock than usual, but as its business was entirely with farmers it was hit harder than many wholesale establishments where a part of the business was done with town people. Business improved somewhat during the summer of 1921, and probably the Exchange is doing as well as many other houses doing a similar line of business.

In the opinion of an experienced and competent observer, coöperative enterprises have never had as much capital as they should have had. This has caused them temporary embarrassment and curtailed the volume of their business. It is true, however, that in all probability the coöperative associations of Nebraska are on at least as firm a footing as are the business institutions with which they enter into competition.[1]

MINNESOTA

Minnesota stands in the forefront of the coöperative movement. There are more than three thousand local associations in the State which are farmer-owned and controlled. Of this number, more than two thousand are strict business enterprises, aiding the farmer in the marketing of his products or in the buying of supplies. The work of local organizations has been coördinated into strong groups, and the second step in coöperation — the establishment of terminal marketing agencies — has been taken.

"The tendency in Minnesota," according to Hugh J. Hughes, Commissioner of Markets of the State, "is to form food groups among the coöperatives. Speaking locally, that means that we are coördinating our local associations into five major commodity groups: live stock, grain, wool, creameries, and potatoes. We have already perfected the group in the case of potatoes. This was done a year ago when the Minnesota Potato Exchange was organized by one hundred local potato shipping associations. The Exchange acts as a central selling agency for all of these local associations, selling their entire output and avoiding duplication of effort and competition between the various associations when they come to market. The crop is handled in an orderly manner, at a minimum expense and effort,

[1] Information from a letter from H. C. Filley, Professor of Rural Economics, College of Agriculture, University of Nebraska, dated October 15, 1921.

and the Exchange has been most successful during its first year of business."

In the opinion of Mr. Hughes, the time is coming within the next few years "when any farmer in Minnesota can sell anything he produces through his own coöperative association. When that time comes, the first step in the coöperative movement will be completed. The next step will be the organization, on the part of consumers, of stores and warehouses for the purpose of cutting out such additional unnecessary expense in the handling of food products as may be possible. The farmer should follow his product, in the process of marketing, up to the very last step before it changes its form. Beyond that point, he should not go as a farmer. As a member of the consumer class, he might properly participate in the formation of coöperative mills, stores, and wholesale houses, but at the present time he is not in a position, either financially or as a matter of good business, to follow his products beyond that point." Mr. Hughes considers it dangerous to the farmers' coöperative enterprises to enter the field which properly belongs to the consumers.[1]

Iowa

Iowa is strong in coöperative elevators and in some parts of the State in coöperative creameries. So far, however, the work in Iowa has been chiefly confined to the development of strong local units. There has been little attempt to build up federations or the strong centralized marketing organizations which characterize some of the other Western States. Such agencies as the Wisconsin Cheese Producers' Federation, the Minnesota Milk Producers' Association, the Michigan Potato Exchange, the Equity Coöperative

[1] "The Minnesota Idea in Coöperation," in *The Iowa Homestead*, August 11, 1921; Hughes: *Marketing Problems of Minnesota Farmers.*

Exchange of North Dakota and Minnesota are not found in Iowa. What is needed is an aggressive leadership that will take up the problem and turn the energies of the Iowa coöperative workers into larger channels. Through the influence of the Iowa Farm Bureau Federation a beginning has recently been made by the organization of a State Federation of Coöperative Live Stock Shippers.[1]

According to the Federal Trade Commission in its report on the grain trade, published in 1920, Iowa ranked third in its percentage of coöperative elevators, having 26.59 per cent as compared with 27.18 per cent for Kansas and 27.14 per cent for Nebraska. Montana, South Dakota, North Dakota, and Minnesota followed with percentages ranging from 25.16 to 21.73.

What has frequently been termed the first coöperative elevator was established at Rockwell, Iowa. The belief of the farmer that "he was being robbed of his just profits through the exactions of the grain trust, the lumber trust, the coal trust, and other combinations with which he had to transact business," prompted about one hundred farmers to meet and discuss their troubles. The result was the organization of a company and the raising of sufficient money to purchase or erect an elevator. There is no available information by which it can be determined whether these early elevators were really coöperative or merely farmer-owned.[2]

According to the best information available, coöperative associations for the shipment of live stock had their beginning in Iowa in 1904 at Postville, Alamakee County. Beginnings were probably made at practically the same time in northeastern Iowa, southeastern Minnesota, and south-

[1] Wallace's *Farmer*, June 3, 1921.
[2] *Report of the Federal Trade Commission on the Grain Trade*, vol. I, pp. 54, 55, 82–83.

ern or southwestern Wisconsin as part of an organization campaign carried out by the American Society of Equity. The chief growth in Iowa was for several years limited to the group of counties in the northeast corner of the State, only nine being formed in other sections during the first ten years of the movement.

Outside of this area growth was very slow, and as late as 1916, twelve years after the first association was established, there were only fifty-seven active associations in the whole State. Development of coöperative shipping arrangements was somewhat increased in 1917 and 1918, but it was only in 1919 and 1920 that popular enthusiasm became general. Clayton County with eighteen associations leads all the counties. Clinton and Story counties come second with fifteen, while Jasper has fourteen, and Fayette and Hardin have thirteen each. Grundy and Ida are the only ones that have no coöperative shipping organizations.

In 1919 there were 130 associations formed, and in 1920 there were 311, making 610 separate associations in active operation by January 1, 1921. Besides independent associations or separate live-stock departments of farmers' elevators, there were fifty-seven shipping points served by coöperative associations at near-by towns and some seventy-five or more farmers' elevators, which bought stock and sold it as part of their business operations. Altogether, there were by the end of 1920 more than seven hundred towns or villages in Iowa where live stock was handled by farmers' organizations on some basis more or less perfectly coöperative in character.

The inadequacy of bookkeeping, the frequent change of managers, or other reasons make it impossible to secure complete and accurate figures of the volume of business. The largest two associations report 507 and 418 cars, but associations handling over one hundred cars of stock annually are exceptional. Estimates based upon figures secured would indicate 49,754 cars for the State. During 1920 there were shipped from all leading points in the State approximately 181,224 cars of stock. A conservative estimate would, consequently, credit coöperatives with the handling of more than one fourth of all the live stock shipped from Iowa.

Estimates of the value of the stock shipped would approximate $100,000,000 for the portion handled by coöperatives. That amount represents a business considerably larger than that of the world-famous California Fruit Growers' Exchange. The California enterprise has had twenty-five years of development, while Iowa's coöperative live-stock shipping business is still in the early formative stage in most localities.

Many of the problems which confront even the local association are by no means local in their character. For meeting these needs a large overhead unit is necessary, and the State Federation of Live-Stock Shippers, already referred to, was organized in March, 1920, and in December, 1920, made an arrangement with the Iowa Farm Bureau Federation, by which that organization lent it both moral support and the funds necessary to develop the services required by local associations. Eventually the Live Stock Shippers expect to finance themselves through a membership fee of ten dollars for each local which joins the State body and a service fee of fifty cents per car for the maintenance of its work. The new organization has been endorsed by the State Officers of the Farmers' Union and the Equity Society.[1]

GRAIN-MARKETING PLANS

In July, 1920, the American Farm Bureau Federation

[1] Nourse and Hammans: *Coöperative Live Stock Shipping in Iowa in 1920.*

called a conference to meet in Chicago for the discussion of grain and live-stock marketing problems. Invitations were sent to the presidents and secretaries of State coöperative Grain Dealers' Associations, coöperative Live Stock Shipping Associations, Farmers' Unions, Societies of Equity, Farm Bureau Federations, and the masters of State granges of various States of the Middle West. All organizations interested in coöperative marketing were invited to be present as well as representatives of the Bureau of Markets, the different agricultural organizations, and the agricultural press.

At the conference Aaron Sapiro, attorney for California coöperative associations, urged the adoption of the California method for the handling of grain. He declared that the farmers were not using the right kind of coöperation in the corn and wheat belts. They were using the Rochdale or consumers' type when they should be using the American or producers' type — the California form of coöperation. At least fifty-one per cent of the wheat produced in the nine most important wheat States should be signed up for a five-year period. There should be State wheat growers' associations and a national wheat growers' association. On the national wheat board which sets the price, there should be representatives from the State associations on a basis of production, three men from the United States Department of Agriculture, and one from the Federal Reserve Bank.

This address made such an impression that President Howard was requested to appoint a special grain-marketing committee which reported as follows: "Resolved, that we recommend that the chairman of this convention appoint a permanent committee, not to exceed seventeen members, representing the various organizations interested, and with the consent and approval of such organizations, to consider, formulate, and submit for consideration a definite plan of organization whereby all organizations of grain producers can conduct coöperative grain marketing through one or more central organizations or grain exchanges, or such other solution of the coöperative marketing problem as may be approved by such committee, and that each organization or interest represented shall bear the expenses of its own delegate or committee members." The report precipitated a lively discussion, but it was finally adopted.

Early in October, 1920, the Committee of Seventeen met and organized for work. C. H. Gustafson, president of the Nebraska Farmers' Union, was named as chairman. He is one of the best-known Farmers' Union men in the country, and has been responsible for a large share of the remarkable record this organization has made in coöperative work in Nebraska. He has also been head of the Farmers' Union Live Stock Commission Company of Omaha, the largest coöperative live-stock marketing company in the United States. The vice-chairman, A. L. Middleton, is a former president of the Iowa Farmers' Grain Dealers' Association and has been a leader in coöperative work in Iowa for years. He has organized a large percentage of Iowa's five hundred and fifty coöperative elevators, and has long been president of an usually successful elevator company at Eagle Grove. J. M. Anderson, manager of the Equity Coöperative Exchange at St. Paul, represented that organization upon the committee.

In February, 1921, the Committee of Seventeen announced its plan for a grain-marketing system controlled by farmers. The plan provides for the concentration of grain selling in the hands of a national sales association with membership and control limited to actual grain-growers. This association will establish branches at all the principal markets, including seats on boards of trade if found desirable. It will establish a complete system of gathering and interpreting statistics of world conditions affecting supply and demand, and provide means for financing orderly grain marketing through a subsidiary corporation. A subsidiary warehousing corporation will provide terminal and district warehouses with clearing and conditioning machinery. An export corporation, also a subsidiary of the national sales association, will find foreign outlets for surplus grain. All money received for grain, less operating and handling costs, will be returned to the growers. Existing farmers' elevator companies, which have done so much valuable pioneer work in coöperative grain marketing, will be made an integral part of the new system.

There are three fundamental elements in the proposed plan: (1) the grain-grower; (2) the local coöperative elevator company or grain-growers' association; (3) the central sales association.

The term "grain-grower" includes any person who raises grain and any landowner who receives all or part of his rent in grain. To become a member of the organization, he must join the national sales association for five years and sign a contract to deliver all surplus grain to the local elevator company or grain-growers' association for the same period.

The surplus grain of the members in any given locality may be handled in any one of three ways to be determined by a three-fourths vote: (1) it may be pooled; (2) it may be sold on consignment; (3) it may be purchased outright from members by the local association.

The local coöperative elevator companies are to be retained as a basic part of the new system; but they must be truly coöperative; stock must be available at a reasonable price to every grain-grower; stock ownership must be limited to grain-growers, and stockholders probably will be required to become members of the national sales association.

Grain can be handled at first with almost no change whatever in the methods that are in use at the present time. While the greatest results will not be apparent until later, when a large portion of the grain of the country is under the control of the national sales agency, the immediate benefits will be great. Farmers will be on the inside of the grain-marketing system, instead of on the outside. A way is provided for the development of grain pooling as rapidly as it is found to be desirable.

The Committee of Seventeen presented its plans to the farmers of the grain States in a series of meetings held late in March, 1921. The purpose of these meetings was twofold. They gave an opportunity for explanation and discussion and provided a means for the election of delegates to the final ratifying convention in Chicago, April 6th. State representation was based on the amount of grain marketed annually. The total number of delegates was one hundred and seven. Of these Illinois had fourteen, Iowa nine, Kansas eight, Nebraska seven, Minnesota six, North Dakota six, South Dakota six, and Missouri four. These States had sixty delegates, or more than half the total number.

Representatives of the grain-producers of twenty-five heavy grain-producing States met, studied, argued, and adopted unanimously the plan proposed by the Committee of Seventeen. Compulsory pooling of one third of the wheat was the big issue before the conference. For a day and a half the debate continued. The final vote was 61 to 38 against adopting it as a part of the plan for the present. Delegates from the West and South were practically unanimous for pooling, while the majority preferred the optional method.

The national sales agency, the United States Grain-Growers, Incorporated, was launched at this meeting. The States were divided into twelve districts and directors chosen to proceed with the work of organization. C. H. Gustafson was chosen president and Frank Myers secretary of the board of directors. The new organization automatically took over the work of the Committee of Seventeen.

The United States Grain-Growers is designed to provide a collective system for marketing grain produced by its members and returning to them the full proceeds minus only the costs of operation. Its success or failure must depend on whether it can prove itself more efficient than the private competitive firms now engaged in grain purchasing and marketing on a national and international scale. The capacity and experience of the men in charge will determine its success or failure. Conflicts in the management and extravagant expenditures have prevented the accomplishment of tangible results. Apparently the hopes of the organizers are doomed to disappointment.[1]

THE AGRICULTURAL "BLOC" IN CONGRESS

Early in the session of Congress which began in April, 1921, several Senators, including Senators William S. Kenyon, of Iowa, and Arthur Capper, of Kansas, took the lead and got together about twenty Senators from the South and West, pledged to stand for agricultural legislation regardless of party lines. Senator Kenyon was chosen chairman and four committees were appointed as follows: Federal Reserve Act; transportation; warehousing and storage; and general agricultural measures. Wisconsin, Iowa, Kan-

[1] *Wallace's Farmer*, July 16, 30, October 10, 15, November 12, December 24, 1920, February 25, March 11, 18, April 1, 15, 1921.
New York Evening Post, July 16, 29, 1921.

sas, Nebraska, North Dakota, Idaho, Wyoming, Alabama, Florida, South Carolina, Louisiana, and Texas were represented upon these committees.

A similar movement was fostered in the House of Representatives among the newer members. Congressman L. J. Dickinson, of Iowa, became the leader of this group. Committees on transportation, tariff, finance, taxation and revenue, and miscellaneous matters were appointed. Indiana, Illinois, Michigan, Iowa, Kansas, Nebraska, North and South Dakota, Colorado, Idaho, Washington, California, Virginia, Georgia, Florida, Louisiana, Texas, Missouri, and Oklahoma were represented upon these committees.

The agricultural bloc transcends party lines. It has its own caucus. Heretofore many bills have been side-tracked simply because of policy and the domination of leaders who would hold up the bills rather than risk a split in the party ranks. The bloc has thus not only kept "new and constructive measures from the cold-storage warehouses of specially appointed Congressional committees; it has also taken measures out of cold storage and passed them." The bloc is not strong enough numerically to pass legislation. Its strength consists in voting as a bloc and adding that strength to one party or the other according to the way the parties favor or oppose a measure. It is the principle of independent voting applied to national legislation.

Commenting upon the results of the Congressional session just after its adjournment late in August, a competent observer declared that it would be called "the farmers' Congress" in normal times, and if foreign affairs, taxation, and the tariff had not overshadowed other matters. Probably more legislation demanded by the farmers and presumed to be in their interest passed from April to August, 1921, than in any five months of Congress in history.

These measures included an act regulating grain exchanges which was the answer to a demand the West had been making for twenty years, a demand which in the beginning was regarded as grotesquely radical. On the same day President Harding signed the bill regulating grain exchanges and one regulating the packers. The latter measure also was the outcome of an agitation that began a generation ago. These laws are not in the extreme form originally demanded, but they are strong bills, and represent an extension of Government regulation analogous to the establishment of the Interstate Commerce Commission.

On the same day these two measures were signed, Congress passed a bill which provided that Government credit should be used, through the agency of the War Finance Corporation, to aid bankers and others carrying agricultural commodities and to facilitate new loans on those commodities as well as to extend old loans.

The War Finance Corporation, which was originally created in April, 1918, to extend Government credit to persons and corporations engaged in business necessary to the prosecution of the war, was granted authority in March, 1919, to make advances to American exporters and bankers who chose to extend credits to foreign buyers. Considerable loans were made under this authority and many applications were pending when the activities of the corporation were discontinued in May, 1920. Congress, in January, 1921, ordered the corporation to resume operations, and President Harding, when he came into office, promptly took steps to restore it to effective activity. Some advances to finance the export of cotton were made, but early in July the corporation found that, through the large cotton coöperative marketing organizations, it could extend the needed financial assistance to American producers on a large scale, and put them in a position to carry their cotton for orderly marketing.

With the passage of the Agricultural Credits Act at the end of August, 1921, the corporation was authorized to expend not to exceed $1,000,000,000 to take up and carry agricultural loans. The task involved the creation of an auxiliary banking system for the agricultural part of the country. Thirty-three agencies were established to receive applications, pass upon the security offered, and make recommendations to the board of directors at Washington.

Up to November 30, 1922, the corporation had authorized loans for agricultural and live-stock purposes amounting to $433,447,000 in thirty-seven States. Of the total, $182,859,000 consisted of loans to banking institutions; $77,671,000 to live-stock companies; and $172,827,-000 to coöperative marketing associations. Repayments received up to November 30, 1922, left a balance outstanding of $155,660,000.

In addition to the help extended in the tangible form of loans, the work developed a better feeling in the business world. One financial institution that received an advance wrote that "since receiving the advance we have renewed or extended several times the amount received." When confidence is restored, banks that have been timid about making loans, buyers who have hesitated to buy, and business men who have been curtailing their operations are encouraged to resume normal activity.

Furthermore, the loans have made it unnecessary for large numbers of farmers to dump their output on an overloaded market in order to pay the notes on which they obtained funds for their producing operations. And they enabled the farmer to undertake that interseasonal carrying of crops which is necessary to a more orderly and evenly distributed marketing.

The War Finance Corporation is a temporary agency at first limited to July 1, 1922, and extended from time to time by Congress. Congress, just before its final adjournment in March, 1923, passed an act establishing twelve institutions to be known as Federal Intermediate Credit Banks. These new institutions are to be located in the same cities as the twelve Federal Land Banks and are to have the same officers and directors. Each bank is to have a capital of $5,000,000 subscribed by the Government of the United States with provisions for its ultimate return out of the earnings. Loans, advances, or discounts may have a maturity of not less than six months nor more than three years. Bonds are to be issued to obtain funds under the same conditions that apply to farm loan bonds.

In addition to the Intermediate Credit Banks, National Agricultural Credit Corporations are also authorized for the purpose of providing credit facilities for the agricultural and live-stock industries. These corporations may be formed by any number of persons not less than five and are to be under the supervision of the Comptroller of the Currency. They are required to have a capital of $250,000.

The same act provides for the increase of the membership of the Federal Farm Loan Board to seven and raises the maximum loan to any one borrower from $10,000 to $25,000. The Federal Reserve Act is amended to allow the admission of smaller banks and the discount of agricultural paper having a maturity not exceeding nine months. The life of the War Finance Corporation is extended to February 29, 1924, when it is expected that the new agricultural credit system will be in complete working order.[1]

The immediate future of our politics seems to be more largely in the hands of the farmers than of any other single

[1] Valgren: "The Agricultural Credits Act of 1923," in *The American Economic Review*, vol. xiii, pp. 442–460 (September, 1923).

group in the country. Their organizations and leaders will be the deciding forces in our political and economic life.

SELECTED REFERENCES

1. Douglas: "A System of Federal Grants-in-Aid," in the *Political Science Quarterly*, vol. XXXV, pp. 255–71, 522–44.
2. Wanlass: "The United States Department of Agriculture," in the *Johns Hopkins University Studies in Historical and Political Science*, vol. XXXVIII.
3. Fisher: *The Farmers' Union*. University of Kentucky, Studies in Economics and Sociology.
4. Weseen: "The Coöperative Movement in Nebraska," in the *Journal of Political Economy*, vol. XXVIII, pp. 477–98.
5. Nourse: "Harmonizing the Interests of Farm Producer and Home Consumer," in the *Journal of Political Economy*, vol. XXVIII, pp. 625–57.
6. *Report of the Federal Trade Commission on the Grain Trade* (1920). 3 volumes.
7. Filley: *Co-Operative Elevators*, Extension Bulletin no. 64, University of Nebraska, September, 1921.
8. Hughes: *Marketing Problems of Minnesota Farmers*, Bulletin no. 11, Minnesota State Department of Agriculture, October 14, 1920.
9. Nourse and Hammans: *Coöperative Live Stock Shipping in Iowa in 1920*, Bulletin no. 200, Iowa State College of Agriculture, July, 1921.
10. Jesness and Kerr: *Coöperative Purchasing and Marketing Organizations among Farmers in the United States*, U.S. Department of Agriculture, Bulletin no. 547, September 19, 1917.
11. Kile: *The Farm Bureau Movement.*
12. Macklin: *Efficient Marketing for Agriculture.*
13. Hibbard: *Marketing Agricultural Products.*
14. *Report of the National Agricultural Conference*, Washington, January, 1922.
15. *Report of the Joint Commission of Agricultural Inquiry*, Washington, 1921–22.
16. Nourse: *Fifty Years of Farmers' Elevators in Iowa.*
17. Burritt: *The County Agent and the Farm Bureau.*
18. Capper: *The Agricultural Bloc.*
19. Wright: *Bank Credit and Agriculture.*
20. Rural Credits: Hearings Before the Committee on Banking and Currency of the House of Representatives, January 31, 1923.
21. Steen: *Coöperative Marketing.*

CHAPTER XV

RECENT SOCIAL PROGRESS

FORTUNATELY social progress in the United States has been largely independent of politics. Successive minor parties from the seventies to the nineties forced the older parties to face the most urgent issues, but the actual accomplishment of the reforms was really due to nonpartisan activity, sometimes the Republican Party and again the Democratic Party being the instrument used.

Since the Civil War no new party has replaced either of the older organizations, but the platforms and issues put forth by the Republicans and Democrats have responded slowly and haltingly to the changing demands of the years. Compare the platforms before and after 1900 and you will measure the social progress that has been made.

THE PROGRESSIVE PARTY PLATFORM

The distinctive feature of the Progressive Party platform of 1912 was the portion devoted to "social and industrial reform." It was the result of a generation of social work and experience. In 1877 the Charity Organization movement began in Buffalo and from thence extended until it embraced in its operations most of the larger cities. Ten years later social settlements inaugurated more constructive social work along broader lines. These two movements gradually developed a social programme. Progress was made from mere relief to prevention. Experience with case work brought out the fact that much relief work as well as preventive work could only be efficiently carried through by means of community action. Social maladjustments were found to play a much larger part in individual problems than had previously been realized.

For three years before 1912 the National Conference of Charities and Correction had had a committee on standards of living and labor. At the close of that year's session, under the chairmanship of Owen A. Lovejoy, those present adjourned as members of the conference (which adopts no resolutions), and as individuals adopted a platform of industrial minimums. There were working-men and employers in the group, but for the most part it was made up of persons actively engaged in what we call social work.

"The standards they set were clear-cut and they offered the public a new conception of the sphere of governmental concern in industry. They held that the human waste which modern large-scale production throws back upon the community in the shape of trade injuries and occupational disease, overwork and overstrain, orphanage and depleted households, gives the public a stake in the human side of industry; that because of this public element, the public is entitled to complete facts as to the terms of work-hours, wages, accidents, etc.; that with these facts and with the advances made by physician and neurologist, economist and engineer, the public can formulate certain minimum standards below which it can be scientifically demonstrated that work can be carried on only at a social deficit; and finally that all industrial conditions falling below such standards should come within the sphere of governmental supervision and control, in the same way that subnormal sanitary conditions, because they threaten the general welfare, are subject to regulation.

"In line with this general principle, certain minimum standards were put out which have won acceptance among those who know labor conditions first hand; and public commissions were called for to investigate wages, factory inspection, social insurance, etc., as a basis for formulating minimums which the public should sanction." [1]

This programme Theodore Roosevelt included in his "Confession of Faith," and on August 6, 1912, presented it to the Progressive Party Convention. In due time it was incorporated into the party platform, where it was referred to as "social and industrial justice." Thus the culmination of the Progressive movement, and its coincidence with the leadership of Roosevelt, gave to this programme, prepared by social workers, a publicity never dreamed of by its framers when they published it in June, 1912. At the same time by a fortunate happening this programme had been wrought out of long experience and contained the ripe results of practical social service. Consequently its value was beyond all comparison with ordinary party platforms. It forms a landmark in the treatment of social and industrial problems in the United States.

Whatever the fate of the Progressive Party, and short-lived as it proved to be, the platform gave standards at which to aim. Since 1912 much progress has been made in the attainment of these standards in spite of the collapse of the Progressive movement.

By 1916 the Progressive Party as an organization had ceased to exist, and when Mr. Roosevelt declined its nomination for President and advised support of Mr. Hughes, he merely accepted the existing situation. The outbreak of the European War had submerged all domestic issues and the proper attitude of the United States and the need of preparedness absorbed party and popular opinions. For the time being social and industrial justice at home became subordinate to the preservation of some measure of justice in international affairs.

[1] Kellogg: "The Industrial Platform of the New Party," in *The Survey*, vol. xxviii, p. 668.

The Democrats in 1916 borrowed wholesale the "social and industrial justice sections" of the Progressive platform of 1912, and "in its planks on labor, conservation, public health, prison reform" the Democratic platform ranked "with the Progressive document of 1912" in the opinion of a trained observer, who also interpreted the similar features of the earlier programme. Such borrowing illustrates very clearly the way by which social progress is made by the permeation of party programmes. By means of this process, the platform of 1912, and the standards of social workers embodied in it, have made considerable progress since that time.

WORKMEN'S COMPENSATION

Three types of social legislation have had a conspicuously rapid record of growth since 1912; workmen's compensation; mothers' or widows' pensions; and minimum-wage laws for women. All workmen's compensation laws have been passed since 1908, and the first law to remain permanently in force in any State after its constitutionality had been settled, went into effect in 1911. In 1920 such laws had been enacted in forty-two States in addition to Porto Rico and the Territories of Alaska and Hawaii. The Federal Government also in 1916 provided such protection for its million civilian employees. During the World War a great system of allotments and allowances, compensation and insurance was created for those in the military and naval service of the country. This has been described as "the greatest step in the social insurance movement made in the United States." [1]

In June, 1920, Congress appropriated one million dollars annually for federal aid to States that made an equivalent

[1] *The American Labor Legislation Review*, vol. x, p. 7; *The Survey*, vol. xxxviii, p. 541.

appropriation for the rehabilitation of industrial cripples. Thus an encouraging beginning of justice for the "battle casualties of peace" has been made.[1] The Federal Government and most of the States are committed to a policy of insurance against accidents. At least thirty of these laws have been passed since 1912.

MOTHERS' PENSIONS

By the close of the legislative sessions of 1919, "mothers' pension" laws had been adopted in thirty-nine States and in the Territories of Alaska and Hawaii. In the remaining nine States — all of which, with the exception of Rhode Island, are in the South — bills were under consideration in at least five. In North Carolina a law of 1919 provided aid not exceeding ten dollars a month to enable poor children to attend school. It was limited to children of school age and applied only during the compulsory school term. Consequently it could not be regarded as a pension law. As in the case of workmen's compensation the first laws were passed in 1911 and the spread of the legislation through the States has been almost as rapid.[2]

MINIMUM WAGES FOR WOMEN

Minimum-wage laws for women had been enacted in 1920 for fourteen States and the District of Columbia. The first of these laws was passed by Massachusetts in 1912 and eight other States adopted similar laws during the legislative sessions of 1913. The slower progress of this kind of social legislation has been due to long litigation over the Oregon State law in the Supreme Court of the United States. That court finally upheld the principle by a di-

---

[1] *The American Labor Legislation Review*, vol. x, pp. 125, 126.
[2] *Laws Relating to "Mothers' Pensions,"* published by the Children's Bureau, 1919.

vided opinion — Justice Brandeis, as previous counsel for the defense, not voting. The Oregon law has been of great importance, and it has served as a model for the bulk of subsequent legislation. It may fairly be contrasted with the original Massachusetts statute as showing the growing definiteness of the living-wage idea.[1]

HEALTH INSURANCE

Health insurance seems to be in a stage somewhat similar to workmen's compensation ten years ago. There is a widespread recognition of its need, but the great obstacle to be overcome is the lack of popular understanding of the subject. The first impulse of employers and wage-earners is to oppose compulsory protection against sickness, and it is difficult to obtain the support of the farmers. Down to January 1, 1920, eleven official State commissions had considered and reported upon it; six favored compulsory health insurance, while four opposed it, and one described the extent and burden of sickness, pointed out the need of action, and recommended a new commission to study health insurance legislation as a solution.[2]

OLD-AGE PENSIONS

Old-age pensions have aroused comparatively little interest so far in the United States. Massachusetts appointed a committee of investigation in 1907 which made a final report in 1910. In 1915 six cities and towns in the State voted four to one in a referendum vote in favor of instructing their representative to support an old-age pension measure.[3] Governor Samuel W. McCall recommended a system of old-age pensions in connection with compulsory

[1] Douglas: "American Minimum Wage Laws at Work," in *The American Economic Review*, vol. IX, pp. 701–38.

[2] *The American Labor Legislation Review*, vol. X, p. 27.

[3] *The Survey*, vol. XXXV, p. 197.

health insurance in his inaugural address to the Massachusetts Legislature in January, 1917. Such legislation was defined and defended by him as "the insurance of society against its diseases, and that society should take wholly or in part upon itself the work of defending against certain well-defined evils which result from our modern system of production, the chief burdens of which have heretofore been left upon deserving people who are least able to bear them."

His specific recommendations for old-age pensions were as follows: (1) that the system should be non-contributory; (2) that the beneficiaries should be persons seventy or more years of age who did not have children able to support them and did not have an income of more than two hundred dollars a year and who had been residents of the State for at least ten years; (3) that the annuity should not exceed sixty-five dollars a year. In his opinion it was "a new field in America" and could "much more easily be broadened," if experience showed that it was wise to do so, than narrowed if a false step had been taken.[1]

The Wisconsin Industrial Commission made a report on Old-Age Relief in 1915 in compliance with an act of the legislature passed in 1913. No further action seems to have been taken.[2]

An Old-Age Pension League was formed at Columbus, Ohio, in the summer of 1916 to prepare a bill to be presented at the session of the legislature beginning in January, 1917. The main features of the measure were that the age limit should be sixty-five; that persons with incomes of less than two hundred and forty dollars a year should be eligible; that property holdings of fifteen hundred dollars should be exempt; persons inmates of public institutions

[1] *Monthly Labor Review*, vol. IV, pp. 206–08.
[2] *Report on Old-Age Relief*, by Industrial Commission of Wisconsin, 1915.

should be ineligible; revenues were to be derived chiefly from inheritance taxes; and the maximum annual pension should be two hundred and forty dollars.[1]

The legislature during the 1917 session directed the Governor to appoint an unsalaried commission of seven members to study health insurance, sickness prevention, and old-age insurance.[2]

The Ohio commission reported in 1919 recommending the enactment of old-age pension legislation and a similar body in Pennsylvania made the same recommendation.[3]

After a number of years of discussion, a compulsory contributory system of old-age and disability insurance was adopted in 1920 by the Federal Government for its 300,000 employees in the classified civil service. The measure provides for the retirement of employees at the ages of sixty-two, sixty-five, and seventy according to the group to which they belong. The pensions range from one hundred and eighty to seven hundred and twenty dollars, according to the salary and length of service. No one who has not been in the service of the Government at least fifteen years is entitled to benefits under the law. The same benefits are provided for those who, after fifteen years' employment, but before the retiring age, become totally disabled because of disease or injury "not due to vicious habits, intemperance, or willful misconduct." The contribution of employees is made through a deduction of two and one-half per cent from all salaries, some of the higher-priced men paying proportionately more for their annuities than those with lower salaries. It is estimated that contributions will cover about one third of the expense, the remainder being paid from general taxation. The interests of those who leave the serv-

[1] *The Survey*, vol. xxxvi, pp. 517, 518.
[2] *The American Labor Legislation Review*, vol. vii, p. 595.
[3] *Ibid.*, vol. x, p. 75.

ice of the Government or die before attaining the age or length of service necessary for retirement are fully protected. Administration of the act is mainly in the hands of the Commissioner of Pensions under the Secretary of the Interior.[1]

The adoption of this law should help the growing movement for old-age pension legislation by the States for workers in both public and private employments as much as accident compensation legislation was stimulated by the adoption of the compensation principle by the Federal Government.

CHILD LABOR

The abolition of child labor is another form of social legislation in which great progress has been made in recent years. Advances in this direction have been very largely due to the work of the National Child Labor Committee which was organized in New York City on April 15, 1904, for the purpose of nationalizing the child-labor movement. The leaders had all been active along State and local lines.

Since its formation the record of the achievements of the Committee has been noteworthy. In furtherance of its object it drafted a Uniform Child-Labor Law which received the endorsement of the American Bar Association. It represented an effort to establish a standard toward which State legislatures might aim. Certain fundamental principles were laid down that could be applied to the varying conditions in the different States.

At the end of ten years' activity of the Committee many States had forbidden child labor under fourteen years, had prohibited night labor for children under sixteen years, had established the eight-hour day for persons under that age, and had limited the employment of minors in the night

[1] *The Survey*, vol. XLIV, p. 271.

messenger service. The regulation of street trades for children was also undertaken. In addition compulsory school attendance laws had been promoted to supplement the restrictions upon the employment of children and to insure the use of the time released from labor for the purpose of education and vocational training.

The very considerable success of the Committee did not conceal the fact that the adoption of uniform State legislation by more than forty different legislatures was a slow method, subject to frequent delay and many setbacks, and requiring constant watchfulness to keep the laws and their administration up to a satisfactory standard. One State with advanced legislation would find itself at a disadvantage in competition with a State having less progressive legislation. Hence there was an almost inevitable tendency to turn to the Federal Government and to try to discover some method by which a uniform law might be passed by Congress, covering the whole country, instead of depending upon separate State legislation, diverse administration, and public sentiment.

In 1907 Senator Beveridge, of Indiana, introduced a bill providing that the carriers of interstate commerce, the railroads and steamboat lines, should not transport the products of any factory or mine that employed children under fourteen years of age. Violation of the law was punishable by a money fine and a sentence in the penitentiary. This bill never advanced much beyond its formal introduction. Its suggestion was probably premature, as progress in State legislation was proceeding rapidly, and the work of the National Committee was still in its early development.

In 1916 a Federal Child-Labor Act was finally passed which provided that "no producer, manufacturer, or dealer may ship, deliver for shipment, or transport in interstate commerce any product (1) of a mine or quarry, situated in the United States, in which within thirty days prior to the removal of the product therefrom children under sixteen have been employed or permitted to work; or (2) of a mill, cannery, workshop, factory, manufacturing establishment, situated in the United States, in which within thirty days prior to the removal of the product therefrom children under fourteen have been employed or permitted to work, or children between fourteen and sixteen have been employed or permitted to work more than eight hours a day, or more than six days a week, or after 7 P.M. or before 6 A.M."

The Attorney-General, the Secretary of Commerce, and the Secretary of Labor constituted a board to make uniform regulations for the enforcement of the act. The Secretary of Labor, or any person duly authorized by him, was allowed at any time to enter and inspect mines, quarries, mills, canneries, workshops, factories, manufacturing establishments, and other places in which goods were produced or held for interstate commerce. The actual work of enforcement was given to the Child-Labor Division of the Children's Bureau of the Department of Labor. Every district attorney, when satisfactory evidence of any violation was presented to him, must cause proceedings to be prosecuted in the proper courts. Any person not complying with the act was liable to a fine of not more than two hundred dollars for each offense prior to his first conviction and to a fine of $100 to $1000, or imprisonment for not more than three months, or both, for each offense subsequent to such conviction.[1]

This act was declared unconstitutional by the Supreme Court of the United States on June 3, 1918, four of the nine judges dissenting. The main objection was that the law invaded the powers reserved to the States. The dissenting

[1] *The American Year Book* (1916), p. 445.

opinion maintained that power to regulate commerce was unqualified and included the power to prohibit, if Congress felt that the national welfare demanded. The case was brought before the Supreme Court on appeal from the United States District Court in North Carolina which had granted an injunction against the enforcement of the law upon the ground of unconstitutionality.[1]

Another effort to attain the same object was made, when the Revenue Act of 1918, approved February 24, 1919, imposed an excise tax on the employment of child labor "equivalent to ten per cent of the entire net profits received or accrued" during any taxable year from the sale or disposition of the products of any mine, quarry, mill, cannery, workshop, factory, or manufacturing establishment, which did not conform to the general requirements laid down in the Federal Child-Labor Act of 1916.

This law was set aside by the same judge who had acted in the case of the earlier act. One week after it went into effect, he granted a permanent injunction forbidding its enforcement in a Charlotte, North Carolina, cotton mill. An appeal to the United States Supreme Court resulted in the declaration of its unconstitutionality as an attempt by Congress to regulate, through the taxing power, something entirely within the jurisdiction of the States.

STANDARDS IN INDUSTRY

The National Consumers' League is another organization which has performed distinct and unique services along the lines of social progress. It originated in the mind of a rich woman in New York City who noticed that the salesgirls in a department store were compelled to stand up all day. She told the management that she would withdraw her account unless seats were provided and the threat

[1] *The American Year Book* (1918), p. 465.

worked. Out of this experience the National Consumers' League developed in 1899 — an organization by which consumers as a group can influence the conditions under which the articles they purchase are made and sold. A "white list" of department stores in New York City, that dealt fairly with the women and children in their employ, was the first undertaking. A little later the early Christmas shopping movement originated in connection with the local League in New York City. Both suggestions came from Josephine Shaw Lowell.

The establishment of standards in industry through labor legislation next occupied the attention of the National League. Child-labor legislation was advocated before the formation of the National Child-Labor Committee. It has continued to spread information as to industrial conditions down to the present time.

The unique service of the League has been the defense of labor and social legislation before the courts. Such work developed logically from its previous activity in urging and getting such legislation enacted. It was useless to have laws passed if they were to be declared unconstitutional by the courts. Evidently the judges must be made to understand the economic facts involved as well as the purely legal principles. Between 1907 and 1915 "briefs" were prepared in twelve cases in defense of the limitation of the hours of work for women, and in each instance these laws were sustained as constitutional by courts in Illinois, Ohio, Oregon, and New York, and three times by the Supreme Court of the United States.[1]

These legal "briefs" were developed by Justice Louis D. Brandeis, assisted by Josephine Goldmark, publication secretary of the National Consumers' League. Instead of

[1] Kelley: "Twenty-Five Years of the Consumers' League Movement," in *The Survey*, vol. xxxv, pp. 212–14.

clinging to precedents and legal arguments, he introduced data to show the facts of working conditions and their effects upon the workers and the community. The testimony of medical and other experts was drawn upon extensively.

Under the title of "The Case for the Shorter Hours," a "brief" of two large volumes, with a total of a thousand pages, was presented to the United States Supreme Court in April, 1916, in defense of an Oregon law limiting the working hours of men and women to ten hours a day. The law declared "that the working of any person more than ten hours in one day in any mill, factory, or manufacturing establishment is injurious to the physical health and well-being of such person, and tends to prevent him from acquiring that degree of intelligence that is necessary to make him a useful and desirable citizen of the State."[1]

The defense in its argument maintained that it had long been accepted by the courts that dangerous trades could be regulated by statute, and that it could be shown by evidence that any occupation which caused excessive fatigue was a dangerous trade — dangerous alike to those engaged in it and to the whole community.

Consequently, the volumes of "the brief" proceeded to pile up evidence "that overwork causes fatigue and that fatigue is poisonous to the bodies of men, to their morals, and the well-being of the Nation." One of the two volumes was devoted to the constructive side showing the need of leisure for the sake of good citizenship, and the advantages secured in foreign countries through the increase of efficiency resulting from shortening the hours of labor. Such an accumulation of scientific testimony can be refuted only by evidence of a similar kind. It is doubt-

[1] *The Survey*, vol. xxxv, p. 531; *The Case for the Shorter Work Day*, Bunting *versus* the State of Oregon, October, 1915.

ful whether there exists competent scientific authority to contradict the main facts set forth. The Supreme Court of the United States sustained the law by a vote of five to three, Justice Brandeis, not participating. This work "The Outlook" aptly described as "the building up of industrial liberty." [1]

Mr. Brandeis has had an unusual career as a lawyer. He came early to a large and profitable practice. He determined to live simply and maintain his personal independence by putting his money into investments yielding returns that would require a minimum of personal attention. His private practice was one of the largest in New England, but nearly half his time was spent in public legal work for which he accepted no compensation. His first services of this kind were in Boston in connection with the street railroad system, cheaper gas, and the merger of the two great transportation systems of New England, the New York, New Haven and Hartford and the Boston and Maine Railroads.

Later he engaged in national controversies which attracted wider attention. Among these were the Ballinger Case in 1909 and the Railroad Freight Rate Inquiry before the Interstate Commerce Commission in 1910 and 1911. In the former he defended the conservation of natural resources against special interests that were trying to use these resources for private gain, and in the latter he maintained that higher rates would not be necessary if the railroads developed greater efficiency through the new science of management. He urged that if the railroads needed more income "they should resort to increase of managerial efficiency, and that it would put a premium on uneconomical management to permit an increase of rates simply because there appeared to be need of greater income." He

[1] *The Outlook*, vol. cxii, pp. 939-41.

believed the railroads might save a million dollars a day by the use of the methods of scientific management.[1]

Early in 1916 Mr. Brandeis was appointed to the Supreme Court and was of course compelled to retire from service as counsel for the public interest. His work was taken up by Professor Felix Frankfurter, of the Harvard Law School. Judge Brandeis, with Professor Frankfurter and Dean Roscoe Pound, of the Harvard Law School, represents the type of lawyers who recognize that law is a social science as well as a legal science. Such recognition is of the greatest importance in a country like the United States where rigid constitutions present serious obstacles to the passage of desirable social legislation. Sociological jurisprudence would remove the need of "the recall of judicial decisions" advocated by Roosevelt in 1912.[2]

AMENDMENTS TO THE FEDERAL CONSTITUTION

Social progress has been made in recent years by amendments to the Federal Constitution. Since 1913 four amendments have been ratified, whereas from 1870, when the Fifteenth Amendment was adopted, to 1913, no change was made in that document. This long interval, and the fact that no amendment of importance had been made except as a result of the Civil War, after those amendments which were really a part of the original Constitution, had led to the establishment of a tradition of its unchangeableness in the country. The "Worship of the Constitution," to which Von Holst referred in his history, was partly the cause and partly the result of this fact. The method of interpretation by the Supreme Court also contributed to this public sentiment, and of course provided a means of

---

[1] Poole: *Brandeis in Business — A Profession*, pp. ix-lvi. Reprinted in 1914 from *The American Magazine*, February, 1911, with revision.

[2] Hard: "Brandeis," in *The Outlook*, vol. CXIII, pp. 271-77.

modification so that the Constitution was bent when it might have been broken. This "worship" of the Constitution is in curious contrast with the bitter controversies over its formation and ratification.

During the Populist agitation one of the leaders declared that "things in this country are in one big mess with the Constitution sitting on top." In 1894 the Populist State Convention of Iowa discussed a resolution proposing "the adoption of a comprehensive amendment" which would "reënact all valuable portions of the Constitution . . . and incorporate therein those necessary reforms which are now constitutionally impracticable, including elective United States Senators, a single term of the Presidency, determined by popular vote, and elective Supreme Court holding office for a definite term, with similar subordinate courts, direct legislation by the people through the initiative and referendum, and such broad extensions of popular rights as shall set the people absolutely free to govern themselves in their own way and to conduct in their national or local capacity such industries as may be withdrawn by monopoly from competition, and such other enterprises as may meet the public approval as properly subject to popular conduct." The resolution closed with a call for "a mass convention of the American people to assemble in . . . Des Moines on the first Monday in December, 1894, to consider the necessary amendment of the fundamental law of the land." The resolution was laid on the table by a large majority.[1]

In 1898 the Iowa Democratic State Convention in its party platform favored the amendment of the Federal Constitution so that "whenever a majority of both houses of the Congress shall deem it necessary the Congress shall

[1] See the writer's *Third Party Movements Since the Civil War*, pp. 349, 351.

propose amendments which shall be submitted to popular vote and shall be valid as part thereof when ratified by a majority of the votes of the people cast at any general or special election at which such question shall be submitted to a vote." [1]

An Inter-State Senatorial Amendment Convention was held at Des Moines in December, 1906, which was attended by delegates from thirteen States. The purpose was to further "the application of sufficient States to require Congress to call a constitutional convention, to the end that an amendment may be submitted providing for the election of United States Senators by direct vote." Governor Cummins strongly endorsed the proposed constitutional convention and favored in addition amendments that would give the voters an opportunity to say "who their President and Vice-President shall be"; make the interstate commerce clause strong enough "to enable Congress to control and regulate things which the developments of commerce have nationalized"; and "unify our marriage and divorce laws." [2]

In August, 1912, Senator La Follette introduced a resolution in the Senate for a "gateway" amendment to the Constitution, which would make all future amendments easier. The amendment provided that a majority of Congress might submit amendments to the States and a majority of the States, together with a majority of all the voting people of the United States, might secure their adoption. If a majority of Congress did not take the initiative in submitting an amendment, the favorable action of ten States, either by legislative or popular action, might require submission. [3]

[1] *Iowa Official Register* (1899), p. 133.
[2] See the writer's *Third Party Movements Since the Civil War*, pp. 464, 465.
[3] *The American Year Book* (1912), p. 46.

Three years later a committee was formed in New York to advocate a more democratic procedure of amending the Constitution. It was pointed out that eighteen years elapsed after the income-tax law was declared unconstitutional before the amendment authorizing such a tax was adopted. It was also noted that the amendment for the popular election of United States Senators was not adopted until long after sentiment was practically united in its favor and the States had found an extra-legal means of accomplishing the same purpose. So small a minority can prevent amendment that the provisions for changing the Constitution cannot be regarded as really functioning in any practicable manner.

"It is hardly going too far to say that we are living under a virtual despotism. . . . We are, indeed, in a worse position in one sense than the people of a monarchy. For our sovereign, or one of our sovereigns, is the letter of a document that was drafted in a time as far removed as possible from the life and thought of our own time, much further removed, it is certain, than is any monarch of to-day from his people." [1]

The Committee proposed a reduction of the vote by which Congress may propose amendments from two thirds to a majority, and of the proportion of States required for ratification from three fourths to two thirds. It also favored substitution for the unworkable method of a constitutional convention the submission to the voters at every fifth presidential election, and at such other presidential elections as a majority of Congress or a majority of the States might determine, of the question of holding a convention to propose amendments, with a majority vote requisite to affirmative action, amendments so pro-

---

[1] *Equity*, July, 1915, pp. 167–72, a quarterly published at Philadelphia and devoted to improved processes of self-government.

posed to be submitted to the voters at the presidential election following the convention, with a two-thirds vote requisite for ratification. Apparently this committee has ceased to exist without attracting any general interest in its work.

Mr. Croly states, in his "Progressive Democracy," that "Professor Munroe Smith is justified in declaring 'that the first article in any sincerely intended progressive programme must be the amendment of the amending clause of the Constitution.' In practice the monarchy of the Law hangs suspended to the nail of this particular bit of writing, and as long as it remains intact the political destinies of the American people will have to rest to an unnecessary and unwholesome extent upon the dicta of a board of judicial trustees." [1]

Such recommendations are not wanting in respect for and loyalty to the Constitution or to the Supreme Court. They merely point the way by which it may be made a little more amenable to changes in public opinion and judgment, but not responsive to mere whims of the people or to gusts of passion and prejudice.

PROHIBITION

The Eighteenth Amendment, the ratification of which was completed in 1919, illustrates the extreme difficulty of changing the Federal Constitution. Indeed, it is very doubtful whether this amendment and the one giving the suffrage to women would have been adopted for a good many years if the world, including the United States, had not been shaken out of its usual state of mind by the Great War.

Agitation for prohibition dates back to the middle of the last century when the Washingtonian Movement for

[1] Croly: *Progressive Democracy*, pp. 230–31.

the reform of drunkards developed and the famous John B. Gough was in his prime as an orator. In 1851 the Society of Good Templars was founded, and it was later the parent of the Prohibition Party and of the Woman's Christian Temperance Union. At the same time Neal Dow campaigned in Maine and succeeded in getting enacted in that State the first prohibitory law. Other States followed the example of Maine, and it seemed as if the entire country might go dry. The absorption in the slavery conflict and the coming of great hordes of immigrants accustomed to the use of liquor overwhelmed this early movement.

In May, 1869, the idea of a National Prohibition Party was suggested during a session of the Grand Lodge of Good Templars and a committee appointed to issue a call for a meeting for that purpose. As a result nearly five hundred delegates, representing twenty States, assembled at Chicago in September, 1869, and organized the National Prohibition Party. The first convention for the nomination of candidates for President and Vice-President was held in 1872 and candidates have been named every four years since that time. The Prohibition Party has done a great amount of propaganda work and has undoubtedly exercised much influence, but its actual political strength has been small. Its popular vote has never much exceeded 250,000, and it has remained nearly stationary in voting strength since 1892, when it reached its maximum. The Prohibition Party has not been the effective force in bringing about national prohibition.

The Woman's Christian Temperance Union began in 1879 its crusade for the introduction of temperance lessons in the schools. The first law was passed by Vermont in 1882. Gradually State laws were enacted until to-day every State has such legislation.

Finally, the American Anti-Saloon League was formed in October, 1895, by a coalition of national, State, and local organizations. The League refused to affiliate with any political party. Its plan was "to gather up into a working whole the many separate temperance forces in all parties and to use them to get legislation against the saloon and the liquor traffic. For years this League was learning how to meet the powerful liquor lobbies of the various States, learning how to play politics."

The Anti-Saloon League became "a giant politician reaching from the Atlantic to the Pacific. . . . It had a powerful lobby at Washington and an enormous publishing house in Westerville, Ohio. It literally turned out its newspapers and its publications by tons weekly. What it realized was that vote-getting is a trade of experts; that votes are made back home in the pleasant summer-time. There in the corner grocery store or the Bible class it silently, year after year, built up the Congress and legislatures that gave us National Prohibition." It bore "the brunt of the non-spectacular drudgery that crystallizes dry sentiment into dry votes."

Kansas, more than any other State of the later prohibition movement, has been the laboratory where the problem of enforcement has been worked out. Its law became effective in 1881, and was enforced in spots, but seldom enforced in cities. The beginning of its enforcement in the cities dates, it is said, from the picturesque crusade of Mrs. Carrie Nation in 1901. Kansas City, Kansas, came into line in 1906. Kansas was an example of prohibition enforced in city and country.

In 1907 there were three prohibition States, Kansas, North Dakota, and Maine. Oklahoma embodied prohibition in its constitution the same year. In 1910, Alabama, North Carolina, Tennessee, and Mississippi were under

State prohibition. In that year "the Anti-Saloon League believed national prohibition was fifty years away, but a State-wide movement seemed possible." Washington, Oregon, and Colorado enacted prohibitory laws in 1914. Before January 1, 1915, there were nine States under prohibition and by 1919 there were thirty-two such States.

Congress, in 1913, passed over the veto of President Taft, the Webb-Kenyon Bill "to prohibit the shipment of intoxicating liquors into any State where they are intended to be used in violation of the State laws." This action was a deadly blow to the liquor interests, for it marked the capture of Congress by a great anti-liquor lobby, and it also revealed to the Anti-Saloon League its power.

The entrance of the United States into the World War ushered in the final scenes of the long struggle. The protection of the men in the national service and the need of saving food forced further limitations upon the use of liquor, and public sentiment developed so rapidly that a constitutional amendment for permanent prohibition passed the Senate in August and the House of Representatives in December, 1917. Forty-five States ratified it in 1918 and 1919, the only States not ratifying being Rhode Island, Connecticut, and New Jersey. National prohibition went into effect in January, 1920. Meanwhile a bill had been passed to become effective July 1, 1919, for prohibition during the war and for the period of demobilization. Since peace had not been officially declared by January, 1920, war prohibition merged into constitutional prohibition without any interval. Legally there has been national prohibition since July, 1919.[1]

---

[1] Calkins: *Substitutes for the Saloon*, pp. 303–18; Appleton's *Annual Cyclopædia* (1883), p. 665.

Equal Suffrage

Like the prohibition amendment the final adoption of equal suffrage for women has come only after a long struggle. As in the case of prohibition the feelings aroused by the World War helped to hasten the granting of the suffrage to women. The great services of women in connection with the war made it seem peculiarly unfair to refuse to them the privilege of voting in the affairs of the country for which they had sacrificed and suffered.

The amendment giving the suffrage to women was passed by the House of Representatives on January 10, 1918, but failed in the Senate on October 1, 1918, and again on February 10, 1919. When the new Congress assembled, the House readopted the amendment almost immediately by a larger majority than before. In the Senate the vote came on June 4, 1919, and resulted in its acceptance. By the end of 1919 twenty-two States had ratified and the thirty-six States necessary were obtained by the action of Tennessee on August 18, 1920.

Fifteen States had granted equal suffrage to women by 1918, but only two of the States, New York and Michigan, were east of the Mississippi, and no Southern State appeared in the list. Suffrage for women has come out of the West. Wyoming in 1869, Colorado in 1893, Idaho and Utah in 1896, Washington in 1910, California in 1911, Arizona, Nevada, Kansas, and Oregon in 1912, South Dakota in 1913, Montana in 1914, had all given suffrage to women before New York granted it in 1917 and Michigan in 1918. Prohibition came from the West and South jointly, but equal suffrage is an exclusive product of the Far West. The fight begun when the Fifteenth Amendment was submitted in 1869 has taken just a half-century to complete.

THE FEDERAL FARM LOAN SYSTEM

On July 17, 1916, President Wilson approved the Federal Farm Loan Act. Its purpose was to supply to American farmers long-term credit for the expansion of their farming operations. It undertook to do for farmers what the Federal Reserve Act did for the commercial classes.

The establishment of a national rural credit system was not the result of a few years of agitation and discussion. The need for such a system had been recognized for many years. During the nineties of the last century the special money and credit needs of the farmers were emphasized by the Populists. The abundance of unoccupied land seemed to make land credit facilities other than the existing mortgage system unnecessary from the point of view of the statesmen, bankers, and economists. At that time, therefore, nothing was done.

As the West has been settled, there has come the rise in land values, which have called for larger amounts of capital and more intensive farming. Attention has consequently been turned to farm finance as a question of greater importance.

The Country Life Commission, appointed by President Roosevelt in 1908, found that among the causes contributing to the deficiencies of rural life was the "lack of any adequate system of agricultural credit whereby the farmer may readily secure loans on fair terms," and suggested that "a method of coöperative credit would undoubtedly prove of great service." Further support was given to this point of view by the report of the National Monetary Commission which contained a suggestive account of German coöperative land-mortgage credit associations.

Public interest in the possibilities of coöperative credit was aroused. Investigations of European systems were undertaken by organizations like the American Bankers' Association and by American diplomatic representatives in different European countries. Later a United States Commission was appointed "to investigate and study in European countries coöperative land-mortgage banks, coöperative rural credit unions, and similar organizations and institutions devoting their attention to the promotion of agriculture and the betterment of rural conditions."

Thus the realization dawned upon the American people that the commercial banking system on which the farmer was dependent was ill-adapted to his needs; that he lacked the financial machinery enjoyed by other classes of borrowers; and that his rate of interest was higher than the rate paid by the commercial and manufacturing communities. Rural credit reform received the endorsement of the three political parties in 1912.

Unlike the Federal Reserve Act, which had been intended to bring about reforms in the banking system with as little disturbance as possible, the Federal Farm Loan Act set aside American traditions in the farm-mortgage business and sought, not only to establish a variety of entirely new land-credit institutions, but also to prescribe new methods in making farm loans. Furthermore, the machinery provided was greatly complicated by the fact that it did not represent the views of any single group of reformers. One group had favored direct Government loans, another coöperation, and a third private enterprise as the basis of land-credit reform. The result of the attempt to reconcile these varied interests was a measure which could hardly be expected to be simple, easily administered, and immediately popular.

The preliminary organization of the system required almost a year. The first task of the Federal Farm Loan Board was to divide the country into twelve districts and to establish in each a federal land bank. Hearings, held in forty-four States and extending over about four months, were devoted to the determination of the districts "with due regard to the farm loan needs of the country." The first bank was not chartered until March 1, 1917. As was expected, most of the stock of the banks was subscribed by the Secretary of the Treasury on behalf of the United States. The total subscription of the United States amounted to $8,891,270 out of the $9,000,000 required to provide $750,000 capital for each of the twelve banks.

As in the Federal Reserve System the twelve land banks formed merely the superstructure and were not intended to deal with individual farmers. Borrowers desiring long-term loans amounting in the aggregate to at least $20,000 might organize national farm loan associations which would deal with the land bank of the district.

The first charter was granted to a national farm loan association March 27, 1917. Since that time there has been a steady increase in the number of associations formed and the volume of loans granted. November 30, 1917, there were 1839 associations chartered; November 1, 1918, there were 3358, and up to December 31, 1920, there were 3966. There is very little agricultural territory not already included within the boundaries of existing organizations. It is, therefore, unlikely that there will be in the future any considerable increase in the number of associations. The rapidity with which farm loan associations have been formed is evidence of the fact that the American farmers will coöperate when they realize that it is to their advantage to do so. Predictions were freely made in advance that the necessary loan associations would not be formed and consequently that the new machinery would not function. In view of the difficulties encountered in the organization of new machinery, the system has made remarkable progress. The alternate plan of designating agents in the failure of the formation of loan associations has been little used.

Naturally the greatest demand for farm loans has come from the West and South where interest rates have been high. The St. Paul and Spokane districts, including the Northwestern States, lead both in the number of associations and in the volume of loans applied for. More associations have been formed in North Dakota than in any other State, except Texas, which is a district by itself. Washington is a close second. At the bottom of the list are the Springfield, Massachusetts, and the Baltimore districts.

Another set of problems developed in connection with the need of keeping the banks supplied with a continuous flow of loanable capital. The act provided that, as a bank invested its capital in mortgage loans, it could pledge the mortgages as security for a bond issue, sell the bonds, and thereby maintain a continuous supply of working capital. The assumption of the act overlooked the fact that the process of issuing bonds involved delay, that a large portion of a bank's capital would be locked up in farm loans at a time when the mortgages were not yet available for bond issues, and that all the capital might be exhausted before bonds could be issued. In addition, it was not fully realized that the bonds would constitute a new type of security to American investors and might not appeal to investors because of that fact.

The entrance of the United States into the European War greatly influenced the interest rates on bonds and mortgages. Between the first and second Liberty Loan issues, nearly thirty million dollars of farm loan bonds were marketed at a premium. The absorption by the Government of nearly six billion dollars of capital within six months, and the rapid rise in interest rates, made it evident that even with a reduction in the premium farm loan bonds could not be marketed in the amount or with the promptness that the farm loan situation required. The Nationwide propaganda to increase the production of foodstuffs created a new demand for the services of the federal farm banks. The rise in interest rates also caused some withdrawal of private capital from the farm mortgage field.

In order to meet the needs of the new situation, the Farm Loan Board submitted to Congress an amendment to the law authorizing the Secretary of the Treasury to purchase farm loan bonds at par and accrued interest to an amount not exceeding $100,000,000 in each of the fiscal years ending June 30, 1918, and June 30, 1919. This amendment was approved January 18, 1918.

By joint resolution in May, 1920, Congress authorized the Treasury to purchase during the years 1920 and 1921 any bonds which it might have purchased during 1918 and 1919 under the preceding grant of power. Under these provisions the Secretary of the Treasury purchased bonds to the amount of $183,035,000 and these bonds are still held by the Government. Their immediate withdrawal is practically impossible except by a complete halting of the system.

Still another set of difficulties arose in connection with the provision for the voluntary incorporation of joint-stock land banks under a federal charter. The status of these banks in the system was peculiar. While they were independent of the formation of national farm loan associations, and were free from many of the restrictions of the federal land banks, they could make mortgage loans in only two States contiguous to one another and could issue bonds only up to fifteen times their capital stock and surplus (the federal land banks could issue up to twenty times their capital and surplus). The joint-stock land banks were under the supervision of the Federal Farm Loan Board. In reality the provision for such banks was intended to satisfy those who favored private enterprise as a basis for land credit reform. The section was carelessly framed and consequently ambiguous and even contradictory on some points.

It was almost a year after the passage of the act before any joint-stock land banks were organized. Up to November, 1918, nine of these banks had been formed and five had issued bonds amounting to $6,875,000. Four had been engaged in the farm mortgage business before their organization as federal corporations. Evidently existing farm mortgage companies were reluctant to come under the law — and for good reason. The business of the larger organization extended over several States and they were under no obligation to limit their loans. Finally, the business of these companies was hardly affected at all by the operations of the federal land banks. The former have confined their activities mainly to the States that rank first in agricultural development, while the latter have found their field of operations largely in the newer agricultural sections.

The farm mortgage bankers became thoroughly aroused by the steady growth in the number of farm loan associations. Although discounting the ultimate success of their new competitors, they endeavored to secure certain changes in the law to enable them to enter the new system and compete with the federal land banks on more advantageous terms. Specific amendments were worked out in a series of conferences, beginning in October, 1917, and lasting until January, 1918, between a special committee of the Farm Mortgage Bankers' Association and the Federal Farm Loan Board. The changes proposed in the law were reasonable and in keeping with the place that private enterprise should occupy in the farm loan system. The proposals, however, failed to receive the endorsement of the Board and the matter made no progress.

Apparently, the Farm Loan Board feared that a rapid increase in number of joint-stock banks, the growth in the volume of their business, and the condition of the investment market might make it impossible to dispose of bonds in sufficient quantities to keep both federal and joint-stock land banks in operation.

The fears of the Board were realized, but for a totally different reason. The institution of proceedings by the farm mortgage bankers to test the constitutionality of the new system seriously affected its operations. Sufficient quantities of bonds had been sold to carry the banks to January, 1920. In anticipation of an early decision by the Supreme Court, some of the banks used their commercial credit and continued lending operations for a time. By March 1, 1920, their funds were entirely exhausted.

Activity against the constitutionality of the Farm Loan Act seems to have started at the 1917 convention of the Farm Mortgage Bankers' Association. The suit was brought in August, 1919, by a stockholder of the Kansas City Title and Trust Company enjoining the officers of the company from investing any funds in bonds issued under the Farm Loan Act. The case was heard in October, 1919, and the court dismissed the bill. Appeal was immediately taken and the case argued before the Supreme Court in January, 1920. Late in April, the court ordered the case reargued and it had to go over to the October term. The decision was announced February 28, 1921. The constitutionality of the act was sustained by the court. In framing the original act Congress had taken pains to insure its constitutionality and the Supreme Court simply adhered closely to time-honored precedents.

In spite of disturbed financial conditions and court litigation, the banks have succeeded in making a large volume of loans. At the close of business November 30, 1921, the net mortgage loans of the federal land banks aggregated $415,173,159. Upon the same date the loans of the joint-stock land banks were $81,734,869. Capital to the extent of nearly $500,000,000 has, therefore, been supplied to aid in agricultural development.

The net earnings of the federal land banks to the end of November, 1921, were $6,476,620, dividends of $2,374,199 had been paid, and a total surplus and undivided profits of $3,870,109 accumulated. The amount of Government stock retired was $2,293,360.[1]

It is evident, therefore, from a review of social progress since 1912, that although the various radical and reform movements have seemed to fail as organizations, very considerable social gains have been made — industrial and social justice have been advanced. The platform of the Progressive Party preceded the programme of the British Labour Party by six years. It was a more conservative document, the outgrowth of American conditions as the other programme was of British conditions. Each document has been the result of a generation of study of social conditions in the respective countries. No single group like the Fabian Society in England has focused the efforts and no single leader like Sidney Webb has been developed in the United States. Political leaders like Weaver, Bryan, La Follette, Roosevelt, and Wilson have coöperated with social workers and teachers like Jane Addams, Edward T. Devine, Robert A. Woods, Richard T. Ely, and John R. Commons to work out a programme and to socialize our politics.

[1] Putnam: "Recent Developments in the Federal Farm Loan System," in *The American Economic Review*, vol. xi, pp. 427–37; Preston: "The Federal Farm Loan Case" in the *Journal of Political Economy*, vol. xxix, pp. 433–54; *Fifth Annual Report of Federal Farm Loan Board*, pp. 13, 14.

The collapse of the Progressive Party, and the submergence of public interest in social issues, due to the World War and its after-effects, make it important to keep in mind actual gains. Immediately after 1918 the prospects of a Labor Government in England in the near future seemed to warrant the conclusion that the British programme was about to be applied to a considerable extent. As the years have passed, such an outcome has receded into the future. Such changes as may be made promise to come gradually as in the past in both England and the United States. England's social needs have been more urgent and her social programme has been more fully developed. The United States has been more backward in social legislation because its social problems on a national scale have been less compelling in demanding attention.

To a considerable extent the Progressive movement and party accomplished their aims. They completed the socialization of our politics begun by minor and third parties and they indicated certain kinds of legislation necessary to meet existing evils. It remains for the future to continue the development of our politics along social lines.

The work of the agricultural bloc in the Congress ending in March, 1923, indicates that progress is still going on in spite of the reactionary tendencies in recent years. The emergency need for agricultural credit has led to the enactment of legislation which meets the demands of the Populists during the nineties for so-called "sub-treasuries," where agricultural products could be put in Government storehouses and advances made upon them pending their actual sale. The impracticable scheme of the earlier period modified by experience, has taken the form of new credit institutions fitted to the needs of agriculture as the older financial agencies are adapted to those of business.[1]

[1] See preceding chapter for the details of the new legislation.

Another indication of the continuance of a progressive movement appeared in the State and Congressional elections of 1922, when in Minnesota, Wisconsin, Iowa, Montana, Oklahoma, Nebraska, North Dakota, and Washington, radical or progressive candidates of both the major parties were helped to victory "by a close combination between organized farmers and union workers." Senator La Follette's reëlection to the Senate has led an experienced newspaper correspondent to describe him as "the leader of the opposition" and to compare him with the leader of the British Labor Party, Ramsay Macdonald. Whatever we may think of La Follette's course since the entrance of the United States into the European War, his leadership is widely regarded as progressive and cannot be entirely separated from the earlier and more constructive part of his career.

SELECTED REFERENCES

1. *Proceedings of the National Conference of Charities and Corrections* (1912), pp. 376–94.
2. *The American Labor Legislation Review,* vol. x, pp. 1–26 (March, 1920).
3. Fisher: "American Experience with Workmen's Compensation," in *The American Economic Review,* vol. x, pp. 18–47 (March, 1920).
4. *Laws Relating to Mothers' Pensions.* Published by the Children's Bureau, 1919.
5. Douglas: "American Minimum-Wage Laws at Work," in *The American Economic Review,* vol. ix, pp. 701–38.
6. Kelley: "Twenty-Five Years of the Consumers' League Movement," in *The Survey,* vol. xxxv, pp. 212–14.
7. *The Case for the Shorter Work Day,* Bunting *vs.* the State of Oregon, October, 1915. 2 vols.
8. Brandeis: *Business — A Profession.*
9. Hard: "Brandeis," in *The Outlook,* vol. cxiii, pp. 271–77.
10. Calkins: *Substitutes for the Saloon,* pp. 303–18 (new edition).
11. Wiprud: *The Federal Farm-Loan System in Operation.*
12. Putnam: "The Federal Rural Credit Bill," in *The American Economic Review,* vol. vi, pp. 770–89 (December, 1916).

13. Putnam: "The Federal Farm Loan System," in *The American Economic Review*, vol. IX, pp. 57–78 (March, 1919).
14. Putnam: "Recent Developments in the Federal Farm Loan System," in *The American Economic Review*, vol. XI, pp. 427–37 (September, 1921).
15. Preston: "The Federal Farm Loan Case," in the *Journal of Political Economy*, vol. XXIX, pp. 433–54 (June, 1921).
16. Moulton: *Financial Organization of Society*, pp. 549–690.
17. Bulletins and Reports of the Federal Farm Loan Board.

THE END

INDEX

INDEX

Accidents, industrial insurance, 368.

Addams, Jane, in Progressive Convention, 184, 185; and social reform, 395.

Agricultural bloc in Congress, formation, operation, 358, 359; accomplished measures, 359–62, 396.

Agricultural College of North Dakota, on exploitation of farmers, 302.

Agricultural Credits Act of 1921, 361.

Agriculture. *See* Farmers.

Allen, William, Brook Farm, 36.

Altgeld, J. P., pardons Anarchists, 69.

Amalgamated Clothing Workers of America, formation, 247–49; and American Federation of Labor, 249; success and strength, 249; structure, 250; Hillman as leader, 260; agreements with manufacturers, 261–63; educational work, 268; standards of production, 270.

Amana Community, history, 23, 24.

Amendments. *See* Federal Constitution.

American Farm Bureau Federation, 337–39; grain-marketing plan, 353–58. *See also* Farm bureaus.

American Federation of Labor, and Socialist Labor Party, 54; beginning as Federation of Organized Trades, conventions, legislative purpose, 97–99; and Knights of Labor, 99–103; general agitation for eight-hour day, 100, 103, 104; reorganized and named, new duties, 102; political movement, collective ownership plank, 104–07; and Farmer-Labor Party, 107, 108; success, reasons, 108, 109; and Western Federation of Miners, 221; radicals criticize, 222; and clothing-industry unions, 244, 246, 249, 264.

American Railway Union, Debs, 190; Great Northern strike, 190; Pullman strike, 191.

American Revolution, influence of frontier, 5.

American Society of Equity. *See* Equity.

American system, and frontier, 7.

Anarchists, and Socialist Convention (1872), 50; Revolutionary Socialist Labor Party, 60; Most, 60–62; convention (1883), Pittsburgh Proclamation, 62, 63; and Socialist Labor Party, 63, 64; Chicago as center, 64; and syndicalism, 65; Haymarket affair and trial, 65–69; influence destroyed, 70.

Anderson, J. M., and grain-marketing plan, 355.

Anti-Federalism, economic basis, 1, 2; and Jeffersonian Republicans, 2, 12, 13.

Anti-Poverty Society, Henry George's, 127, 128.

Anti-Saloon League, work, 385.

Arbitration, conductors' union and, 112; in clothing-workers' agreements, 250, 252, 254, 255, 257, 258, 261.

Arthur, P. M., as head of Engineers' Brotherhood, 110.

Baker, N. D., and reform in Cleveland, 177.

Baltimore, city central union (1833), 84; clothing-industry agreements, 262.

Bank of North Dakota, created, 318, 320, 321; fall, 326–29.

Banking, State guarantee of deposits, 316. *See also* preceding title, and Rural credit.

Beard, C. A., on economic causes of Federal Constitution, 8–12; and of Jeffersonian Democracy, 12, 13.

Bebel, August, on Most, 61.

Beecher, H. W., on Henry George, 122.

Bellamy, Edward. *See* Nationalism movement.

Bennett, W. M., war-time mayoral campaign, 285.

Benson, A. L., as presidential candidate, 201–03, 277; Social Democratic League, 281.

Berger, V. L., and origin of Socialist Party, 73; and Debs, 193; and

lation and formation of Federal Constitution, 10.
Public opinion, influence of Chautauqua, 172.
Public ownership, Nationalism movement and, 139, 148–50; of municipal utilities, 176.
Pullman strike, 190.

Railroad brotherhoods, insurance, 109; engineers, 110, 111; conductors, 111, 112; firemen, 112–14; trainmen, 114; other unions, 114.
Railroads, strikes, 55, 92–94, 114, 115, 190–92; Nationalism movement and government ownership, 148; result of Granger movement, 159, 161; La Follette's programme, 169–71; Pingree and taxation, 175; freight-rate legislation, 316, 320.
Rand's School of Social Science, and education of laborers, 265.
Ratification, economic division, 1, 10.
Raymond, H. J., and Fourierism, 33.
Recall, election in North Dakota (1921), 329, 330.
Red Special in campaign of 1908, 196.
Referendum, on declaration of· war, 278; on conscription, 280. See also Initiative.
Republican Party (first), as successor of Anti-Federalists, 2, 12, 13.
Republican Party (second). See Elections; Politics; Progressive movement.
Revolutionary socialism in United States, 289–97. See also Anarchism; Industrial Workers of the World; Socialism.
Revolutionary Socialist Labor Party. See Anarchism.
Riley, J. W., on Debs, 203.
Ripley, George, Fourieristic convention, 34; Brook Farm, 35–38.
Rochester, clothing industry agreements, 262.
Rockwell, Iowa, coöperative elevator, 351.
Roosevelt, Theodore, mayoral campaign, 125; and social reform, 167, 365, 395; and La Follette, 183, 186; campaign of 1912, 183–86; on Haywood, 221.
Rural credit, in Nonpartisan League programme, 307, 309; problem, 341;

Populist scheme, 341; local banks in grain States, 343–46; Federal subvention, 360–62; Federal Loan Act, 388–90; its operation, 390, 391; marketing loan bonds, Federal purchase, 391, 392; joint-stock land banks, 392–94; business of Federal land banks, 395; constitutionality of Federal act, 394.
Russell, C. E., and presidential nomination, 200, 201; Social Democratic League, 281.

Sabotage, as American idea, 218.
St. John, Vincent, and direct action, 222.
St. Louis, Folk's fight against corruption, 180; Socialist Convention and declaration on war (1917), 278–80.
San Diego, I.W.W. agitation, 231.
Sanitary control board in clothing industry agreements, 250, 251, 255.
Sapiro, Aaron, and coöperative grain marketing, 354.
Sayer, W. N., in Firemen's Brotherhood, 113.
Schaffner, Joseph, and labor problems, 259.
Schwab, Michael, Haymarket affair, trial, 66–69.
Seidel, Emil, candidacy, 200; as mayor of Milwaukee, 208, 209.
Senators, direct election, 172; Oregon Plan on election, 179.
Shearman, T. G., and term "single-tax," 127.
Sherman, J. S., death, 186.
Silver, free coinage agitation, 165.
Simons, A. M., Social Democratic League, 281.
Sinclair, Upton, Social Democratic League, 281.
Single tax, in Nonpartisan League programme, 307, 309, 316, 319. See also George, Henry.
Slavery question, effect of frontier, 7, 15; and democracy, 15, 16; absorbs other agitations, 30, 46, 384.
Social Democracy of America, and colonization, 72, 73; split, 73.
Social Democratic League, formation, 280; reconstruction programme, 281–84.
Social Democratic Party, formation, 73; and faction of Socialist Labor

Veteran compensation in North Dakota, 319.

Wabash Railway, strike (1885), 92.
Wages, standardization in clothing-industry agreement, 254; minimum, 368, 377.
Walker, F. A., attack on George's doctrine, 122.
Walla Walla, I.W.W. agitation, 230.
Wallas, Graham, on future of socialism, 297.
Walling, W. E., Social Democratic League, 281.
War Finance Corporation, and rural credit, 360.
Wars, as check to democratic movement, 15–17, 46, 366, 396.
Washington, George, land speculation, 10.
Washington, D.C., city central union (1833), 84.
Weaver, J. B., and Socialist Party, 59; on Federal powers, 154; as presidential candidate, 161, 162, 164; and social reform, 395.
Webb, Sidney, as Socialist, 289, 395.
Webb-Kenyon Bill, 386.
Weinstock, Harris, I.W.W. investigation, 231.
Weitland, William, career, in America, 43–45.
Wenatchee, Wash., I.W.W. agitation, 230.
West, as seat of Socialist strength, 204, 207; as seat of I.W.W., 218. See also Frontier.
Western Federation of Miners, type, development, 218, 221; strikes and direct action, 221; and I.W.W., 226.
White, W. A., on Progresive movement, 181.
Wholesale Clothiers' Association, labor agreements, 261.
Wholesale Tailors' Association, labor agreements, 261.
Wilson, Woodrow, and social reform, 395.
Wisconsin, economic conditions and politics, 5; as Socialist State, 214; Nonpartisan League, 326.
Wisconsin Idea. See La Follette, R. M.

Witt, Peter, and reform in Cleveland, 177.
Woman labor, Nonpartisan League measure, 319; minimum wages, 368, 377.
Woman suffrage, in North Dakota, 316; State and Federal, 387.
Women's Christian Temperance Union, work, 384.
Wood, F. B., and Nonpartisan League, 308, 309.
Wood, Howard, and Nonpartisan League, 308.
Woods, R. A., and social reform, 395.
Workers' International Industrial Union, 227.
Workers' University, in New York, 266.
Working-Men's Party of Philadelphia, 79–81.
Working-Men's Party of the United States, 52.
Workmen's Circle, educational activity, 265.
Workmen's compensation, Nonpartisan League measure, 319; movement, 367.
World War, attitude of I.W.W. considered, 237–39; European Socialists and outbreak, 272; declaration by American Socialists on outbreak, 273, 274; Socialists and Lusitania, 273, 274; Socialist peace programme, 275; Socialists in election of 1916, 276–78; Socialists and break with Germany, 277, 278; Socialists' St. Louis convention after American entry, declaration of policy, 278–80; Social Democratic League's reconstruction programme, 280–84; Socialist Party's reconstruction programme, 284; Socialists in elections during, 284–88; National Party, 286, 287; veteran compensation, 319; and industrial reform, 332, 366, 396; service insurance, 367.
Wright, C. D., on great strikes, 115.
Wright, Frances, negro community, 29; and labor agitation, 81.

Young, A. N., on Henry George, 117, 118.